297

EXAMINING RELIGIONS

Islam

Ruqaiyyah Waris Maqsood

Heinemann Educational Publishers
Halley Court, Jordan Hill, Oxford OX2 8EJ
a division of Reed Educational & Professional Publishing Ltd

MELBOURNE AUCKLAND FLORENCE PRAGUE
MADRID ATHENS SINGAPORE TOKYO
SÃO PAULO CHICAGO PORTSMOUTH (NH)
MEXICO IBADAN GABORONE JOHANNESBURG
KAMPALA NAIROBI

First published 1989
New edition 1995

99 98
10 9 8 7 6 5 4

British Library Cataloguing in Publication Data

A catalogue record for this book is available from the British
Library

ISBN 0 435 30319 8

Designed and typeset by Gecko Ltd, Bicester, Oxon
Illustrated by Barry Rowe and Gill Bishop
Printed and bound in Spain by Mateu Cromo

Acknowledgements

To my publisher, Sue Walton, my picture editor, Amanda
Davidge and to all those who helped the production of
this book run so smoothly; to my agent Carolyn Whitaker,
for her staunch faith in me, which has kept me going
through some very hard times; to Rahmat Aziz Salik, the
Imam of Hull Mosque, for his constant support both in my
professional and personal life, and for his gentle wisdom;
to Hussain Abbara of 'Iqra' Trust Resources Evaluation and
Assessment, for his detailed criticism of my original text
and to E H Bladon for her careful criticism and observation
– many improvements in this new edition are thanks to
their efforts on my behalf; any remaining errors or
weaknesses are not their responsibility; to Dawud Price of
Madinah Distribution, 586 Harrow Road, London W10 4NJ
for his prompt support; to Fazlun Khalid for helping me
with information regarding the Murabitun Sufi
movement; to Gayur Ahmad Butt, a Naqshbandi Sufi of
Settlements Consultants, 64 Aslett Street, Wandsworth,
London SW18 2BH (tel: 0181–871 9156) for his constant
support, prompt help and the supply of much information
concerning the Naqshbandi Sheikh Nazim, whose contact
address is 277 St Ann's Road, London N15 5RG (tel:
0181–802 0754; to the Chisti Order of Sufis, Sufi House,
Barton Farm, Bradford-on-Avon, Wiltshire (tel: 01225
4174); to my dear friend Zarina Choudry who never ceases
to help and support me; to my loyal correspondent Reg
Hale, and to other friends who have given me help in
ways they do not even realize – Salman, Mustafa, Shakil,
Faiz, Nadeem and Ismail; my husband Waris Ali and my
long-suffering helpers at the Hull Library, Trevor Norman
and Ann Willey.

'Oh You who created me,
Show me truth as truth, and lead me toward that,
Show me falsehood as falsehood, and help me avoid that,
and whichever way of life is most loved by You
guide me in that best of ways so that I may love that way,
and make it clear for me.'

(Prayer of the Prophet)

The publishers would like to thank W Owen Cole, our
religious studies consultant. Thanks are also due to E H
Bladon for reading and advising on the manuscript.

The publishers would like to thank the following for
permission to reproduce copyright material.
Muslim News for the articles on pp. 128 and 129, with special
thanks to Zaineb Latis (aged 14) for the cartoon on p. 128;
Octagon Press Ltd for the extract from *The Elephant in the
Dark* by Indries Shah on p. 37.

The publishers would like to thank the following for
permission to reproduce photographs.
Abbas/Magnum Photos pp. 22, 54, 66, 73 (both), 74
(bottom), 77; the J Allan Cash Photo Library pp. 6 (top),
110 (bottom), 111 (top right, bottom left and right); Circa
Photo Library p. 58; Donna DeCesare/Format Partners
p. 105; Sally and Richard Greenhill p. 102; Robert Harding
Picture Library pp. 93, 143; The Hutchison Library pp. 6
(bottom), 34, 51, 89 (left), 110 (top), 112 (bottom), 122; Barry
Lewis/Network Photographers p. 85; Dr Jean Lorre/Science
Photo Library p. 28; Mohamed Abu Mustafa p. 80 (right);
Ann and Bury Peerless pp. 111 (top left), 112 (middle); Rex
Features Ltd p. 127; Peter Sanders pp. 5, 8, 25 (right), 38,
44, 60, 61, 62, 67, 74 (top), 75, 76, 87, 89 (right), 90, 94, 96, 98
(left), 112 (top left and top right); Frank Spooner Pictures
p. 147; Telegraph Colour Library p. 98 (right); Topham
Picturepoint p. 21; Zefa p. 25 (left), 69, 113. All other
photographs were supplied by the author.

Cover photographs by Peter Sanders

The publishers have made every effort to trace copyright
holders. However, if any material has been incorrectly
acknowledged, we would be pleased to correct this at the
earliest opportunity.

CONTENTS

1 INTRODUCTION

SURRENDER

Islam is an Arabic word which means 'submission', 'surrender' or 'obedience'. Another meaning of the word is 'peace'. It stands for a person's decision to surrender totally to the will of God. Followers of the religion are known as Muslims, and they believe that submission and obedience to the will of God is the *only* way in which a person can ever achieve real peace in the heart and mind, and in society as a whole.

Their knowledge of the will of God comes through the Qur'an, a series of revelations or messages from God, given over a period of 20 years to the Prophet Muhammad, who lived in the sixth century CE (Common Era).

Submission to God is not passive, but a positive act of bringing your likes and dislikes, attitudes and behaviour into harmony with God's will. Both belief (**iman**) and action (**amal**) are absolutely vital. One is worthless without the other.

Muslims believe that God exists. They submit to God's will as revealed in the Qur'an where He revealed His name as 'Allah', the Merciful, the Compassionate One. They believe that the Qur'an consists of messages revealed by God to Muhammad, and keep the Five Pillars of the faith-bearing witness, praying five times a day, giving one-fortieth of savings to the poor, fasting the 30 days of Ramadan and making the pilgrimage to Makkah (see p. 66).

> 'It is not righteousness to turn your faces towards east or west; but this is righteousness – to believe in God and the Day of Judgement, and the Angels, and the Book, and the Messengers; to give from your wealth out of love for God to your family, to orphans, to the needy, to the wayfarer, to those who ask, and for the freeing of slaves; to be steadfast in prayer, and practise regular giving; to fulfil all the promises which you have made; to be firm and patient in pain (and suffering) or any other adversity, and through all periods of panic. Such are the people of truth, the God-fearing.'
>
> (surah 2:177)

Islam is often misunderstood in the West, due not only to ignorance but also to bad publicity. People have reacted to newspaper reports concerning the strict penalties given for theft, drunkenness, adultery and treason, and the terrorist activity carried out by various extremists throughout the war-torn Middle East.

The spirit of Islam is totally against acts of violence and oppression, although Muslims believe in defence of the weak and the constant battle against evil. Islam is a religion that offers God's compassion and guidance to all people, a spiritual system based on mercy, peace, forgiveness, modesty and happiness.

> 'He is not a believer whose neighbour cannot feel safe from his harm.'
>
> (Hadith)

A **Hadith** is a saying or tradition of Muhammad.

That Islam is misunderstood is particularly sad, as it is a world religion of over 1000 million followers (of whom perhaps some two million live in Britain).

People often confuse 'Muslim' with 'Arab'. This is misleading, for although Islam has its roots amongst the Arabs, there are now millions more non-Arabic than Arab Muslims.

In Britain, some people confuse 'Muslim' with 'Asian'. This is also wrong since Asians might be Hindus, Buddhists, Sikhs, Christians or not religious at all – and less than half of Muslims in Britain are of Asian origin.

MAKKAH AND THE KA'BAH

The Prophet Muhammad was born in **Makkah** in the land of Arabia. Makkah was famous as a sacred city because it contained an ancient temple known as the **Ka'bah** or 'Cube' because of its distinctive plain cube shape.

There is a legend that the original Ka'bah was built by **Adam**, the first man, and was therefore the first house of God on earth.

At the time of Muhammad, the Ka'bah contained a collection of over 360 altars, statues and cult objects of various gods. Many idols were meteorites, slabs of rock, or pillars. Some were worshipped as gods, but most were considered to be focal points that somehow contained the 'home' or 'power' of a god. Many were symbolic – for example, pyramid shapes symbolized the sun breaking through the clouds, and therefore the power and blessing of the Supreme Force reaching earth. Deeper thinkers said they symbolized spiritual awareness breaking through the 'blank' world of matter, touching the soul and bringing it to life.

Pilgrims at the Ka'bah, Makkah

In the Ka'bah, the most important gods were **Ilah**, the 'Strong One' or 'Most Powerful', and three goddesses said to have been his daughters – Al-Lat the sun (the life-force); Al-Uzza the planet Venus or Evening Star (the force of purity and love); and Manat or Fortune (the decider of fate).

THE QURAISH

The most important tribe living in and around Makkah was the **Quraish**, merchants who organized and gave protection to the vast numbers of traders who came through Makkah from many countries. The Quraish had control of the Ka'bah and the water supply of Makkah, and so made a profit not only out of the traders, but also by supervising provisions for the thousands of pilgrims who came there to see and worship the idols.

THE HANIFS

With so many visitors coming to Makkah, the Quraish became extremely wealthy, but many honourable tribesmen were not entirely happy with the greed, selfishness and corruption that seemed to come with the money.

These upright people known as **hanifs**, would often go off alone to pray and refresh their longing for purity in the silence and solitude of the desert and mountains.

They believed that there could only be one Supreme Power, who must have created the universe. Since He created it He must therefore be quite separate from it and exist outside it. This Almighty God, who had sent revelations many times

in the past to such prophets as Musa (Moses) and Isa (Jesus), was a spiritual power that could not have physical sons and daughters. He entered the heart, and was not to be found in rocks and idols.

One hanif, a man highly respected for his devout life of prayer and fasting, who often used to spend an entire month praying in a cave near Makkah, was **Abd-al-Muttalib**.

Abd-al-Muttalib was famous for his visions. According to legend, in one of these visions an ancient water supply which had been lost for centuries was revealed to him. This was said to have been the spring which God's angel had shown to Ibrahim's wife **Hajar**.

In the year 570 CE Abd-al-Muttalib's son **Abdullah** died suddenly, shortly after marrying, leaving his young wife **Aminah** pregnant. The boy who was born in due course was to change the whole history of the world. That boy's name was **Muhammad**.

FOR YOUR FOLDERS

▶ Look at surah 2:177. Make a list of (a) the things Muslims are called to believe in, and (b) the practical duties of Muslims.

▶ How would you answer a person who said that Muslims were Arabs or Asians?

FOR DISCUSSION

▶ Does ownership of property and possessions **always** make people selfish? If a rich person lives alongside a poor one, what might this suggest about the character of the rich person?

▶ Why do you think people worshipped stone pillars and statues, or the sun, moon and stars? What did these things represent?

A bedouin and his camel

'By the glorious light of morning, and by the
stillness of night! Your Lord has not forsaken you,
and He is not angry with you.
Surely your hereafter will be better for you
than the present, and in the end
God will be kind to you, and you be satisfied.
Did He not find you an orphan, and give you a
home?
Did He not find you [lost and] wandering,
and showed you the way?
Did He not find you in great need,
and took care of you?
As to you, therefore, do not wrong the orphans,
do not turn away those that ask your help,
but proclaim the goodness of your Lord.'

(surah 93)

LEGENDS

There were many legends about Muhammad. One
said that before his birth his mother Aminah heard a
voice telling her the child would be a great leader.
Another told of a heavy shower of rain, a blessing
that ended a long drought.

Yet another legend was that two angels removed
Muhammad's heart, washed it clean, then weighed
it against first one man, then ten, then a hundred,
then a thousand. Finally they said: 'Let it be. Even if
you set the whole community in the scale, he would
still outweigh it.'

Muhammad himself disapproved of all untruths,
especially the spreading of any stories suggesting he
had miraculous powers other than the ability to
receive the Qur'an. He insisted that it was the
Prophet Isa (Jesus) who was the miracle worker, and
not himself. He was no more than a simple and
devout man, through whom God had chosen to
speak (see surah 7:188, page 13).

EARLY TRAGEDIES

It was customary for Quraish women to entrust their
babies to **Bedouin** women (wandering tribespeople),
to take them away from the towns and raise them in
the desert where the air was pure and free from
disease. Muhammad was taken by **Halimah** the
Bedouin until he was six, when he returned to his
mother.

Sadly, she died that year, and he became an
orphan. He was not abandoned to the streets,
however; his devout grandfather, Abd-al-Muttalib,
then an old man of 80, took him in.

Two years later he also died, and Muhammad
passed into the protection of his uncle **Abu Talib**, a
wealthy merchant.

MUHAMMAD GROWS UP

Muhammad first worked as a shepherd. When his
uncle found him to be trustworthy and
hardworking, he began to take him on business
journeys. At this time Muhammad earned the nickname al-Amin, the Trustworthy One.

The Prophet worked as a shepherd

Muhammad grew up to be a fine man, with dark eyes and hair, a piercing expression, a thoughtful intelligent face, and a decisive manner. He was very kind and had a lively sense of humour.

MUHAMMAD GETS MARRIED

Muhammad continued to impress the merchants by his hard work and fair dealings. One of these merchants was **Khadijah**, a wealthy widow. She employed young Muhammad to supervise her caravan (camel train) trade.

When she was about 40 years old, she found the courage to ask Muhammad – who was then only 25 – to consider marriage to her. He was young, handsome and devout, and no doubt any woman would have been honoured to marry him, so she may have been afraid he would reject her, or feel embarrassed because of her possessions.

However, she became his only love until she died 25 years later, standing by him through all his trials and persecutions, and even after her death she remained close to him in his mind and heart.

They had six children – two sons, Qasim and Abdullah, and four daughters, Zainab, Ruqaiyyah, Umm Kulthum and **Fatimah**. The two boys died in infancy.

ALI AND ZAID

Muhammad's uncle Abu Talib fell on hard times, and Muhammad repaid his kindness by taking responsibility for his little son **Ali**.

Another child in the house was **Zaid ibn Haritha**, a slave boy given to Khadijah as a present. One day Zaid's father, who had been searching for him for years, discovered where he was and offered to buy him back. Zaid was asked what he wished to do, and chose to stay with Muhammad. Muhammad

was so moved that he freed the boy instantly, and raised him as his own son.

'Everyone begins the morning by trading with his soul; he either wins it or ruins it.'

'There are four qualities in a hypocrite:-
when they are trusted they cheat;
when they talk, they lie;
when they give promises, they break them;
when they argue, they are abusive.'

'Those who show the most perfect faith are those who are kindest to their families.'

(Hadiths)

THINGS TO DO

▶ Look at the Hadiths (sayings of Muhammad) given below. What do they tell us about his character?

▶ Explain what parts were played in the life of Muhammad by – Halimah, Abu Talib and Khadijah.

FOR YOUR FOLDERS

▶ Imagine that you are the father of Zaid, finding your son again after years of searching. Describe your feelings:

a on finding him

b on discovering he chooses to stay with Muhammad

c when Muhammad frees Zaid and raises him as his own son.

▶ In what ways do you think Muhammad proved he was a fine man, worthy to be used by God as a prophet? What do his sayings reveal about his character?

▶ Why did Muhammad disapprove of flattering legends about himself?

TALKING POINTS

● Muhammad's feelings would have been quite different if he had not suffered himself, and if people had not been kind to him.

● What do Muslims believe surah 93 teaches about God's feelings towards those in trouble? What kind of people do they believe stir God's compassion?

'Truly, We have revealed this [Message] on the Night of Power…. The Night of Power is better than a thousand months; on that night the angels and the spirit descended by permission of God, and all is peace till the breaking of the dawn.'

(surah 97)

THE SPIRITUAL SEARCH

Muhammad spent more and more time in solitude and prayer, often going to the hills to be alone. Sometimes he stayed out all night and, like his grandfather, he liked to spend the whole month of Ramadan in prayer (see pages 50 and 64).

Although he could not read or write (surah 7:157–8 calls him 'unlettered') he was respected as a man who was close to God, who thought deeply and was kind and wise. Muhammad had known the Ka'bah all his life, with its many shrines and altars. He had also known the greed, exploitation, lack of compassion and corruption of the rich merchants. Oppressed people prayed hopefully to their idols, but how could objects of stone help or understand?

Muhammad spent his life searching for spiritual guidance, drawing ever closer to God.

THE REVELATION

One night, when Muhammad was 40 years old, something happened that changed his life. This night became known as the Night of Power, or **Laylat-ul-Qadr**. It was the year 610 CE, in the ninth month (Ramadan). Muhammad had gone to pray alone in a cave on Mount Hira (later called **Mount Nur**, or Hill of Light). Suddenly he heard a voice calling his name, and the command '**Iqra!**' which means 'Proclaim!' or 'Recite!' He saw a roll of silk with writing on it in fiery letters, but could not read what it said.

The angel who appeared to Muhammad was **Jibril** – the same angel who had appeared to the prophet Ibrahim and to Maryam (Mary) the mother of Isa (Jesus), the founder of the Christian religion. Now Muhammad had also been chosen to be God's messenger or Prophet.

Three times the angel ordered him to read aloud, and each time he replied that he could not do so. A tension or pressure began building up inside him, then something seized his body and throat, gripping him so tightly that he felt he would die.

Suddenly the Prophet knew in his heart what the words said, and began to utter them.

THE MESSAGE

'Proclaim! In the name of your Lord and Sustainer who created Man from a clot of congealed blood, speak these words aloud! Your Lord is the Most Generous One – He who has taught the Pen, who reveals directly things from beyond human knowledge.'

(surah 96:1–5)

Mount Hira, where the Prophet received his first revelation

THE WAITING

After this shattering experience came the temptation of doubt. The Prophet struggled home to Khadijah, trembling with shock. He had always been a good man, but how did he know what he had seen was not some trick of the devil, trying to make him claim something about himself that was not true, something he was unworthy of?

He told Khadijah everything and repeated the words to her carefully. She wrapped him in the thick cloak he used as a blanket and helped him sleep. She had a cousin called **Waraqa ibn Nufal** who had always been a seeker after truth. He had become a Christian and produced a translation of the Gospels in Arabic. He was now nearly 100 years old, and blind, but Khadijah respected his judgement above all others. Waraqa was quite sure that this was no evil demon, but that God had indeed sent His revelation to her husband.

Knowing him so well, and seeing the effect the revelation had on him, Khadijah became the first to believe the Message he revealed. The second was little Ali, then only ten years old, and the next was Zaid. Soon Muhammad's friend **Abu Bakr** was also convinced, but at this stage the Prophet did not talk about his experiences openly.

THE WAIT

Now the Prophet's faith was tested. He had no further revelations for about two years, and became fearful and anxious of what it might mean. At last the angel came again.

> 'O you wrapped [in your cloak] – arise and warn! Glorify God! Make your garments pure! Give up all uncleanness. Give, without expecting any return. For the sake of your Lord, endure with patience!'

(surah 74:1–7)

The time of personal contemplation was over. Now Muhammad had to go out and proclaim the messages he was receiving, in public.

From that time on, for the rest of his life, Muhammad continued to receive messages and instructions from God.

> ' "O people, your companion is not one possessed. He saw him without any doubt in the clear horizon; he keeps nothing back of what was revealed to him; it is not the word of an accursed spirit." '

(surah 81:22–5)

(See also surah 68:1–4, page 11.)

FOR DISCUSSION

▶ Muhammad had always been a devout man. In what ways, therefore, do you think his life was different after the Night of Power from his life before?

FOR YOUR FOLDERS

▶ Imagine that you are one of the characters in this unit. Write a brief account of what happened on the Night of Power, and what convinced you that what the Prophet told you was genuine.

▶ In what ways could doubt have tempted or discouraged the Prophet? What would have been the outcome if the Prophet had given in to doubt?

▶ Explain what the surahs quoted in this unit teach about God and His relationship with the Prophet.

QUICK QUIZ

▶ What age was the Prophet when he received the first revelation?

▶ What was the name of the angel?

▶ What is the meaning of the command 'Iqra!'?

▶ What was the name of Khadijah's Christian cousin?

▶ Name the first four Muslims.

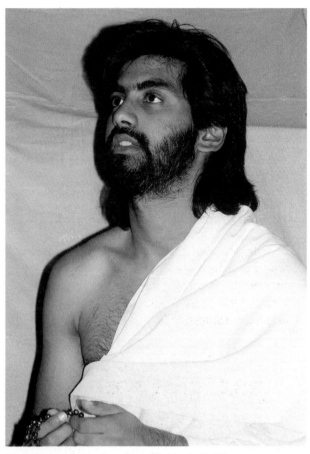

'God chooses those whom He will' (surah 42:13)

The Prophet was not a theologian, or a learned man. He did not have a set of rules or theories about God. He was simply a very devout person to whom God had chosen to make Himself known.

TAQWA – AWARENESS OF GOD

The closest experience a non-religious person can get to religious awareness is probably love. Imagine you have been happy and contented as a child, enjoying life and play. Suddenly you fall desperately in love, and discover a new range of overwhelming joy, belonging, and agonized suffering that you never knew existed. Your whole life takes on a new meaning, and you can never go back to being unaware and contented as you were before. A door has opened, and you have gone through it. You cannot explain your experience to a child who has no awareness of it.

There are other moments of truth in life: the realization that you are totally alone and no one can help you but yourself (and God); childbirth; the discovery that you are going to die. All these moments are flashes of enlightenment, and after experiencing them your life is totally changed and you can never go back.

For Muslims, discovery or awareness of God is the most shattering moment of all, and is often spoken of as being 'born again', because the experience is so devastating. Everything becomes different, everything has a new meaning, everything falls into place. New believers look at everything in a completely new light, and the whole motivation and interest of their life changes.

You can be good and honourable and kind without ever experiencing this awareness, but when it comes, perhaps the most obvious change that comes over a person is conviction.

For Muslims, to know God is to submit. To accept Him is to hand over ordinary life and begin to live a guided life.

> *'Wait with patience for your Lord's commands; and don't be like the prophet Jonah who cried out in agony. If grace from his Lord had not reached him he would indeed have been cast off on the naked shore, in disgrace. But your Lord chose him, and placed him among the righteous. Unbelievers might well stare at you, and call you mad when they hear the Message – but it is nothing less than a Message to all the world.'*

(surah 68:48–52)

RECEIVING THE MESSAGES

The Qur'an consists of messages 'sent down'. The word 'nazala' (sent down) is used over 200 times, to distinguish it from other forms of revelation. The insight needed to understand the meaning of the messages is known as 'wahy'.

The prophet related the messages to his friends, whose duty it was to memorize them and write them down, so that nothing of the message might be lost. It is important to realize that all Muslims accept without question that these messages were not just the thoughts and teachings of the Prophet, which were a different matter altogether, but the words of God that were sent down to him.

- The special revelations were always attended by dramatic phenomena, like shaking or trances.

- The Prophet always knew when they were about to happen.

- Sometimes he lay down covered in his cloak.

- Sometimes he seemed to loose consciousness.

- Sometimes he became very hot and would be soaked in sweat, even in cold weather.
- Sometimes the voice did not come through clearly. One tradition claims that he said 'Sometimes it is revealed like the ringing of a bell. This form of revelation is the hardest of all. This state passes after I have grasped what is inspired.'
- Sometimes the message came instantaneously, while he was out riding, or being questioned by the public.
- On a few occasions the angel Jibril appeared in the form of a man in order to transmit revelations.

The Prophet's visions always appeared to make him feel close to death, and that he was leaving his body and might not re-enter it. At the end of the experience he would appear as usual again, sit up, and repeat what he had been taught.

'Not once did I recieve a revelation without thinking that my soul had been torn away.'

(Hadith)

- Muslims believe, therefore, that the Qur'an is not a book written by the Prophet, but the word of God exactly as he received it. The Prophet was simply the instrument by which the words were revealed.
- The Qur'an is not a book *about* the Prophet, although sometimes, when the events and problems of his personal life caused difficulties, a revelation would come to him with specific instructions for dealing with that problem.
- The Prophet faced many people in his lifetime who did not believe in him. They challenged him to work a miracle like the Prophet Isa (Jesus) in order to prove that God had really spoken to him. This he could not do. He retorted that it was quite unnecessary, as the Qur'an itself was the supreme miracle. If anyone doubted it, let them try to compose ten verses that would bear comparison with it (see surah 11:13).
- Those who did not believe in God or his desire to communicate in this way explained the messages as being no more than the product of the Prophet's mind, and even suggested that he was mad or possessed by evil spirits.

Certainly the Prophet's mind and body were 'receiving equipment', and there is no way of proving whether or not that equipment was 'faulty' other than by examining the content of the messages and the life and influence of the Prophet.

Certain individuals have claimed 'divine guidance' who have been either quite mad, or deluded by evil influences. When you examine their words and actions, it is immediately obvious that what they did or said was not 'from God'.

'Those without knowledge say "Why doesn't God speak to us, why can't we have a sign?"...But the signs are clear to any people who hold firmly to faith [in their hearts].'

(surah 2:118)

The Qur'an was quite clear about these matters:

'You are not mad or possessed, by the grace of your Lord. Your character is above the standard that can be slandered. Soon everyone will see which of you is really mad...Take no notice of despicable slanderers.'

(surah 68:2–6,10)

FOR YOUR FOLDERS

▶ List the kinds of things the Prophet's family and friends observed when he was receiving revelations.

▶ Explain why believers became irritated if too much stress was laid on such things as these phenomena, or the desire to see miracles.

▶ Explain the difference between 'nazala' (sent down revelations) and personal inspiration.

FOR DISCUSSION

▶ How might a person judge whether their conviction that they are doing God's will is really right, not wrong?

▶ God cannot be 'seen' or 'proved'. Neither can the existence of love. What evidence would you use to prove that love exists?

▶ Why is it impossible to give a 'sign' to someone who is not ready to believe?

THE MESSAGE

As soon as the Prophet was ordered by Allah to go out and preach in public he began to do so with great urgency. He had to make people realize not only that there *was* a True God, but that life after death was real too, and there could be a time of judgement when they would be rewarded or punished according to how they had lived.

The Prophet tried to convince everyone that even if they did not believe in life after death, they would be forced to do so once they had experienced it. When that happened, they would be sorry for all the things they had done wrong and would beg for forgiveness – but it would be too late. Their lives were tests, and if they failed, they failed.

God was indeed merciful, and knew everyone's background and motives – and if people were truly sorry for their bad thoughts and actions they would be forgiven. But God was also perfect justice – if people who had passed a lifetime doing bad things were still not sorry about them when they died, they would not be forgiven. That was not fair, and God was always fair.

The prophets, like Ibrahim (Abraham), Musa (Moses) and Isa (Jesus), had all given the true message, and now he, Muhammad, was also putting God's commands before them. People had the freedom to choose whether to listen and obey or not, and they had been told what the outcome would be. If they refused to listen, it was their own fault.

The Prophet insisted that their duty to God, who saw everything, was much more important than any links with family or tribe – and their first duty was to become aware of the difference between God and the useless idols that had no powers.

The Prophet taught that God required dignity for all people, including women and slaves – two groups who had very few rights in those days and were often badly treated.

THINGS TO DO

▶ Make a list of reasons why you think the Quraish merchants of Makkah were so against their kinsman Muhammad and his message.

▶ Explain why you think the Prophet's message was particularly successful with poor people, women and slaves.

THE REACTION

It must have been very difficult for the Prophet to go out for the first time to the people of Makkah, who knew him very well, and preach openly. Everyone was amazed. His kindness and gentle wisdom had shown him all his life to be a noble and devout man – but now he was claiming that he had received messages from God, and that he had been sent to change their lives.

Crowds gathered, but most people didn't take him seriously, and ridiculed him. Few wanted to give up their selfish ways. The Prophet's own tribe was in charge of the Ka'bah with its idols, and when they realized that he was trying to stop people worshipping there they were furious because they thought their profit was in danger.

They did not hurt the Prophet, but they threatened, ridiculed and insulted him. When this had no effect, they accused him of being a sorcerer, insulting the gods, and trying to split up families by making young men rebel against their fathers. The Prophet's uncle **Abu Lahab**, one of the tribal chiefs, tried argument, bribery and threat against him, but nothing would make him give in.

The people who braved the opposition and joined the Prophet became known as 'Muslims'. Many of them were hurt, including a negro slave **Bilal** who was left to die in the sun with a huge rock on his chest. He was rescued by Abu Bakr.

The bravery of the Muslims impressed others, however, including people like the Prophet's uncle **Hamza**, a famous and highly respected warrior, who decided to join them. The Prophet's enemies grew more worried when they realized that important people were beginning to believe his message.

'By the star when it sets, your fellow man [Muhammad] is not mistaken, neither has he been misled. He does not speak from mere impulse. The Qur'an is nothing less than inspiration sent down to him. One mighty in power taught him, one full of wisdom…He revealed to his servant what he revealed. The [servant's] heart did not falsify what he saw.'

(surah 53:1–11)

'In His service'

ABU TALIB'S PROTECTION

The Prophet was under the protection of Abu Talib. Abu Talib's brother, Abu Lahab, tried angrily to make him disown him. Abu Talib was very distressed by the rift growing in his family, and begged the Prophet to go back to private life, and to give up his mission.

He said, 'Spare me and yourself; do not put a greater burden on me than I can bear.' The Prophet answered, 'O my uncle, by Allah, if they put the sun in my right hand and the moon in my left in return for giving up this cause, I would not give it up until Allah grants victory to the Truth, or I die in His service!'

Abu Talib was deeply moved, and swore he would always protect the Prophet, come what may.

FOR YOUR FOLDERS

▶ 'Ridicule is one of the most destructive forms of torture, but it is also a refining fire.' Discuss the truth of this statement with particular reference to the Prophet's experience.

▶ How true do you think it is that the most difficult people to impress are those in your own family? Why do you think this is so? Is it a good thing?

THINKING POINTS

'I have no control over what may be helpful or hurtful to me, but as God wills. Had I the full knowledge of the Unseen, I should increase the good and evil should not touch me. I am only a warner, and an announcer of good tidings to those who believe.'

(surah 7:188)

● The Prophet's critics claimed that if he was a genuine prophet God would protect him, or at least he would be able to see suffering coming and avoid it. How does the above passage answer this criticism?

THE YEAR OF SORROW

Ten years after he had received his call, when the Prophet was 50, his uncle Abu Talib died. Immediately he lost his strong protector and his life was in danger. At the end of the year, his beloved Khadijah also died at the age of 64. Without their support, the Prophet went through a time of bleakness and sorrow, though he accepted, of course, that death must come to all.

The persecutions got worse, his enemies taking advantage of this difficult time.

The Prophet was despised and humiliated by those who did not believe in him. Abu Lahab's wife used to take sharp thorns and rubbish and throw them down outside his house every day. (Later, she was taken ill, and the Prophet did housework for her until she recovered.)

REJECTION AT TAIF

As much as three years before, some of the Prophet's companions had acted on his suggestion that they should move away to Abyssinia, which was a Christian country. The Prophet tried to preach in **Taif**, but the people there just laughed at him and incited the youths to throw stones at him. The Prophet said this was the saddest day of his life.

LAYLAT-UL-MI'RAJ

It was probably during this period of persecution that the Prophet had his next extraordinary experience. It is known as the Mi'raj. This means 'ladder' or 'ascent', and refers to what Muhammad saw on his Night Journey, or **Laylat-ul-Mi'raj**.

The Qur'an does not reveal much about this incident. It states only that glory should be given to

'Him who made His servant travel by night from the sacred place of worship to the farthest place of worship.'

(surah 17:1)

The 'farthest place of worship' is taken to mean either the holy city of Jerusalem, or the presence of God in heaven.

Since it was a miraculous journey, it is not clear whether the event was supposed to have really happened physically, or was a vision. According to one tradition the Prophet (who had remarried) never left his sleeping wife's side. His body remained in Makkah while his spirit journeyed to heaven. The things he experienced on the Night

The place from where Muslims believe the Prophet ascended to heaven

Journey were a profound influence on the rest of his life.

THE JOURNEY

As the Prophet lay sleeping, the angel Jibril shook him into wakefulness and took him to Jerusalem on a strange animal like a horse with wings, named al-Buraq, the Lightning.

From Jerusalem he was taken through the seven heavens and was shown paradise and hell. In each of these heavens he met and spoke to earlier prophets, including Aaron, Musa, Ibrahim and Isa. The Prophet was particularly surprised when he met Ibrahim, 'Why, I never saw a man who looked so much like myself!'

THE PRAYERS

One very important detail the Prophet was given was the number of times per day a devout Muslim should pray. The Prophet thought 50 times to be about right, but Musa said the burden would be too great for ordinary humans. The number was finally settled at five, and that has remained Muslim practice ever since.

THE LIGHT

Gradually, the Prophet and the angel approached the highest heaven and the throne of God. Muhammad was aware only of great peace and the brilliance of pure light. Neither he nor the angel could approach any closer. Time, thought and feelings were all stilled as the Prophet experienced the overwhelming blessings of the presence of God, an experience that he could never put adequately into words, for it was beyond all human knowledge and understanding.

> *'No vision can grasp Him, but His grasp is over all vision; He is above all comprehension, yet Himself knows all things.'*
>
> (surah 6:103)

> *'Those round the throne of God sing glory and praise to the Lord and believe in Him, and implore forgiveness for those who believe. Our Lord, Thy reach is over all things in mercy and knowledge.'*
>
> (surah 40:7)

All too soon the experience drew to a close, and the Prophet was brought back to earth. To his amazement, when he finally arrived back in Makkah he found that the place where he had lain was still warm, and a cup he had tipped over was still emptying. It had all happened in a flash.

THE MEANING

For Muslims, the real meaning of this night was not the making of a journey from Makkah to Jerusalem, but the inward and mystical experience of the Prophet's spiritual ascension from earth to heaven.

Sufi mystics (see pages 148 and 152) stress that it is an experience that can be shared by all believers – the soul's journey to God as it abandons the weakness and corruption of the human body and rises to the heights of mystical knowledge, a state of pure spirituality.

The experience brought great comfort and strength to the Prophet, and convinced him that God was with him always.

◇

THINGS TO DO

▶ Copy out surah 6:103 with a decorative border, and explain why one of the names of God is al-Latif – the One unable to be imagined or understood.

▶ Explain why Muslims regard the night of the Night Journey as the second most important time in the Prophet's life.

TALKING POINTS

● Many believers experience a time they describe as a 'dark night of the soul' before times of great spiritual awareness. Is it necessary to go through the depths of sorrow and helplessness before one can fully know joy?

● Believers are often described as having seen the light. What do you think is meant by the 'darkness'?
After experiencing something like this, do you think the 'darkness':

   a would seem darker;

   b would not matter at all; or

   c would be regretted, but would no longer affect the believer?

FOR YOUR FOLDERS

▶ What was the inner meaning of the Night Journey? In what way do all Muslims believe they can share in it?

▶ Why would a Muslim be suspicious of anyone who claimed direct knowledge of God, or to be able to describe God?

THE CONVERTS OF YATHRIB

The Prophet returned to his preaching in Makkah. One day he was heard by some pilgrims from **Yathrib**, a town inhabited by three Arab and two Jewish tribes. The visitors were very impressed by what he had to say, and invited him to go to their town and judge their disputes.

They made a pledge in which they agreed:

- to obey none but Allah
- never to steal
- never to commit adultery
- never to do evil
- to protect the Prophet against all odds.

The Prophet warned of the dangers they would face if they responded to his call. They said: 'We take the Prophet, despite all threats to property, wealth and life. Tell us, O Prophet of Allah, what will be our reward if we remain true to this oath?'
The Prophet answered: 'Paradise'.
The Prophet eventually agreed to leave Makkah, and go to their town.

THE HIJRAH

The Prophet's followers were sent on ahead, and he stayed behind, still waiting for the final guidance from God that he should leave. Everyone knew that once he started out and was isolated in the desert, he could easily be ambushed by the enemies who wanted to kill him. According to tradition, there was a plot that one member from each tribe should stab him, so that no individual could be blamed.

Ali insisted on staying behind as a decoy, while the Prophet left the city. The Prophet doubled back and hid in a cave on **Mount Thawr** for four days. Food supplies were brought to him by Abu Bakr's daughter, Asma. His enemies were soon on his trail, and at one point they came right to the mouth of the cave; but a spider had woven its web across the front, and a pigeon was nesting there, so they suspected nothing.

THE ARRIVAL

When the Prophet arrived at Yathrib he was amazed and delighted at the welcome he received. Here he was accepted as an honoured and respected leader. Everyone wanted to take him into their homes. Not wishing to give offence, he said that he would leave the choice to his camel, al-Qaswa. The animal knelt at the place where the dates were dried out. Here the Prophet bought land and built a house. It is preserved to this day as the first mosque or **masjid** (see page 110).

THE CALENDAR

Yathrib took the new name of Madinat-an-Nabi, or **Madinah**. The year was 622 CE, and this became year one in the Muslim calendar.

The journey to Madinah was known as the **Hijrah** or Hegira, meaning migration. The Muslim calendar therefore makes all its dates **AH** – after Hijrah.

ANSARS AND MUHAJIRUN

The Muslims who had gone with the Prophet were refugees. They had left everything behind them and had no homes, little money and no employment. They were called the **muhajirun** or emigrants. The Prophet asked the people of Madinah if they would share their homes and belongings with the new arrivals, and they did so without hesitation. These kind people were known as **ansars** or helpers. Many 'adopted' a stranger, or a complete family.

ORGANIZATION

The Prophet became the city's political chief as well as its religious adviser. For the next ten years he worked to unite the tribes under the rule of God. Faith in God had to come before loyalty to the tribe or family.

- He drew up a written constitution outlining all the rights and duties of Muslims and non-Muslims in Madinah.
- He built the first mosque, or meeting place for the faithful, on his own premises.
- He taught the regular prayer times.
- He organized collection of money for the poor, and taught regular fasting.

CONFLICTS

The Prophet's life was still in danger from the Makkans, who demanded that he should be handed over, and also from some Jews who were angry because part of his revealed message disagreed with their own holy books.

The Prophet accepted that all the Jewish prophets had received revelations from God just as he had, and expected the Jews of Madinah to accept his message and become Muslim. The Treaty of Madinah recognized the rights of Jews as a protected minority, and they were allowed to practise their religion with complete freedom, as followers of the Prophet Moses (Musa). However, Allah had requested that Muslims prayed facing Jerusalem, and many Muslims fasted on Yom Kippur, the Jewish Day of Atonement.

> '*Say – "We believe in the revelation which has come down to us and also in that which came down to you;*
> *Our God and your God is one, and it is to Him that we bow." '*

(surah 29:46)

However, the Prophet soon received the revelation that Muslims should turn towards Makkah for prayer (surah 2:142–50), and that the fast on the Day of Atonement was only voluntary. The Muslim compulsory fast was to last the whole of Ramadan.

This tested whether or not the Jews really believed in Allah, and whether they were willing to obey the voice that spoke to Muhammad, or their own traditions. Many Jews would not accept the new revelation, so there was conflict between them and the Muslims. They began to side with the idol-worshippers of Makkah, to sabotage the Muslim state in Madinah from within.

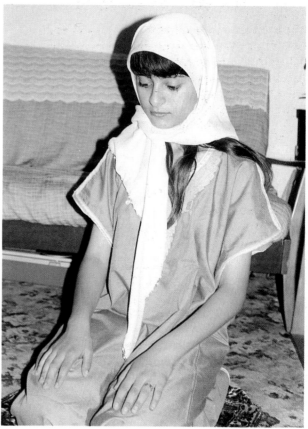

'O believer! Bow down and worship your Lord, and do good, that you may prosper.' (surah: 22:77)

FOR DISCUSSION

▶ Muslims believe that they should place loyalty to God before loyalty to their families. How could this

a   split families up

b   bind them more closely together?

THINKING POINTS

● Why do you think Muslims decided to count the year of the migration to Madinah as year one of their calendar?

● Why do you think the Prophet might have expected the Jews of Madinah to support his mission? Why do you think they finally decided against him?

FOR YOUR FOLDERS

▶ Write out the promises made by the converts of Madinah (Yathrib).

▶ Make a list of the ways in which the Prophet began to organize the Muslims of Madinah.

The Prophet's family lived in simple, mud-brick houses

Although the Prophet was now ruler of Madinah, and eventually became the supreme head of a nation commanding the loyalty of thousands of believers, he continued to live like a poor man. He used to work alongside his friends, mend his own clothes, repair his shoes, do the shopping and milk the goats.

He could have lived like a king, taking taxes and tribute from all his subjects and using them to build palaces to keep himself and his friends in luxury. He could have worn a golden crown and dressed himself in the finest garments – but he believed with all his heart that there was no king but God, and that to keep more for himself than he needed was a sign of greed, deprived somebody else, and showed a lack of faith in God the Provider.

Everything belonged to God, not to any individual; therefore when the Prophet was given money or goods, they were instantly given away again, to be shared amongst the needy.

God must come first, before any earthly possessions; a Muslim had to be willing to give up all material things for the sake of God and keep nothing back. To do less meant that love of another thing came before the love of God. This was not true submission; that person had not truly found God.

The Prophet taught that self-discipline was not a matter of 'going without' or 'giving things up' – that was the wrong attitude. It should never be a burden, but be done out of great love for God.

The Prophet's 'kingdom' was one in which God was king, and all the subjects agreed to accept His laws and not the wishes of any human ruler. Some of the laws are given here:

- Control your anger, then forgive your brother. Do you not wish to be forgiven?
- Do not hate each other, envy each other, or provoke each other.
- Do not spy on each other, or betray each other's trust.
- Do not speak ill of your friend behind his back.
- Give the labourer his wages before his sweat dries.
- Do not drink alcohol, and do not gamble – it opens the door to the devil.
- Do not steal the property of another.
- Do not cheat each other.
- Do not defile the honour of a woman.
- Do not charge interest on money loaned to those who have need of it.
- Do not take part in corrupt practices, or do anything of which you would be ashamed if it became known.
- Do not reveal your friend's weaknesses. Cover their failings if you wish God to cover yours.
- Do not pay bribes to get what is not lawfully yours.
- Do not commit adultery, or practise homosexuality.
- Do not be cruel to slaves, or forbid them to marry or buy their freedom.
- Do not force slaves into sexual relationships they do not desire.
- Do not kill unwanted babies, either before or after birth, because of poverty.
- Do not be cruel to animals.
- Gladden the heart of the afflicted, feed the hungry, give comfort to the sorrowful, and remove the wrongs of the injured.

Slavery, as such, was not forbidden, for it was accepted by many poor people as a way of saving themselves and their families from debt, or even starvation. People could put themselves into slavery for agreed lengths of time in order to pay off what they owed. The Prophet did, however, look forward to a time when slavery would no longer be necessary, because no one would take interest on money lent, and all the needy would be taken care of by the community. He urged Muslims to release their slaves, and suggested that slaves who could read could earn their freedom by teaching ten others.

The Prophet's life was extremely simple. He regarded it as a weakness to give in to urges to comfort the body. He would never allow his stomach to become full, and existed mainly on a diet of dates and parched barley. He sometimes went without lighting a fire in his hearth for days, and ate raw food only. Some days he took nothing but water.

He owned only one change of clothes, carefully mending and patching them, and using his only cloak as his blanket at night. One story tells of a cat which brought her kittens and settled down on the corner of his cloak. Rather than disturb or deprive them, he cut off the piece of material, and made sure they stayed warm and cosy.

It was quite usual before the Prophet's time for men, including prophets, to have as many wives as they liked. The prophet **Dawud** (King David of Jerusalem) had ten; his son **Suleimen** (King Solomon the Wise) maintained 1000 women. In practical terms, most men took as many women as they could afford, and if they were not pleased with them, they could just throw them out. Under guidance from the Qur'an, the marriage laws were changed to care for the many defenceless women who had lost their families and protectors.

After the death of Khadijah, the Prophet took into his household twelve other women – daughters of his friends, widows of his close warriors and daughters of defeated enemies. Other Muslim men were allowed to support up to four women, but only if all were willing, it did not cause hurt, and they were treated equally (see pages 103–4).

The Prophet's dwelling was no more than a row of tiny rooms for himself and his wives, alongside the place of prayer. The only furniture in the Prophet's bedroom was a leather sack filled with twigs and palm branches to lean against when sitting, and a rush mat to sleep on. The Prophet never slept in a soft bed. He often spent the whole night standing up in prayer, sometimes accompanied by his youngest wife **Aishah**.

The Prophet's wives were devout women, able to accept this life of extreme simplicity, and total devotion to God. They were known for their kindness, unselfishness and generosity, and were held in very special regard by the Muslims as 'mothers of the faithful'.

The Prophet loved children. Another story tells how one of his little grandsons ran up to him while he was kneeling in prayer, climbed up on to his back, and rode him like a horse. Instead of being angry, he allowed the game, and continued his prayers afterwards. Sometimes, when he saw his grandsons coming, he would interrupt his prayer to go and fetch them.

The Prophet's words, actions, and way of life reveal him as a man of gentleness, kindness, humility, good humour, and excellent common sense, who had great love for all people, especially for his family. The Prophet's way of life, or example, is known as the **Sunnah**, and Muslims who take the Qur'an and Sunnah as their only guides are known as **Sunni** Muslims (see page 146).

FOR YOUR FOLDERS

▶ Explain what is meant by the Sunnah. Why do you think the Prophet did not take advantage of all the riches and luxuries he could have had? Do you think his attitude is to be admired?

▶ Look at the list of laws the Prophet expected Muslims to obey. What would you say were the main principles that he revealed to be the will of God?

THINGS TO DO

▶ List the laws for Muslims which you think would be particularly difficult to keep:

a for a nosy, bad tempered person

b for an employer

c for a wealthy business person

d for you.

FOR DISCUSSION

▶ In what way would a love of material comforts and possessions reveal that a person was not truly Muslim?

The new Islamic state of Madinah made no distinction between its ruler and subjects. Every citizen belonged to Allah and had equal rights. There was no discrimination on the grounds of colour, class, sex or family. God judged a person's worth or nobility according to his or her heart.

'The most noble among you in the sight of God is the one who is most virtuous.'

(surah 49:13)

Few in the community were wealthy, because the migrants from Makkah had arrived with nothing. The people of Madinah took them into their homes and shared their possessions with them. But the Prophet was full of hope and confidence – what mattered was the strength of their faith, not their wealth.

THE BATTLE OF BADR

The Makkans were still determined to harm the Prophet. They tried to bribe the Madinans to hand him over. They persecuted the relatives of the Muslims that remained in Makkah, and took away their property. In 623 CE a small group of Muslims raided a camel train in the old pagan month when warriors usually kept a truce. Although the Prophet had not sanctioned this attack, he understood their grievances. Sadly it provided the Makkans with an excuse to attack Madinah with a full army.

In 624 CE the Prophet's relative **Abu Sufyan** set out with a force of 1000 men. The Prophet only had 313 warriors, including young boys. They marched out of the city expecting to die, and camped at **al-Badr** – determined to die for God if they must.

To everyone's amazement, their faith and courage won the day. The Makkan army fled, leaving 70 killed and another 70 prisoners. In those few hours the Muslims changed from being a despised and persecuted group into a victorious military power, whom Allah had protected.

THE BATTLE OF UHUD

The Makkans longed for revenge, and a year later a much larger army attacked the Muslims at **Mount Uhud**. This time the Muslims were confident, but things went wrong. There was lack of discipline and confusion over tactics, and the Muslims lost the battle. The Prophet was wounded – he lost two teeth.

Now the Muslims were depressed, and wondered if God had deserted them. Later, however, it was seen as additional proof of the Prophet's mission.

'Your courage failed, there was chaos, and they disobeyed the Prophet. God allowed you to be defeated in order to test you.'

(surah 3:152)

When Muslims acted on revelation, they were always right, but when they acted on a human level, mistakes were made (see surah 3:152).
It was revealed to the Prophet that:

● defence against those who were challenging the faith was acceptable
● Muslims who died fighting for God would go straight to paradise
● The wars were God's will and the Muslim soldiers were God's army.

'Fight in the cause of God those who fight you, but do not go beyond the limits. Slay them whenever you find them, and remove them from the places they forced you to leave; for tyranny and oppression are worse than murder. Don't fight at the sacred mosque unless they fight you there [first] – but if they do, then slay them. Such is the reward of those who suppress faith. But if they stop, remember God is the Forgiving, the Merciful. Fight [only] until there is no more tyranny and oppression, and justice and faith in God prevail: if they stop let there be no more hostility – only to those who are tyrants.'

(surah 2:190–3)

After several other battles, in 629 CE the Prophet had a dream telling him to go unarmed on a pilgrimage to Makkah. He went with 1400 men, and the Makkans came out to fight. When they realized he came in peace they settled for a ten-year truce known as the Treaty of Hudaibiya. However, this truce was broken by the Makkans a little over a year later – but not until 2000 Muslims had been able to make their pilgrimage.

MUHAMMAD TAKES MAKKAH

In 630 CE the Prophet marched on Makkah with a force of 10 000 men. No one could withstand him. He rode into the city on his camel, circled seven times round the Ka'bah, touched the Black Stone set in a corner of the Ka'bah (see page 72), and then called everyone to midday prayer. He had conquered in the name of Allah, and Makkah was his. Only eleven people had been killed, in a skirmish outside the city.

As a conqueror, he was lenient and forgiving, and declared a general amnesty. Soon everyone in Makkah accepted the faith and became Muslim. After this, Makkah became the holy city dedicated to Allah, and anyone who was not a Muslim was forbidden to enter it. This ban is still in force today.

Out of the chaos and wickedness he had known when he first started his mission, the Prophet had created a well-disciplined state in the name of Allah. There was justice instead of oppression and compassion for the poor instead of callousness. The energies of the Muslims were directed into longing for the submission of the whole world to Allah.

'You shall not enter Paradise until you have faith, and you cannot have faith until you love one another. Have compassion on those on earth, and God will have compassion on you.'

(Hadith)

True Muslim warriors fight against oppression until justice prevails

TALKING POINTS

- Belief in peace at all costs might be no more than a temptation to cowardice.
- Humans are the only animals which wage war on each other.
- Defence is not the same thing as attack.
- Being prepared to sacrifice yourself because of your beliefs in non-violence is not the same thing as bringing about a just peace.

FOR YOUR FOLDERS

▶ Muslims do not believe in peace at all costs, but accept that people should fight in order to establish a 'just peace'. What is meant by the phrase 'just peace'? Under what conditions do Muslims accept that war is justified?

▶ The battles of holy war are not against people, but against evil. How far do you think this true?

▶ Muslims cannot be expected to fight for Allah if they are ill, old, infants or disabled – and yet they would like to think they are not left out of the fight against evil. How might such people show that they, too, are 'warriors for God'?

THINKING POINTS

People often talk of total pacifism as if it is a good and noble thing, but Muslims consider it sometimes wrong *not* to fight. Here are some examples of when action would be thought necessary:

- someone was beating up an old person or a child
- someone was attacking your mother, brother or sister
- a teacher was watching a bully torment a child.

What principles do you think lie behind Islamic action?

The Mount of Mercy, where the Prophet gave his final sermon

'Today I have perfected your religion for you, completed My favour upon you, and have chosen for you Islam as the way of your life.'

(surah 5:4 the last revelation given to the Prophet)

In 632 CE the Prophet became aware that his great mission was drawing to a close. He went back to Makkah on a pilgrimage along with a vast crowd of some 140 000 people. Going up to the Mount of Mercy he addressed them in a sermon charged with high emotion.

THE SERMON

'O people, listen to my words carefully, for I do not know whether I will meet you again on such an occasion as this. You must live at peace with one another. Everyone must respect the rights and properties of their neighbours. There must be no rivalry or enmity among you. Just as you regard this month as sacred, so regard the life and property of every Muslim in the same way. Remember, you will surely appear before God and answer for your actions.

All believers are brothers...you are not allowed to take things from another Muslim unless he gives it to you willingly. You are to look after your families with all your heart, and be kind to the women God has entrusted to you.

You have been left God's Book, the Qur'an. If you hold fast to it, and do not let it go, you will not stray from the right path. People, reflect on my words... I leave behind me two things, the Qur'an and the example of my life. If you follow these you will not fail.

Listen to me very carefully. Worship God, be steadfast in prayer, fast during Ramadan, pay alms to the less fortunate.

People, no prophet or messenger will come after me, and no new faith will emerge. All those who listen to me will pass on my words to others, and those to others again.'

(Hadith)

At the end of the speech he looked round at the vast array of people. 'Have I fulfilled my mission?' he cried. The crowd roared their approval. 'You have fulfilled it, O messenger of God.'

The Prophet raised his eyes to heaven and called out three times, 'O God, You are Witness, You are Witness, O God You are Witness.'

There was a moment's silence broken by the call to prayer from the powerful voice of Bilal. Then, shoulder to shoulder, they joined in worshipping God.

DEATH OF MUHAMMAD

When Muhammad returned to Madinah he fell ill with a fever and violent headaches. Becoming weak, but still mindful to the last of fairness to his household, he asked permission of all his wives to move into Aishah's room to be nursed until he died.

He still tried every day to reach the praying place outside, but he knew his death was not far off and asked Abu Bakr to lead the prayers in his place.

On his last day, after the dawn prayer, he was helped back exhausted, and lay in Aishah's arms. She felt his head grow heavy, and heard him say, 'Lord, grant me pardon'. His last words were said to have been, 'I have chosen the most exalted company, in paradise'.

With his head in Aishah's lap, the Prophet died. Instantly there was shock and panic. **Umar**, who became leader of the Muslims after Abu Bakr, refused to believe that it was possible the Prophet could die. He thought he would live for ever, and began to raise false hopes.

Abu Bakr took control. 'O people,' he cried, 'don't worship the Prophet, for the Prophet is dead. Know that God is alive and never dies!' He then recited the verse of the Qur'an:

'Muhammad is but a messenger; there have been many prophets before him, and they all died. If he dies, or is killed, will you now turn back?'

(surah 3:144)

Tradition suggests the Prophet died on 8 June 632 CE (12 Rabi'ul-Awwal 11 AH) at the age of 63. He was buried where he died, in Aishah's room, and his grave is still a place of pilgrimage to this day. Muslims regard him as the greatest of all men – the seal of the prophets, the servant and messenger of God.

'If all [the waters of] the sea were ink [with which to write] the words of my Lord, the sea would surely be drained before His words are finished, even if we were to add to it sea upon sea.'

(surah 18:109)

THINKING POINT

- Why do you think Muhammad was called the 'seal' of all prophets? (A seal is the 'stamp of approval', or the guarantee that everything in a document is in order.)

FOR YOUR FOLDERS

▶ What do you think are the qualities of truly great people? To what extent do you think the Prophet possessed those qualities?

▶ Why were Abu Bakr's words after the death of the Prophet important? How did this incident show that he was worthy to succeed the Prophet as leader of the Muslims?

TALKING POINT

- Do you think the Prophet Muhammad would have been equally successful if he had lived in our time? Give reasons for your answer.

WHAT DO MUSLIMS BELIEVE ABOUT GOD?

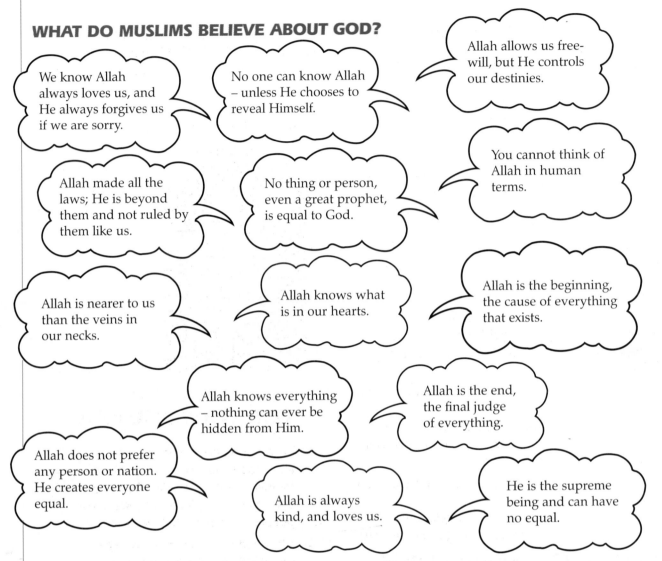

We know Allah always loves us, and He always forgives us if we are sorry.

No one can know Allah – unless He chooses to reveal Himself.

Allah allows us free-will, but He controls our destinies.

Allah made all the laws; He is beyond them and not ruled by them like us.

No thing or person, even a great prophet, is equal to God.

You cannot think of Allah in human terms.

Allah is nearer to us than the veins in our necks.

Allah knows what is in our hearts.

Allah is the beginning, the cause of everything that exists.

Allah knows everything – nothing can ever be hidden from Him.

Allah is the end, the final judge of everything.

Allah does not prefer any person or nation. He creates everyone equal.

Allah is always kind, and loves us.

He is the supreme being and can have no equal.

To be a Muslim, you must have thought about the vital question – is there or is there not a God? Either God does exist, or He doesn't. Many people seem to pass their entire lives without ever thinking about the reason for their existence, or whether there is any point to their lives, or any goal to be aimed for. They think this universe is all there is, and there is nothing beyond it. Their lives are just chains of happenings until everything stops at death.

Muslims think it is impossible for anything to come into existence from nothing, or exist without being caused. They believe that certain people (the prophets) have been given 'insights' from God, and guidance, throughout history. Muslims acknowledge the urge to improve themselves and to stop themselves doing wrong that is triggered off by conscience. From all this, they conclude that *there is a god.*

To recognize that God does exist, and is unique – above and beyond all the things He has created – is the recognition that Muslims believe will bring a person to paradise. Without this awareness, you cannot be admitted to paradise. It is not that God refuses to forgive a person, but if a person refuses to accept God's loving presence and 'puts up a wall' then nothing can be done until the 'wall' is taken away.

THE LIGHT

'God is the light of the heavens and the earth; His light may be compared to a niche in which there is a lamp; the lamp is in a crystal; the crystal is, as it were, a glittering star kindled from a blessed olive tree neither of the East nor of the West. Its oil would burst into flames even though fire had hardly touched it; Light upon Light!'

(surah 24:35)

'Those who believe in the Qur'an and those who follow the Jewish scriptures and the Christians and the Sabians and [any] who believe in God and the Last Day and work righteousness shall have their reward with their Lord; on them shall be no fear, nor shall they grieve.'

(surah 2:62)

'It is He who sends down blessings upon you, as do His angels, that he may bring you out of the darkness into the light. He is full of mercy to those who believe; on the day they meet Him the cry will be of "Peace", and He has prepared for them a generous reward.'

(surah 33:43–4)

'He will provide for you a Light by which you will walk [straight on your path]; He will forgive [your past], for God always forgives and is most merciful.'

(surah 57:28)

'The light shines into many courtyards, all separated by walls. Take away the walls, and you will see the Light is the same.'

(Jalal ud-Din Rumi, a Muslim teacher)

'O Lord! Illumine my heart with light, my sight with light and my hearing with light. Let there be light on my right hand and on my left and light behind me and light going before me.'

(Prayer of the Prophet)

'O God, who knows the innermost secrets of our hearts – lead us out of the darkness into the light.'

(Prayer of the Prophet)

Allah, the name of God

FOR YOUR FOLDERS

▶ Why do you think some people never think about God, or the possible reasons for their existence, while others are quite convinced that God exists? Are some people more 'religious' than others?

▶ What sort of events or experiences might lead some people to an awareness of God?

THINGS TO DO

▶ Read the words about light. Why do you think God is so often compared with the symbol of light?

▶ Make a list of events, experiences or emotions that could come under the headings 'light' and 'darkness'.

▶ Choose five of the statements about God which you most agree with, and write them out on a decorated scroll or a poster. Say why you agree with them.

God's guidance is often compared to light

TAWHID

The most basic Muslim belief about God is Tawhid. This means 'one-ness', 'unity', 'the absolute' or 'the alone'. This is one of the hardest concepts to grasp of all. It means accepting that God by definition is supreme. If God exists at all, there can be nothing that can rival Him as a source of power or love. It means that there is nothing remotely like Him.

'He is Allah, the One, Allah is Eternal and Absolute. None is born of Him, He is unborn. There is none like unto Him.'

(surah 112)

TRANSCENDENCE

Tawhid means that God alone is the creator, the power behind the universe and the sole source of its guidance. He knows everything, sees everything and is able to do anything.

God is transcendent, which means that He is outside and beyond everything that He created. God is outside time, whereas all created things are part of time. Things which are part of time have beginnings and ends, but this is not true of God.

When Muslims talk of God being 'eternal' or 'infinite', they are admitting that He is beyond human knowledge and reasoning.

'No vision can grasp Him, but His grasp is over all vision; He is above all comprehension, yet is acquainted with all things.'

(surah 6:103)

IMMANENCE

Muslims also believe that God is immanent, which means that He is closer to each human than their heartbeat and knows even our unspoken thoughts, fears and hopes.

'When My servants ask you about Me I am close [to them]; I listen to the prayer of every suppliant who calls to Me. Let them listen to my call and believe in Me, that they may walk in the right way.'

(surah 2:186)

'It was We who created man, and We know even the secret suggestions his soul makes to him; for We are nearer to him than [his] jugular vein.'

(surah 50:16)

Muslims believe God is close and listens to every prayer

IMPLICATIONS OF TAWHID

To think that you own any object, or any person, breaks Tawhid. Everything in the universe belongs to God. You may only 'borrow' possessions, or even your own bodies, for as long as God wills.

Pride or arrogance breaks Tawhid. You were given your talents or brain capacity before birth, and did not choose them for yourself.

Ignorance of God's supremacy breaks Tawhid. No other power in the universe can act except as God wills it. Superstition breaks Tawhid.

Complaining to God, or begging for favours, or trying to change His will as if your own was better, breaks Tawhid. God already knows everything and is supreme compassion. If tragedy strikes it is for a reason, even if we do not understand it.

Thinking God can be fooled or deceived breaks Tawhid. He knows even the thoughts you conceal from yourself in your subconscious mind.

A false pride, or sense of holiness, breaks Tawhid. God is not fooled by hypocrisy. He knows all our weaknesses, our lack of faith.

SHIRK

When a person tries to liken God to any created thing, or to suggest that other things in the universe somehow share in God's creative power, or have His knowledge or ability to guide or forgive – this is known as the sin of **shirk**.

God is beyond the world of matter, and the idea of His somehow mingling with matter to become the father of a human being, or produce a being that is half human and half divine, is blasphemy to a Muslim.

To a Muslim, the Holy Spirit is the action of God and not a separate entity, and Isa – 'the miracle worker' who even raised the dead – was in his humility a supreme Muslim and not in any way a divine being.

A prophet cannot *be* God. No prophet ever claimed this. Muslims insist that this is true of Isa also, one of the greatest and humblest prophets. They think that the claims made about him by later Christians were not the claims made by Isa himself. They believe that Isa would have recoiled in horror from the suggestion that he was God.

The traditions that Isa (Jesus) was born of a virgin mother and worked miracles are accepted by Muslims without question – for God revealed this to the Prophet in the Qur'an. But these two beliefs do not lead Muslims to assume that God has any equal or partner (see also pages 36–7).

RESULTS

Belief in Tawhid results in:

- *faith*, and surrender to the will of Allah
- *self-respect* and *confidence*. No other power (king, employer, relative or friend) has any rights over Muslims. They depend on and fear no one but God
- *humility* and *modesty*. Whatever Muslims are or own is from God, so how can they be proud or boastful?
- *responsibility*, because Muslims know they are answerable to God for their actions
- *trust*, because they believe that everything must be God's will, and therefore planned
- *courage*, because they accept that they will face tests as God wills, and not die before the appointed time for them to do so
- *unity with the universe*, because they act for God in taking care of the planet
- *determination, patience* and *perseverance*, because Muslims have dedicated themselves to pleasing God, and it is no easy task.

'They do blaspheme who say that "God is Christ the son of Mary." For Christ himself said "O children of Israel, worship God, my Lord and your Lord." '

(surah 5:75)

'O people of the Book! Do not commit excess in your religion. Of God speak only the truth. The Messiah, Isa, son of Maryam, was [only] an apostle of God, and His word which He conveyed to Maryam, and a spirit proceeding from Himself. Say not "Three". Do not do it. God is only one God. Far be it from His glory that He should have a son.'

(surah 4:171)

FOR DISCUSSION

▶ Why do Muslims believe it is impossible to describe God in human terms?

FOR YOUR FOLDERS

▶ Explain how Muslims believe Allah to be both transcendent and immanent. Why is hypocrisy completely pointless?

▶ Make a list of what Muslims believe are the most important results of Tawhid in their lives. You could do this as a diagram or table, using just the key words.

▶ In what ways do pride, envy, hatred or selfishness break Tawhid?

▶ Explain what is meant by the sin of shirk.

THINGS TO DO

▶ Copy out one of the surah quotations given in this unit and explain in your own words what you think it means.

'Allah is Lord of all the worlds.' (surah: 1:2)

THINKING ABOUT CREATION

Interviewer: Ali, why do you think Allah created all this? How can you prove it?

Ali: This universe did not just spring into being by chance or accident. Some scientists say that sort of thing because they do not want to believe in God. None of them can give the answer. They're only guessing.

Interviewer: But they know what they're talking about.

Ali: Look, isn't it possible that this whole universe might never have existed at all?

Interviewer: I suppose so.

Ali: Of course. *You* might never have existed. That table might never have existed. Nothing exists without a cause. Therefore, if the universe *does* exist, it must be because of a reason. If you take away the cause, how can anything happen?

Interviewer: We ought to be able to prove God exists, then, from the laws of nature. Couldn't God just have evolved?

Ali: How can God be under the same rules as that which He created? He is above and beyond them. There is this difference between Allah and everything else in the universe.

Interviewer: Don't you think the scientists will ever prove the existence of God, then?

Ali: How can a creature who sees only in black and white ever understand what is meant by blue? You can show a monkey all the rules of science, but it will never understand them. Likewise, a human being will never fully understand the universe, let alone Allah who made it.

Interviewer: Do you think the scientists are just wasting their time?

Ali: No, no. They make discoveries all the time. Allah wants us to be intelligent and to love Him. But look, all the rules the scientists discover – they are nothing new, are they? They have been there all the time, waiting to be found. Science just suddenly sees what has always been there. But the true scientist realizes that he or she doesn't know very much.

Interviewer: I think that's true. Our great scientist Sir Isaac Newton once said that after the whole of his lifetime's study, he had been just like a boy playing with pebbles on the beach while a whole vast ocean lay before him.

Ali: And in any case, the universe contains far more than our earth and its solar system; it contains more than the whole of the 'space' that is waiting for the astronauts. There are whole regions of existence, whole 'heavens', which are quite beyond physical space.

Interviewer: Will we ever know the truth, Ali?

Ali: One day, one day – insha Allah [if God wills].

> *'There is no God but He, the Living, the Self-Subsisting, the Eternal. He neither slumbers nor sleeps…No person can grasp anything of His knowledge, except as God wills it.'*
>
> (surah 2:255)

> *'God has the key of the unseen, the treasures none know but He. He knows whatever is on land and in the sea: no leaf falls without His knowing it; there is not a grain in the darkness of earth, or a green or dry thing, but it is carefully noted.'*
>
> (surah 6:59)

> *'If you think that you can control your own destinies, then try to stop your souls leaving your bodies at the time of your death.'*
>
> (Hadith. See also surahs 3:168, 56:83–7)

> *'To God belong the East and the West; wherever you turn, there is the Presence of God; for God is All-Pervading, All-Knowing.'*
>
> (surah 2:115)

> *'False gods cannot create a fly – nor could they ever get back what a fly could take from them.'*
>
> (surah 22:73)

> *'The value of this world in comparison to the hereafter is like a droplet in the ocean.'*
>
> (Hadith)

THE SEVEN HEAVENS

Muslims believe there are seven heavens beyond our universe. The Prophet Muhammad saw this revelation in his lifetime. In the heavens he met Adam, Ibrahim, Musa and Isa, all still living.

As he approached nearer to God, he found himself surrounded by 'Oceans' of light, and felt a sense of perfect peace (see page 14).

FOR YOUR FOLDERS

▶ Explain why a Muslim could never accept that:

  a the universe came into being by chance

  b there was no evidence for the existence of God

▶ Read the surahs given here, and explain carefully in your own words what each one teaches about God.

THINGS TO DO

▶ Look up the meanings of these names of Allah, and list them carefully:

  Compassionate; Supreme; Omnipotent; Omnipresent; Omniscient; Beneficent.

▶ Work out the chain of cause and effect for the existence of a table. (The table exists because…)

▶ Love and conscience are known by their effects. Write down some of the effects of these two concepts that prove they really do exist, even though they are not physical things.

TALKING POINTS

● Why do Muslims believe a created being can never understand that which created it?

● Does a living cell in your body know that you exist?

● Could it be true that there is no such thing as mind or conscience, and these are just the workings of the physical brain?

'He sends forth guardians [to watch] over you, and when death overtakes you, the messengers will carry away your soul.'

(surah 6:61)

'Behold two guardians appointed to learn his doings, one sitting on his right and one on the left. Not a word does he utter but there is a sentinel by him, ready to note it.'

(surah 50:17–18)

'Angels are appointed over you to protect you; they are kind and honourable, and write down your deeds. They know and understand all that you do.'

(surah 82:10–12)

BEINGS IN THE UNIVERSE

Muslims do not accept that humans and animals made of matter are the only beings in the universe. They believe in at least two other kinds of beings, the **jinn** and the **angels**. Neither are human, and so they are beyond real human understanding. Muslims object strongly to any attempts to draw pictures of them based on imagination, as these can be very misleading.

Jinn are usually thought of as elemental spirit forces, neither good nor evil. The Qur'an describes them as being made from fire. They usually cause upset and disturbance to human beings but they can also be benign and friendly. Surah 72 mentions some who were converted to Islam.

Angels are the messengers of God, the channels by which humans become aware of Him.

Neither angels nor jinn have physical bodies, but both can affect the world of matter and people with whom they come in contact. Both humans and jinn are endowed with free-will, but angels never vary from the will of God.

ANGELS

The word 'angel' means 'messenger', and this is the chief function of these beings.

Muslims believe angels are creatures of light who pervade the whole universe. They are not far away, and are in constant contact with humans, present all the time, but especially whenever a person prays or thinks about God. Then they gather round and join

in. Their presence can be felt as a sensation of peace and love and it helps to build up the atmosphere of worship.

PROTECTING FRIENDS

'Surely those who say: "Our Lord is Allah" and then go straight, the angels descend upon them, saying: "Fear not and do not be sad, and hear the good news about the Garden which you have been promised. We are your protecting friends in the life of this world, and in the next world. There you will have all that your selves desire, and there you will have all that you ask, a gift of welcome from the Forgiving, the Compassionate."'

(surah 41:30–2)

Humans only see angels on very rare occasions, but Muslims believe that they are sometimes seen by specially chosen people, or at times of great crisis. However, many sensitive people do become aware of loving and guiding presences watching over their lives, and those who become constantly aware take their presence almost for granted, so that it becomes quite hard to remember that other people do not share the same awareness.

An angel may take human shape, as Jibril did to the prophet Ibrahim, and to Maryam, the mother of Isa – but this is not its true form. It can materialize in any shape it chooses. According to Hadith Muhammad first saw Jibril as a huge creature covering the horizon between heaven and earth with several thousand wings.

NAMED ANGELS

- **Jibril** – the messenger of God who gives revelations to the chosen ones
- **Azra'il** – the angel of death who is present at deathbeds to receive souls
- **Israfil** – calls all souls on the Day of Judgement
- **Mika'il** – the protector of the faithful and guardian of places of worship
- **Munker and Nadir** – will question souls
- **Iblis** – the devil or Shaytan – chief of the jinn

THE DEVIL

Muslims believe that both angels and jinn existed before the human race at a stage when the universe was perfect and evil did not exist. The urge to do evil was caused when humans were created. God intended the first man, Adam, to rule the earth and look after it. He ordered all the angels to respect His decision and so they did. But Iblis (also called Satan or Shaytan) refused to do this because he considered himself a superior creature.

For this he was punished, and therefore became the enemy of all humans. Since that time he has done his best to get revenge by leading people's hearts and minds away from God.

'Iblis' means 'desperate' and the word 'Satan' conveys the idea of rebellion and perversity.

> 'The Lord said to the angels… "When I have created Man and breathed My spirit into him, then fall ye down and worship him." So all the angels bowed down in worship, all of them together. But not so Iblis (the chief jinn): he refused to be among those who bowed down.'

(surah 15:28–31)

THE RECORD

Muslims believe that every person has two special angels, or guardians, who keep a record of their good or bad deeds. If you thought nobody saw you do a bad thing, and you have got away with it, you are wrong. It was seen and recorded. Likewise, if you thought no one had noticed your good deed and it was not appreciated, again you are wrong. Nothing a person ever does or thinks is ever unknown, unseen, forgotten, or left out.

At the end of formal prayers Muslims turn to the right and the left and bless their two angels as they hover near their shoulders (see page 57).

(see page 57)

THINKING POINTS

- Why do Muslims believe that evil is possible in a universe created by God?
- Pride and disobedience are real causes of evil in the universe. Do you think this is true? Give reasons.
- If there was no such thing as 'evil', would such a thing as 'good' exist?

TALKING POINTS

- Do you think believing in guardian angels makes life easier or more difficult for Muslims?
- The universe only contains the creatures proved to exist by science. The Muslim belief in angels is no more than imagination. Do you agree?

FOR YOUR FOLDERS

▶ Think through the last two days. Make a list of some of your thoughts and actions that might have gone into your record book.

▶ How might a Muslim be helped in life by the belief in guardians?

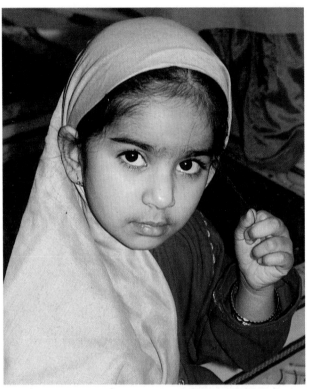

It is the soul and not the body the soul lives in, that is the real person

'We created Man from the essence [of clay], We made out of that lump bones and clothed the bones with flesh; then We developed out of it another creature. At length you will die; and on Judgement Day you will be raised up.'

(surah 23:12–16)

'O Humanity, be mindful of your duty to God, who created you from a single soul, and from it created its mate, and from the two spread widely many men and women.'

(surah 4:1)

THE SOUL

Human beings are the highest physical creations of God, with the most capacity for shaping their own futures. They have freedom of will and action. Like other species, they can reproduce themselves from their own living cells. However, although human bodies are living, they are not conscious.

Muslims believe that God gave to each reproduced human form a quite distinct individual soul, called **ruh**. It is the soul, not the body the soul lives in, that is the real person.

SOIL

Muslims believe that all human beings are descended from one original couple, Adam and Eve, who were created by God. The word 'Adam' means 'soil' or 'dust', and 'Eve' comes from a word meaning 'living'.

Our physical bodies are made of 'clay'; the human aspect totally dependent on humus (the living part of the soil). Bodies are what they eat. If they cease to take in matter from the soil, they die.

GOD'S IMAGE

Muslims do not believe that God made humans to look like Him. There is no reason to suppose that the creator of the universe should have the form of *any* of the things He has created.

Muslims do not believe that humans have descended by evolution from apes or that both were descended from the same ancestor. Apes were created in their own image, and still exist, as apes. Humans were created as humans. The modern 'theory of evolution' is only a theory, and not a proved fact.

THE TIME SPAN

Muslims believe that God allows each soul to inhabit a body for a certain time, until it is taken away again. They believe that each soul remains the soul of that individual person, and does not travel into the body of another human, or animal, or live again on earth in a future reincarnation.

Although corpses break down after death, a person's soul and body will eventually be reunited when the Hour of Judgement comes.

'Some say, "What is there but our life in this world?; we live and we die, and only Time destroys us." In this they have no knowledge, it is merely their own guesswork. God gives you life, then causes you to die; then He will assemble you again on the Day of Judgement. There is no doubt of this – but most people have not arrived at this knowledge.'

(surah 45:24)

ALL EQUAL

During earthly life we all have different sets of experiences. Some are fortunate, others are not. Life is not a purposeless wander towards death, or a game. It is a test, in deadly earnest.

Because humans have conscious souls, they have the great ability to love and be kind – or to hate and be destructive. This means that humans do not remain equal.

The spiritual faculties of human beings raise them above the animal kingdom, and make them responsible for it. Some humans behave so badly, they sink below the level of the animal kingdom.

'We have honoured the sons of Adam, provided them with transport on land and sea, given them for food things good and pure, and conferred on them special favours above a great part of Our creation.'

(surah 17:70)

KHILAFAH – STEWARDSHIP

Muslims believe that Allah not only granted consciousness and a sense of responsibility to human beings, He also required them to be the guardians of the planet on His behalf as His deputies or **khalifahs**.

Muslims make a deliberate effort to look after and make the most of His wonderful creations (see page 92). Muslims accept the duties of caring for other people, especially the less fortunate; of sustaining all the earth's species; and of working for the proper use of the earth's resources.

'Be steadfast in prayer and regular in charity; and whatever good you send forth from your souls, you will find it with God; for God sees all that you do.'

(surah 2:110)

THINGS TO DO

▶ Read the passages in this unit from the Qur'an. What do they teach about the beginning, lifetime and end of humans?

▶ What is meant by 'khalifah'. How could you be a khalifah in your own life?

THINKING POINTS

● Think about the life cycle of a physical body. How is it kept alive? What happens to it after death? Is any part of it not dependent on the earth itself?

● How is it that a fat person can slim off pounds of weight, or an accident victim lose a limb, or a tiny baby grow into a huge adult – and yet still be the same person? What is it that makes a 'person'?

FOR YOUR FOLDERS

▶ Explain what Muslims believe about the uniqueness of each species.

▶ Why do Muslims believe the physical body is not actually the real person?

▶ What do Muslims believe happens to a person after death?

QUICK QUIZ

▶ Who was the first man?

▶ What do the names Adam and Eve mean?

▶ Why was Adam created?

▶ What was Adam made out of?

▶ What is the ruh?

▶ What is the soul's time-span?

▶ When are soul and body reunited

Some people become aware of the closeness of God and are chosen as prophets

GOD'S DUTY

Muslims believe that it is a human's duty to love and serve God, and submit to His will. Obviously, no one can do this if God does not let them know what His will is. How is human life to be guided? How can a person decide whether an action is right or wrong?

Since God is just, it is obvious that He has a duty to reveal His will to us, and give us a code of conduct by which to live.

Risalah is this channel of communication between God and humanity. A **rasul** is a prophet. A message communicated directly to a prophet's mind in this way is called a revelation.

THE MESSENGERS

Muslims do not believe that the Prophet was the first to receive such revelations, or that he was the founder of their religion. God Himself is the founder, and long before the Prophet had ever lived He had communicated with many other people.

Muslims believe the first prophet was the first man, Adam, and that between Adam and Muhammad there had been thousands of other messengers of whom at least 24 are mentioned in the Qur'an. In other words, God has always revealed Himself to those who had the necessary spirituality to understand His messages.

The messengers did not choose to do this work. On the contrary, God chose them – much to the surprise and reluctance of some of them! God did not pick the great and famous, the wealthy or influential – but those who lived virtuous and honourable lives.

The five major prophets before Muhammad were **Adam**, **Nuh** (Noah), **Ibrahim** (Abraham), **Musa** (Moses) and **Isa** (Jesus).

> *'God chooses for Himself whoever He pleases, and guides to Himself those who turn [to Him].'*
>
> (surah 42:13)

THE SEAL

The Prophet Muhammad holds a very special place for Muslims, because he was the last of the long succession of prophets to whom specific revelations were made. He was the final seal of all who had gone before.

THE BOOKS

The holy books include the

- **Sahifa** – scrolls given to Ibrahim
- **Tawrah** – the revelation to Musa (the Torah)
- **Zabur** – the psalms given to Dawud (David)
- **Injil** – the teachings given to Isa (the Gospels).

Each of these was originally a complete revelation, but Muslims believe the books and teachings were not preserved properly. Some, like the Sahifa, were lost completely.

Others, like the Zabur, Tawrah and Injil, were changed in various ways. Bits were left out and forgotten, and many additions made.

Muslims do not believe that the Injil is the same thing as the Gospels now kept by the Christian Church, or that the Tawrah is the same thing as the present Torah of the Jews.

If you extracted all the specific teachings from God and laid aside all the comments, opinions, notes, legends and so on that were added afterwards by editors, you would get nearer to the truth, but even then Muslims do not accept that all the sayings are genuine.

'Those who say "God does not send down [revelations] to humans", do not judge rightly. Who sent down the Book which Musa brought – a light and guidance for humanity? But you have made it into [separate] books for show, and you conceal much of its contents.'

(surah 6:91)

The Jewish and Christian scriptures are therefore accepted by Muslims only as edited versions of the revelations, altered according to the beliefs or motives of the various writers and editors involved, and the guidance given in them – since it is no longer in its original form – cannot be relied on.

THE QUR'AN

What the Prophet saw and heard was quite different. It was the *complete guidance*, the last 'revealed book', the eternal book giving guidance for human lives. Muslims call it **Umm-ul-Kitab** or 'Mother of Books' – meaning the greatest of all books.

Therefore, the revelations given to the Prophet were to be preserved exactly and were intended to put right any errors in previous holy books, and set the standard by which to judge all these earlier revelations – a message not just for Arabs but for the whole of humanity.

All the sections of the Qur'an were put into writing during the Prophet's lifetime and carefully checked on numerous occasions. The Qur'an still exists today in its original form, unaltered.

THE ORDER

The order of the surahs in the Qur'an is not the order in which the Prophet received them during his ministry. Muslims believe that the order set by God was specifically told to the Prophet towards the end of his life. Tradition states that in order to keep a check the Prophet was made to repeat all the surahs to the angel Jibril, in the order God required, once every year, and just before he died he had to repeat it twice.

So, to Muslims, the Qur'an is itself the greatest of miracles, the exact message of God, and the words must never be altered. That is why they try to make all believers study it in Arabic, the original language, and not from a translation – since all translations differ, and none can give the exact meaning of the original.

'O people of the Book, you have no ground to stand on unless you stand fast by the Law, the Gospel, and all the revelation that has come to you from God.'

(surah 5:68)

THINKING POINTS

- Is the fact that certain people feel themselves to be called by God in fact a good proof of the existence of God? Why?

- How could you use the examples and messages of the prophets to build up a picture of God? Do you think the qualities and values of the prophets tell us anything about the things God values?

FOR YOUR FOLDERS

▶ Explain why Muslims feel the traditions given to the Jewish and Christian scriptures to be unreliable. How is the Qur'an thought to be different from these other scriptures?

▶ Explain why it is important to a Muslim:

  a that a copy of the Qur'an is made exactly, with no alterations, not even of one letter; and

  b that the Qur'an should be studied and learnt in Arabic, its original language.

FOR DISCUSSION

▶ Should there be new prophets for every generation, or in every geographical location – or should people have the faith to accept and rely on that which has already been written?

17 ISA (JESUS)

DISCUSSING ISA (PEACE BE UPON HIM)

Interviewer: Tell me, Hassan, is it true that Muslims believe in Jesus?
Hassan: Yes, it is true, but not in the same way that a Christian does. We find it quite amusing, really, that Isa does not seem to be reverenced as much in a so-called Christian country as he is by Muslims.
Interviewer: What do you mean?
Hassan: Because of the revelations in the Qur'an about Isa, no one would ever mock him, or doubt his miraculous birth, or treat his name lightly. You will never hear the name of Isa used as bad language by a Muslim.
Interviewer: You believe in the virgin birth of Isa?
Hassan: Certainly. Maryam is actually mentioned in the Qur'an more times than in the New Testament. The accusation that Maryam was not a virgin is blasphemy to a Muslim. Such a charge is bad enough when made against any woman, but to make it against Maryam brings into ridicule the power of God.
Interviewer: Why?
Hassan: God can do whatever He likes – there is no limit to His power.
Interviewer: And yet you don't believe that Isa was the son of God, do you?
Hassan: Only in the sense that we are all God's children. Isa is not God, but one of us, our brother. Don't forget that Adam had no father or mother, so his birth was an even greater miracle – yet no one claims he was equal with God or part of a Trinity.
Interviewer: Do you believe in the crucifixion?
Hassan: Yes, there was a crucifixion, but we do not think it was Isa who died. We think that God took him up to Heaven without dying at all, the Ascension. We do not believe that God allowed the Jews or the Romans to kill him.
Interviewer: So you don't accept that he died to save people from their sins?
Hassan: Certainly not. We reject this. It seems to us as though Christians might think that they will only be forgiven because Isa has 'paid the price' for them. We do not accept this. God is the Compassionate, the Merciful – how can He be wheedled, or persuaded, or bribed to become more merciful than He already is? To us, such a thought is blasphemy. It means that the person pleading or sacrificing is more merciful than God! How can that be so? We say that if we turn to God for forgiveness, He will surely forgive us – He is our dear Lord. This is what Isa himself taught in the Parable of the Prodigal Son

(Luke 15:11–32). But if we die unrepentant, then we will have deserved our punishment. Justice requires it. That is why we have free will – to accept or reject God as we choose. But we must pay the penalty ourselves. We cannot be bought off. How can God send Himself to earth and then kill Himself to save us? That does not make sense to us.
Interviewer: But what about the teachings of Isa? Don't you accept them, if you believe in him, as you say?
Hassan: Yes, of course; but we believe the Christian holy books were not written by Isa himself but by disciples who misunderstood his relationship to God, and were then altered by editors. If there is a clear revelation in the Qur'an, we prefer that – because it is straight from God. We think Saint Paul taught things about Isa that Isa never claimed for himself.
Interviewer: One of the sayings of Isa is *'No man cometh to the Father except by Me'* (John 14:16).
Hassan: There is also the saying *'No man can come to me except it were given to him by the Father'* (John 6:65). This may perhaps have been the original saying, which was altered by a later editor.
Interviewer: I think I see what you mean.
Hassan: I like to read the prayer of Isa best – *'Our Father, who art in Heaven'* – that is pure Islam. Our Father. We worship God *with* Isa. He is our brother. You know Islam means 'submission to God'. That is how Isa was – the most pure and holy Muslim, and one of the greatest prophets before Muhammad.

ISA SUBMITS TO GOD

'She said – "How, O Lord, shall I have a son, when no man has ever touched me?"

He said – "Thus: God creates what He wills. He says no more than 'Be!' and it is so." '

(surah 3:47)

'His name shall be Messiah Isa, the son of Maryam, held in honour in this world and the next; one of those who are nearest to God.'

(surah 3:45)

'And they crucified him not, but only one who was made to appear to them like Isa… They did not really kill Isa, but God took him up to Himself.'

(surah 4:157–8)

'Isa said: – "I have come to you with wisdom, in order to make clear some of the points about which you argue. Fear God, and obey me – for God is my Lord and your Lord. Worship Him. That is the straight path." '

(surah 43:63–4)

'We sent Isa the son of Maryam, confirming the Law that had come before him; We sent him the gospel, wherein was guidance and light, and a confirmation of the Law, a guidance and a warning to those who fear God.'

(surah 5:46; see also surah 57:26–27, surah 2:87)

ISA THE HEALER

'Isa, on whom be peace, saw a blind leper who was saying: "Praise be to God, who has saved me from so many things." "From what are you free?" Isa asked him. "Spirit of God," said the wretched man, "I am better off than those who do not know God." "You speak truly," said Isa. "Stretch out your hand." He was instantly restored to health, through the power of God. And he followed Isa and worshipped with him.'

(story preserved by the Muslim teacher al-Ghazzali, from *Elephant in the Dark* by Idries Shah, Octagon Press, 1978)

THINKING POINT

- How is it possible that some people do suffer because of the sins of others? Is it possible for one person to pay the penalty for another?

FOR YOUR FOLDERS

▶ Why do Muslims not believe that Isa's death could have been a sacrifice for the sins of humanity, or that Isa should be called Saviour or Redeemer?

THINGS TO DO

▶ Copy out these statements and tick the ones Muslims would agree with:
- Isa was miraculously born of the Virgin Maryam.
- Isa was God made man.
- Isa was the expected Messiah.
- Isa died on the cross.
- Isa died to save us from our sins.
- Everyone pays the penalty for their own sins.
- Isa ascended into heaven.
- Isa was *'of one substance with the Father, by whom all things were made'* (from a Christian creed).
- Isa was a pure prophet, the miracle worker.
- Isa prayed to *'Our Father in Heaven'*
- Isa could have said, *'Not my will, O God, but Thine be done.'*
- Isa could have said, *'No man can come to the Father except through me'.*

CAUSE AND EFFECT

Every single thing in our universe is the effect of something that caused it – but the causes are not always instantly obvious. Suppose you did not know what an acorn was, and had never seen an oak tree. You could not possibly guess what the acorn would become. If you saw the tree, you could never guess what it had come from.

The whole universe is like that. We might happen to know a little bit about it, but we don't know much.

Think about yourself – who would have guessed that the whole 'programme' or 'package' that is you was once just a microscopic 'seed' and a 'seed receiver' in two separate bodies? And who knows how your 'self' – and the stage of life after this one – will compare to this?

Muslims believe the whole creation was caused by God. If it had no cause, it would never have existed.

AL-QADR

Muslims believe that Allah is responsible for even the minutest details of human life, and knows everything in the greatest detail. He knows how many leaves are on a tree, or how many hairs are on your head.

Everything that exists or happens is an expression of His will, everything has a purpose and meaning, and all things are part of His plan for His creation, and are under His control.

Al-Qadr (destiny) really means all that is ordained by God. There cannot really be such a thing as a chance or random event.

> *'Whatever God grants to humanity out of His mercy, no one can withhold; and what He withholds no one can grant apart from Him. He is the [source of] Power, the All-Knowing.'*
>
> (surah 35:2)

> *'If God lay the touch of trouble on you, no one can deliver you from it save God alone; and if He wills good for you, no one can prevent His blessing. He confers them on His servants as He chooses.'*
>
> (surah 10:107)

We do not know our destiny and have the free will to choose

INSTINCT AND MIND

All humans are given an instinct (called **nafs**) which can be an influence for good or for evil. Everyone has the freedom to choose, and the part that makes the choice is the mind.

Muslims believe that God does not control anyone's mind by force, but has allowed *free will*.

Nothing can happen without the will and knowledge of Allah. He knows the present, past and future of all His created beings. Our destiny is already known. Whether we will obey or disobey His will is known to Him – but that does not affect our freedom of will. Humans do not know what their destiny is, and have the free will to choose whatever course they will take.

> *'On the Day of Judgement no step of a servant of God shall slip until he has answered concerning four things:*
> *– his body and how he used it*
> *– his life and how he spent it*
> *– his wealth and how he earned it*
> *– his knowledge and what he did with it.'*
>
> (Hadith)

FREE WILL

Freedom of choice brings enormous responsibility. It would be quite possible for God to make us all into robots, but He does not do so. We may choose how to act, how to respond to each challenge. It is usually quite obvious whether a particular deed is good or bad, and Muslims believe that if we deliberately choose to act *against* our consciences and do evil instead of good, then it is our own fault if one day we have to pay the penalty.

The devil and his followers are always eager to gain control of a person's mind, so people should be on the alert at all times. If we do not control our instincts, we are in grave danger – for the path towards evil is always attractive and tempting, and the path towards good is usually hard and full of difficult decisions and sacrifices.

POINTLESS SUPERSTITION

Since God alone is the source of benefit or harm, it is pointless superstition to turn to anything else for protection or help. This wrongfully suggests that lucky charms and such-like have more power than God. (See page 133.)

DANGERS OF FATALISM

If God knows in advance everything a person might do, how can Muslims believe they have freedom of choice and free will?

Islam does *not* teach Fatalism – which is rather the basis of materialistic science. Fatalism suggests that people are helpless, and so it weakens their sense of responsibility.

Since God allowed humans to have conscious minds and the freedom of making choices, Muslims believe our choices are not meaningless but are the very things on which we will face our future judgement.

If there was no possibility for making free choices, there would have been no point in Allah sending messengers or prophets.

'It is not poverty which I fear for you, but that you might come to desire the world as others before you desired it and it might destroy you as it destroyed them.'

(Hadith)

ALLAH'S RULES

- He imposes on no soul a duty or test beyond his or her ability.
- Whoever does good or evil does it for the benefit or harm of their own souls.
- Allah does not force changes on people; He waits until they change themselves.
- No one will bear our burden for us but ourselves.
- No one may intercede with Allah for us on our behalf.

FOR YOUR FOLDERS

▶ Muslims do not believe it would be a better universe if we did not have free will, or the dangerous possibility of making wrong choices. Do you? Give reasons for your answer.

▶ Obeying without question might be unreasonable or even dangerous. Can you think of examples when it might be? In what ways do Muslims consider trust to be vital in their relationship with God?

THINKING POINTS

The Big Bang Theory is the belief that the whole universe started expanding when a colossal first atom exploded.

- What was this atom?
- Where was it?
- How did it get there?
- Why did it explode?

Muslims believe the causes were already there.

THINGS TO DO

▶ At first sight the doctrine of al-Qadr looks like a fatalistic belief. Argue the case that this cannot be so in Islam.

THE TEST

All Muslims believe in **akhirah** – life after death. They accept that human life is divided into two sections – each individual's life on earth, and the eternal life that follows. Since our earthly lives are short by comparison to the eternal, it is obvious that eternal life is far more important.

If people wander aimlessly through this life, they are wasting it. Muslims consider that life on earth has a very important purpose – it is a test. We may be born

- wealthy or poor
- healthy or sick
- strong or weak
- beautiful or ugly
- generous or mean

It is a complete waste of time moaning about our circumstances. We do not know the reasons why, or what we are intended to learn. We can be bitter or resentful, or we can accept. To a Muslim it is all God's will.

Muslims believe that nothing can happen that is not God's will, and nothing is ever an accident – but we have been given the free will to react to the things that happen to us in all sorts of ways. It is up to us to choose.

IS THERE A 'POINT' TO IT?

If – God can do anything He wishes, He could easily have made everyone exactly the same. Why didn't He?
If – wealth is not a reward for the rich, and poverty is not a punishment for the poor;
If – sickness and misfortune are not punishments either;
Is God unfair?

WHAT IS IT THAT IS TESTED?

- Our characters – are we greedy, selfish, lacking in sympathy, mean, spiteful or cowardly?
- Our reaction to misfortune – are we frightened, full of complaint, a burden to others, depressed?
- Our reaction to good fortune – are we selfish, conceited, arrogant, proud, miserly?
- Our way of life – are we dishonest, disrespectful, hurtful, unforgiving?

GOD KNOWS

'A poor man owned nothing but a fine white stallion. One day, he found his paddock empty. "What terrible fortune!" said his friends. "Maybe yes, and maybe no," he said.

The next day the stallion returned, fetching with him five beautiful wild mares. "What wonderful fortune!" said his friends, amazed.

"Maybe yes, and maybe no," he said.

The next day his only son tried to tame a mare, and was thrown down. He broke his legs and became a cripple. "What dreadful fortune," sighed the friends.

"Maybe yes, and maybe no."

The king came by, and took away all the young men of the village to fight in the army – all except the cripple. The army lost, and all the young men were killed…'

(a Muslim story)

THE RECORD

Muslims believe that:

- All people earn, or are responsible for, their own salvation.
- How we respond to our tests is our own business, and by our lives and actions we earn our place in the next life.
- Whatever we do will have a direct effect on ourselves alone.
- Our actions can neither help nor harm God, they only help or harm us.
- Everything we do or think is known by our guardian angels, who keep the full record on which our judgement will be based. This record is to show us, not God – who already knows everything.
- God cannot be bought or bribed.

  'Your good actions will benefit only you, while evil harms only the person who does it.'

  (surah 41:46, 45:15)

'Every person's judgement is fastened round his neck; on the Day we will bring forth a book which shall be shown wide open. Read your book; you have no need of anyone but yourself to work out your account.'

(surah 17:13–14)

JUDGEMENT

There is a time limit for everyone. Muslims believe that the test takes place in this earthly life, and when it is over and they face God, it will too late to beg forgiveness.

After death comes judgement. No one else's love or sorrow can free another from their sins. All people stand alone before God, answerable only for themselves.

In every generation God sent witnesses or messengers to stir consciences and tell people what to do. If they chose to reject the warnings and not believe in them – when it was so obviously right to reject unkind and depraved living and do their best to live well – then that was their free choice from their free will.

Just as the people they hurt had to bear the consequences of their unkindness in this life, they must accept the consequences of their actions in the next life.

All a person has to do to gain God's forgiveness is to ask for it while there is still time, in this life. But if the person is determined to persist in evil and refuses to repent and accept God's mercy, then hell is the inevitable consequence.

'On no soul does God place a burden greater than it can bear.'

(surah 2:286, 23:62)

'One burdened soul shall not bear the burden of another. And even if the heavy-laden [soul] should cry out for its burden [to be carried] not one bit of it shall be carried, not even by the next of kin.'

(surah 35:18)

'It is the Day when one soul shall be powerless to plead for another.'

(surah 82:19)

'To God belongs the mystery of the Heavens and the Earth. The Decision of the Hour [of Judgement] [will be swift as] the twinkling of an eye, or even quicker: for God has the power over all things.'

(surah 16:77)

'At evening, do not expect to live till morning, at morning, do not expect to live till evening. Take from your health for your illness, and from your life for your death.'

(Hadith)

TALKING POINT

- If there is a God, should He interfere with the laws of nature to protect people from such things as floods, earthquakes and famines? Why do you think God does not protect humans from such things?

FOR YOUR FOLDERS

▶ What is the Muslim attitude to fate and free will? How does the way you exercise free will affect your future eternal life?

▶ Choose two of the passages from the Qur'an or Hadith. Write them out and explain what you think each of them means.

▶ People in despair often cry out 'Why is this happening to me?' or 'What have I done to deserve this?' How might a Muslim answer these questions?

FOR DISCUSSION

▶ It is harder to pass the test of life if one is born fortunate with little hardship to face.

▶ People who believe in God should accept everything without question, and do nothing about it.

▶ It would be a better universe if we did not have free will, or the dangerous possibility of making wrong choices.

'The companions of the right hand shall ask of the wretched – "What has cast you into hell fire?" They will say, "We were not of those who prayed, nor those who fed the poor, and we wasted our time with empty arguments, and we rejected as a lie the Day of Reckoning – till we were forced to accept the Reality."'

(surah 74:39–47)

Since Muslims believe they will be accountable after death, it affects the way they behave while living. It creates a sense of God-consciousness (taqwa, see pages 10, 82–3), and helps them to live decent and generous lives on earth. If they act in a cruel, depraved or selfish manner, they know they will not escape God's punishment on the Day of Judgement.

BELIEFS

- The knowledge that we will die makes humans different from all other animals.

- Death is not the end of existence.

- Once people die, they cast off the limitations of the body, and awareness is greatly increased.

- Even those who did not believe in God or life after death will have to accept it once they become aware of it.

- Unbelievers will beg for a second chance, to return to life and try again, but it will not be allowed.

BARZAKH

For those who die before the Day of Judgement, Muslims believe that Azra'il, the angel of death, takes their souls to **barzakh**, a state of waiting that comes between the moment of death and the Day. The word 'barzakh' means 'partition' or 'barrier' and it may not be crossed by those who wish to go back and warn others.

'When death comes, one may say "O my Lord, send me back [to life] in order that I might put right the things I neglected [and did wrong]." By no means! This is no more than an excuse. Before them is a Barrier until the Day of Resurrection.'

(surah 23:99–100)

THE END OF THE WORLD

Descriptions of the end of the world in the Qur'an are vivid. There will be a blinding light, the sky will be cut through, the moon shall cease to appear and the stars be scattered, the mountains shall be reduced to dust, the oceans boil over with explosions of fire…all the contents of the tombs will come back to life, and people will be asked what kept them away from their God? (See surahs 81 and 82.)

THE REWARD

The reward will be paradise, a state of joy and beauty, happiness and peace. The Qur'an describes it symbolically as a green garden, full of foliage and flowers and the sound of water and birdsong.

'In gardens of delight [they shall enjoy honour and happiness] facing each other on thrones: a cup will be passed to them from a clear-flowing fountain – delicious to drink and free from intoxication or headaches: and beside them will be innocent women, restraining their glances, with eyes wide [with wonder and beauty].'

(surah 37:43–8, see also surah 38:52)

'They will hear no unworthy talk there, or any mention of sin, but only the cry "Peace, peace".'

(surah 56:25–6, see also surahs 43:70, 48:5, 56:17–25)

The vision is of peace and purity, contentment and love.

THE PUNISHMENT

Hell, or **jahannam**, is the reward for unbelievers. It is also described symbolically, in lurid terms – a horrible place of torment under the earth's crust, a place of scorching fire, where the damned will be chained amid hot winds, boiling water and black smoke (see surahs 14:16–17, 38:55–8, 56:42–4, etc.).

Many people find the idea of God punishing evil people hard to reconcile with His mercy – but no one will go to jahannam unless absolutely determined to do so.

'I warn you of the flaming fire. None shall be cast into it but the most wretched, who has called the Truth a lie and turned his back.'

(surah 92:14–16)

'If God punished people according to what they deserved, He would not leave on [earth] a single living thing.'

(surah 16:61)

THE AFTER-LIFE

All the descriptions of the after-life, including such things as youth, beauty, dress, food, and so on are intended to be understood symbolically since in eternal life the faithful are not subject to physical limitations at all.

It is a completely different dimension, and we are created afresh in a form beyond our knowledge. Marital and family bonds do not necessarily continue, since individual eternal souls outside time are not bound by the relationships that belong to the world of time. Old relationships of the present world will be dissolved, and each soul will stand on its own merits.

'When the trumpet is blown, there will be no relationships between them that day, nor will they ask after another.'

(surah 23:101)

'We have decreed Death to be in the midst of you, and We will not be prevented from changing your forms and creating you [again] in [forms] you know not.'

(surah 56:60–1)

It is impossible for the real nature of heaven and the presence of God to be understood by human minds with their limited awareness, until the time comes.

'In Paradise, I prepare for the righteous believers what no eye has ever seen, no ear has ever heard, and what the deepest mind could never imagine.'

(Hadith, see also surah 32:17)

THINKING POINTS

- Is the idea of hell with its punishments compatible with the Muslim idea of God's compassionate justice? Could God be called just if there were no punishments, only rewards?

- Is it possible that certain people could become so depraved or evil that they could never be forgiven?

- Is belief in life after death a weakness or a strength?

- Does the burning fire suggest eternal punishment, or simply that the evil will be burnt up and cease to exist?

FOR YOUR FOLDERS

▶ Explain the idea of the Day of Judgement, and the ways in which this belief can:

  a alter the character of an individual

  b affect the way people treat each other, and

  c affect the way a Muslim practises faith throughout an average day.

▶ What do the passages from the Qur'an given in this unit and the last unit reveal about

  a individual life after death

  b judgement

  c the future state of existence?

▶ Explain why all descriptions of paradise and hell can only be symbolic, not literal.

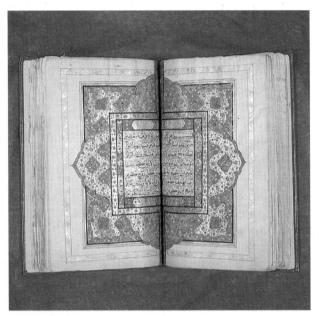

The art of calligraphy – an eighteenth-century handwritten Qur'an from North India

SOME COMMANDMENTS

- Show kindness to your parents, particularly in their old age.
- Do not be either wasteful or mean – all your possessions belong to God.
- Do not commit adultery.
- Do not kill, except for just cause.
- Always keep your promises and agreements.
- In business and daily life be honest.
- Avoid gossip and slander.
- Whatever your life, remain humble.
- Do not take advantage of poor people or orphans.

(from surah 17)

The Qur'an has 114 surahs, or chapters. All except one of them begins *'In the name of Allah, the Most Merciful, the Most Kind'*.

The first surah in the Qur'an – the **Fatihah** or the opening – is given on page 56. It was not the first message revealed to Muhammad but he was told to put it first. The first revelation the Prophet received was the first part of surah 96, and the second was number 74.

Each surah is named after some striking incident or word in it, so some have very strange names, like the Spider, the Bee or the Cow. The Cow is actually about religious duties, divorce laws, and rules governing warfare!

THE EFFECT

The Qur'an was intended to be heard, and Muslims believe that blessings flow from the sound of it. From the beginning it made a profound impression on those who heard and believed. Some were overwhelmed with fear and trembling; warriors would burst into tears; some people would fall into a state in which they lost all consciousness of the world around them.

Many people, both men and women, learned all the surahs by heart and many still do. Such a person is called a **hafiz** (plural huffaz).

Others wrote the messages down on pieces of paper, date leaves, shoulder blades, ribs, bits of leather, and tablets of white stone.

Muslims were taught to recite it, and it must still be learnt in Arabic. Although it can now be read in at least 40 languages, all translations lose part of the inspiration and meaning, and are not treated with the same respect as the original.

THE QUR'AN COMPILED

Muslims were involved in much persecution and warfare because of their beliefs, and after one battle about 70 huffaz died. The Prophet's companion Abu Bakr began to worry about how the accuracy of the recitations would be checked after the Prophet's death. On the advice of the Prophet's other close companion Umar, he asked the Prophet's secretary **Zaid ibn Thabit** to make a special book of all the revelations, in the order the Prophet had taught him. This was done in the Prophet's lifetime.

Zaid, who was himself a hafiz, did not attempt to shape the book into a connected sequence, or fill in gaps, or suppress details not flattering to the Prophet. No editorial comment was added to the text, nothing removed, nothing altered. Zaid accepted that every word was the word of God, the belief shared by every Muslim today.

Au Bakr passed this volume to Umar, and it was kept by Umar's daughter **Hafsah**, who had been one of the Prophet's wives. Under the next caliph **Uthman**, the Qur'an began to be recited in different dialects, and this created confusion for new converts whose mother tongue was not Arabic. Uthman prohibited the variant readings and made sure that copies of Hafsah's book were sent to the chief places as the standard text.

Two of these very early copies still exist today, one in Istanbul (Turkey) and one in Tashkent (Uzbekistan). Modern technology has now taken over – the Tashkent original has recently been photocopied.

The Qur'an is always treated with respect

THE QUR'AN HONOURED

The Qur'an is considered to be so holy that Muslims treat it with enormous respect. While it is being read:

- you must not speak
- you must not eat or drink
- you must not make a noise
- you must not touch it unnecessarily.

Before reading or touching it:

- you must wash carefully, or take a bath
- you must be in the right frame of mind
- if you are a woman, you should not be having a period.

When not in use, it should be

- placed high up, so that nothing is put on top of it
- kept covered and free from dust.

During use, it is often placed on a special stool called a **kursi**, so that it is handled no more than necessary. It is never allowed to touch the ground.

The art of calligraphy (or beautiful writing) grew up because it was an honour to copy the Qur'an, and this task was done as beautifully as possible.

THINGS TO DO

▶ If possible, listen to a tape recording of the Qur'an being recited. Do not do this surrounded by people who will laugh at its strangeness. Try to listen alone, for at least five minutes. Make a note of your impressions.

▶ Make a decorative card or poster, using the laws of surah 17.

▶ Explain why Muslims believe the Tashkent Qur'an (and all others) to be the exact words revealed to the Prophet.

QUICK QUIZ

▶ What is a hafiz?

▶ What is the Fatihah?

▶ What is a kursi for?

▶ Why is calligraphy important to a Muslim?

▶ Who compiled the Qur'an in writing?

▶ Which woman kept the book?

▶ Where could you now find an original copy?

▶ Where is the Qur'an kept when not in use?

FOR YOUR FOLDERS

▶ In what ways do Muslims show their deep respect for the Qur'an by

a their behaviour, and

b the way they take care of the book?

'He is not a believer who eats his fill while his neighbour is hungry.'

'Do not shut your bag, or God will hold back His blessings from you.'

'The warrior who truly fights for God's cause is he who looks after a widow or a poor person.'

'If you think of God, you will find Him there before you.'

(Hadiths)

Hadiths, often referred to as 'traditions', are the recorded words, actions and instructions of the Prophet Muhammad. The word 'Hadith' comes from the verb 'haddatha', meaning 'to recount' or 'to tell'. After Muhammad's death, many collections of reports about him appeared, accounts of things he had said or done. These are held in enormous respect, but are quite separate from the Qur'an.

There are actually two sorts of Hadiths – sacred and prophetic.

The Prophetic Hadiths are the wise words and teachings of the Prophet himself, who is loved and respected because of his outstanding character, and devotion to God and humanity. His sayings reveal him as a man of enormous compassion and kindness, and great practical wisdom.

The Sacred Hadiths, or **Hadith Qudsi**, are so named because Muslims believe their authority is traced back beyond the Prophet to God Himself. They are further insights that God revealed to the Prophet but which were not part of the Qur'an. Muslims hold these sayings in very great reverence.

SOURCES

The two chief sources of reliable Hadiths are the very early collections made by the scholars Muhammad ibn Isma'il al-Bukhari, which lists 2762 traditions, and Abul Husayn Muslim ibn al-Hajjaj, which lists another 4000. The other chief collections are Abu Dawud, Tirmidhi, Ibn Majah and an-Nisai.

The earliest biographies of the Prophet (i.e. stories of his life) were made by Zuhri and Ibn Ishaq. Zuhri knew the Prophet's scholarly wife Aishah, and Ibn Ishaq was Zuhri's disciple.

When Muslims want guidance over a particular course of action – especially in today's complicated society – if there is no clear answer in the Qur'an, they turn to the Hadiths to support their actions, or decide their differences.

However, by the third century after the Prophet there were some 600 000 Hadiths in circulation, and many of these – although no doubt well-intentioned – were not genuine. One pious inventor, for example, admitted claiming the Prophet to be the source of no less than 4000 sayings of his own! This kind of fraud caused so much confusion and was taken so seriously that the writer was executed for his deception (see page 141).

THE CHAINS

Muslims base their judgement of the reliability of the Hadiths on the reputations of the people through whom the quotations can be traced back to someone who had actually been with the Prophet. Each saying is transmitted along a particular chain. The most famous transmitters of Hadiths were the Prophet's wives Aishah and Umm Salamah, and his companions Anas ibn Malik, Ibn Umar and Abu Hurairah.

HADITH QUDSI

Hadith Qudsi are messages from God communicated to the Prophet through revelations or dreams, but which the Prophet explained using his own words or expressions. In other words, the meaning is from God, but the words are those of the Prophet. They are not part of the Qur'an.

On the whole, the Sacred Hadiths are concerned with various aspects of belief, worship and conduct, and not the more practical aspects of everyday living, which are dealt with in the Prophetic Hadiths.

The style is usually very moving, either commands direct from Allah to His servants, or through conversations with them.

INTERPRETATIONS

When a Hadith does not seem to 'ring true' with the general principles of Islam, or contradicts the revelation of the Qur'an, then the memory or understanding of the transmitter could be at fault.

Scholars examine the chain of transmitters very carefully to establish how reliable a Hadith is. Even the most close companions could make a mistake – and some were occasionally corrected by the Prophet's scholarly wife Aishah.

The companions of the Prophet went to enormous lengths to check the Hadiths, and were reluctant to preach them in case they accidentally falsified his words – a very different attitude from those who took pride in reeling off many hundreds 'from their memories'.

SELECTION OF HADITHS QUDSI

'I am with him when he makes mention of Me. If he draws near to Me a hand's span, I draw near to him an arm's length.'

'On the Day of Judgement Allah will say: "O son of Adam, I fell ill and you did not visit Me." The man will answer, "O Lord, how could I have visited You when You are Lord of the Worlds?" He will say – "Did you not know that My servant had fallen ill, and you did not visit him? Did you not know that if you had visited him, you would have found Me with him?"'

'A man said of another – "By Allah, Allah will never forgive him!" At this Allah the Almighty said – "Who is this who swears by Me that I will never forgive a certain person? Truly, I have forgiven him already."'

'If he has in his heart goodness to the weight of one barley corn, and has said There is no God but Me, he shall come out of hell-fire.'

'O son of Adam, so long as you call upon Me and ask of Me, I shall forgive you for what you have done.'

(from Ezzedin Ibrahim *et al.* (eds) *Forty Hadith Qudsi*, Dar al-Qur'an al-Kareem, Beirut, 1980)

'If you think of God, you will find Him there before you.' (Hadith)

THINGS TO DO

▶ Look through the Hadiths in this unit and choose any three of them. Write them out carefully on a decorated page. Explain why you choose these three in particular.

▶ Some Muslims regard the Hadiths as vital information for the guidance of life. Others regard them with caution. Explain why this is so.

FOR YOUR FOLDERS

▶ Explain what is meant by the word 'Hadith'. How do Muslim scholars decide which of the Hadiths are reliable and which are not?

▶ What is the difference between Prophetic Hadiths and Hadith Qudsi?

THINKING POINTS

● How far do the Hadith Qudsi bear out the suitability of giving Allah the titles 'the Compassionate, the Merciful'?

● Although Muslims treat the Hadiths with enormous respect, and refer to their teachings when a matter not covered by the Qur'an is in dispute, why do they nevertheless not regard them as sacred in the same way as the Qur'an?

All sane human beings are aware that they are not as perfect as they might be. Worship is based on this feeling – that above and beyond all humans there is a higher standard which they should be trying to reach in their lives. Those who believe in God feel that awareness of His presence changes the entire way they live – and it is a change towards good, not evil.

Turning to God in reverence, submission and wonder is called **Ibadah,** from the word **abd** meaning 'servant' or 'slave'.

WHY WORSHIP?

If someone asks 'Why should I worship God?' it is like asking 'Why should I think this is beautiful?'. You cannot really give the answer to someone who is not aware of God, or of something's beauty. You may see beauty, and be lost in wonder and appreciation of it, or you may not see it at all. It is the same with awareness of God.

THE FAILINGS

To a Muslim, pure worship has to be free of three 'sins', which are really matters of awareness:

- **kufr** – disbelief, ingratitude
- **shirk** – association
- **tughyan** – arrogance, tyranny.
- If you choose to deny God, and are not aware of His existence by reason or intuition, feel no responsibility or obligation through conscience, and no purpose in life – these are forms of kufr.
- If you question the nature of God, believe that He is not supreme or alone, or that some other entity or person shares His power and has the right to judge or forgive sins, and therefore no longer trust in God alone – these are forms of shirk.
- If you become over-confident and arrogant, so 'religious' that your presence makes others feel small or uncomfortable or stupid, become oppressive or unkind, over-do your devotions and rituals to a fanatical extent or force your own laws or opinions on people in defiance of the Law of God – these are forms of tughyan.

'God does not accept beliefs if they are not expressed in deeds; and your deeds are worthless if they do not back up your beliefs.'

(Hadith)

Turning to God in prayer

TRUE WORSHIP

Ibadah, or worship, involves a complete way of life, and consists of:

- **iman** – belief
- **amal** – action
- **ihsan** – realization.

Realization is the heart of religion, and can begin even when faith is weak. No religious leader or teacher can *make* it happen, although they do their best to guide people towards God. When faith enters the heart it causes a certain mental state – a feeling of love and gratitude towards God.

You cannot be made to feel faith, any more than you can be made to feel love. It is a matter of awareness.

When the Prophet was asked to describe ihsan, he said:

'Ihsan is to worship Allah as if you are seeing Him; for He sees you, even if you do not see Him.'

Muslims believe that we are created by God and belong to God, and to Him we shall return and give account of ourselves. Submission to God is not a passive, but a positive act of bringing all your likes and dislikes, attitudes and behaviour into harmony with God's will. The Arabic word for religion is **din**. It refers to the complete way of life from birth to life after death.

Whenever any act is done to within the limits set by Him to please God, it is worship. This covers everything – going to school or work, eating and drinking, enjoying all the pleasures of life, every aspect of our behaviour. Muslims aim to:

- reform their lives
- develop dignity
- develop patience and courage in the face of hardship and difficulty
- enjoy and appreciate God's gifts to the full
- strive for good and try to defeat evil.

In extreme cases, the Muslim faith requires that they must actually fight in order to be a witness, and perhaps even die for what they believe in.

JIHAD

Someone who dies for the faith is called a **shahid** or martyr. The fighting of a war for the sake of God is known as **jihad.**

The word 'jihad' actually means 'striving'. It implies a readiness to give up everything that you have, including your own life, for the sake of Allah, but the real jihad is the struggle to keep on the pathway of God. It means putting in your full effort, exerting yourself to the very limit in order to live correctly, and working as hard as possible to see God's principles established in society.

'Those who do not believe take their comfort in this life, and eat as cattle eat; fire will be their future abode.'

(surah 47:12)

◇

INTENTION

Muslims believe your intentions are vital. People are not all saints, and often they fall short, or fail completely. It is easy then to get depressed, and give up. Muslims believe that God judges us by our intentions or **niyyah,** and is merciful, even when we do not succeed.

Nevertheless, our intentions should be honest, and our efforts as great as possible.

TALKING POINTS

- Is living as if God existed worth as much as actually being aware of His presence? Could it be worth more? Give reasons for your answer.

- History has given many examples of tughyan – people who have believed in God and yet acted badly or oppressively. Can you think of any examples? What do you think was missing from their faith?

THINGS TO DO

▶ Draw and decorate a poster to illustrate the theme 'every act done to please God is an act of worship', or 'every sincere act is a prayer'.

FOR YOUR FOLDERS

▶ Can belief in God really alter a person's life? Is it possible to be a good religious person by belief in God alone? What is wrong with worship that does not include all the elements of iman, amal and ihsan?

▶ Explain what is meant by

a kufr   c jihad

b shirk   d niyyah.

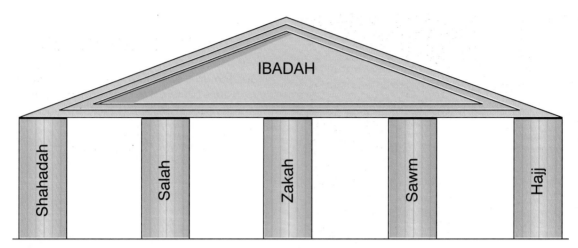

The five pillars or arkan

PILLARS

Muslims often think of the practice of their faith as a kind of temple for God held up by five pillars, called **arkan.** These are the five basic duties which all Muslims must perform. They are:

● **Shahadah** – the bearing of witness, or declaration of faith, that there is truly one Supreme Being and that Muhammad was His genuine messenger
● **Salah** – prayer five times a day
● **Zakah** – the giving of money for the poor
● **Sawm** – fasting during the month of Ramadan
● **Hajj** – making the pilgrimage to Makkah, at least once in a lifetime, if physically and financially possible.

These pillars are not the whole of Islam, but without them Islam would not really exist. If any one of the 'pillars' is weak, the whole 'building' suffers.

SHAHADAH

Shahadah is the first pillar of Islam, without which the rest is meaningless. It comes from the word 'Ash-hadu' which means 'I declare' or 'I bear witness'.

Islam does not demand a great number of complicated things to believe. No religion, in fact, has a shorter or more dramatic creed. It states, quite simply:

'Ashadu an la ilaha il-allahu wa Muhammadar rasulullah.'

'I believe there is no God but Allah, and Muhammad is the Messenger of God.'

A longer declaration of faith is the Iman-I-Mufassal – the 'faith in detail'.

'I believe in Allah,
in His angels,
in His revealed Books,
in all of His prophets,
in the Day of Judgement,
in that everything – both good and bad –
comes from Him, and
in life after death.'

THE SACRIFICE

When people make this declaration and truly believe it in their hearts, they have entered Islam. But being a good witness involves far more than words – your whole life must back up what has been declared.

Muslims lay down their lives as sacrifices to God. Your life is your most precious possession; but if you are **shahid** (ready to die for your faith) you recognize that your life does not belong to you, but to God.

THE CALL TO PRAYER

Muslims repeat the shahadah first thing on waking and last thing before sleeping. They are the first words whispered into the ears of a new-born baby, and if possible, the last words uttered to the dying.

It was with these words that Bilal, the freed Ethiopian slave, first summoned the faithful to prayer, when the call to prayer was instituted by the Prophet after his arrival in Madinah in 623 CE.

*The man who calls is the **Mu'adhin** (Muezzin); he calls the **adhan***

THE MUSLIM CALL TO PRAYER

'Allahu Akbar. (said four times)
Ash-hadu an la ilaha illallah (twice)
Ash-hadu ana Muhammadar rasulullah. (twice)
Hayya alas salah (twice)
hayya alal falah (twice)
Allahu Akbar (twice)
La ilaha illallah.' (once)

'God is Great! (said four times)
I bear witness that there is no God but God (twice)
I bear witness that Muhammad is the Prophet of God (twice)
Come to prayer! (twice)
Come to success! (twice)
God is Great! (twice)
There is no God but God. (once)

At dawn prayer this phrase is added:

'Asalatu khairum min an-naum'
'Prayer is better than sleep' (twice)

FOR DISCUSSION

▶ Should a Muslim living in a non-Muslim community make his or her religion obvious to everyone, or not?

▶ Bearing public witness is too embarrassing. Religion should be a private matter.

THINGS TO DO

▶ If possible, listen to a recording of the call to prayer. Do you have any personal reaction to the sound of it? Try to imagine it piercing the sky at the break of dawn.

▶ Make a survey of your local area to discover what visible signs of Muslim commitment there are, e.g. mosques, special shops, people in Muslim dress (for instance prayer caps, women wearing scarves and long coats, etc.).

FOR YOUR FOLDERS

▶ Make a list of the seven sections in the Iman-i-Mufassal. You could present this as a diagram, or perhaps a flower with six petals, with 'I believe in Allah' at the centre.

▶ Do you think it takes courage to make a public declaration of faith and if so in what ways? How might commitment and bearing witness affect someone's life?

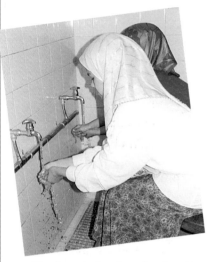

Hands washed to the wrists three times

Water snuffed into the nostrils

Face washed three times

Arms washed to the elbows three times

Head, ears and back of neck washed

Feet washed up to the ankles three times

THE DISCIPLINE

It is not easy to live all your life as a witness for God. People are very busy, they have lots of things to do. It is all too easy to forget God, and then disobey Him by either doing things that should not be done, or by not doing things that ought to be done.

Muslims believe that a deliberate conscious effort must be made, that is trained and disciplined.

THE MEANING

You can, of course, pray to God at any time and anywhere, but five times a day Muslims perform **salah,** a special kind of prayer that is not on the spur of the moment or spontaneous, but follows a deliberate preparation of the heart to receive God.

During salah, everything else in life is set aside for a few moments, and Muslims concentrate on God, praising Him, thanking Him, and asking for His forgiveness and blessing.

Salah is regarded as a duty that must be performed at work, at home, on a journey or even at war. If Muslims are too ill to stand or kneel, they can go through the motions in their hearts while sitting or lying down. It is not a burden to do this, but a great comfort.

Muslim children begin to practise salah around the age of seven; by the age of ten it is expected of them as a duty.

PREPARATION

- The place chosen should be clean (a special mat is often used).
- The mind should be attentive.
- The body and clothes should be clean.
- A man's clothes should cover his body from the navel to the knees.

- A woman's entire body should be covered, except for her face and hands.
- A woman should not be wearing make-up or perfume.
- Prayer begins with the ritual wash, or **wudu**.

WUDU

Wudu is part of the discipline. This wash is not because Muslims are dirty, but as part of the preparation for the prayer that follows. They may take a complete bath (called **ghusl)** or go through the procedure outlined below. If no water is available, as in the desert, then a wash with clean sand will do. This symbolic wash is called **tayammum.**

The wudu follows a set pattern:

1 Declaration of intent **(niyyah).** The heart must turn to God as a deliberate act.
2 The hands must be washed up to the wrists three times.
3 The mouth is rinsed three times.
4 Water is snuffed into the nostrils and blown out three times.
5 The face is washed three times.
6 The arms are washed up to the elbows three times.
7 The wet hands are passed over the top of the head and round the back of the neck. The ears are wiped out with the index finger, and the back of the neck with the thumbs.
8 The feet are washed up to the ankles three times. (See surah 5:6.)

This washing will do for more than one prayer, providing there has been no 'breaking' action in between. Wudu is 'broken' if anything has come out of the body (e.g. blood, wind or urine) or if the mind has lost conscious control (e.g. in sleep or unconsciousness). After a sexual act, or after a period, a complete bath is required.

QIBLAH

After these preparations, Muslims face the direction of Makkah, standing on a prayer mat, or alongside other Muslims in orderly fashion at the mosque.

The direction of Makkah is called **qiblah.** If Muslims are in a mosque, there is a special alcove in the qiblah wall called a **mihrab** which locates the direction. Outside a mosque, many Muslims use a small compass in order to be accurate.

QUICK QUIZ

Explain what is meant by:

- wudu
- tayammum
- qiblah
- mihrab.
- niyyah

FOR YOUR FOLDERS

- If Muslims believe that a person can pray to God at any time and in any place, why do you think they go to such trouble for formal prayers?
- Which part of the washing do you think requires the most effort, and why?
- Give an outline of what preparations you would have to make if you were a Muslim about to perform salah.

THINKING POINTS

- How would praying at regular intervals affect someone's thoughts and activities during a normal day?
- Is making prayer an obligation for all Muslims over the age of ten reasonable?

THINGS TO DO

- Draw a series of diagrams (pin-people will do) to illustrate wudu.
- Explain how the intention of salah is quite different from 'spur of the moment' prayers.
- Make a list of the sort of activities during the day that might stop a person thinking of God.

THE AIMS OF SALAH

- to bring people close to Allah
- to combine soul and body in divine worship
- to keep them from indecent, shameful and forbidden activities
- to calm down dangerous passions and master the baser instincts
- to bring a sense of peace and tranquillity
- to show equality, unity and brotherhood
- to promote patience, courage, hope and confidence
- to develop gratitude and humility
- to demonstrate obedience
- to train in cleanliness, purity and punctuality
- to develop discipline and will power
- to remind people constantly of God and His greatness
- to draw the mind away from personal worries and problems towards God – who could at any moment change the entire course of a person's destiny.

TIMES

The five set prayers have special names and are performed at special times.

- Salat-ul-Fajr – between first light of day and sunrise
- Salat-ul-Zuhr – after the sun has left the midst of the sky
- Salat-ul-Asr – between mid-afternoon and sunset
- Salat-ul-Maghrib – between sunset and the last light of day
- Salat-ul-Isha – between darkness and dawn.

Salah should *not* be said at sunrise, noon or sunset as these times have pagan associations of sun-worship.

CONGREGATION

It is not necessary to go to the mosque. Prayers can be said equally well at home, and in Muslim countries it is not uncommon to see people praying in the street, or wherever they happen to be when the call to prayer is sounded. However, Muslims feel it is preferable to pray the compulsory prayers together, whenever possible.

When Muslims pray together, they stand before God in a real sense of brotherhood, shoulder to shoulder in a line, facing the Ka'bah sanctuary in Makkah.

Muslims at prayer in the street

PRAYER START TIMES

Islamic month	Day	Calendar date	Sehri ends – Fajr starts	Sun rise	Zuhr	Asr	Sunset Maghrib	Isha
21 Muhrm	**Fri**	**1st July**	**2.55**	**4.35**	**2.56**	**6.47**	**9.40**	**11.00**
22 Muhrm	Sat	2nd July	2.55	4.35	1.15	6.47	9.40	11.00
23 Muhrm	Sun	3rd July	2.56	4.36	1.15	6.47	9.39	10.59
24 Muhrm	Mon	4th July	2.57	4.37	1.16	6.47	9.39	10.59
25 Muhrm	Tue	5th July	2.58	4.38	1.16	6.46	9.38	10.58
26 Muhrm	Wed	6th July	2.59	4.39	1.16	6.46	9.38	10.58
27 Muhrm	Thu	7th July	3.00	4.40	1.16	6.46	9.37	10.57
28 Muhrm	**Fri**	**8th July**	**3.01**	**4.41**	**1.16**	**6.46**	**9.36**	**10.56**
29 Muhrm	Sat	9th July	3.02	4.42	1.16	6.45	9.35	10.55
30 Muhrm	Sun	10th July	3.03	4.43	1.17	6.45	9.35	10.55
1 Safar	Mon	11th July	3.04	4.44	1.17	6.45	9.34	10.54
2 Safar	Tue	12th July	3.05	4.45	1.17	6.44	9.33	10.53
3 Safar	Wed	13th July	3.06	4.46	1.17	6.44	9.32	10.52
4 Safar	Thu	14th July	3.08	4.48	1.17	6.43	9.31	10.51

Prayer times for two weeks in July 1994, Hull

PRAYER MATS

Although mats to kneel on are not compulsory, they are a way of making sure you are kneeling on a clean space. Any mat will do, but Muslim prayer mats usually have a geometrical design or pictures of famous mosques. They never have designs including living things or representations of God, angels or the Prophets. When not in use they are folded up and put away. They are not used for walking on, as fireside rugs or general room decorations.

The Muslim husband is imam for his household

FOR YOUR FOLDERS

▶ What are the main aims of salah?

▶ Why do you think Muslims feel it is preferable to pray *together*?

THINKING POINTS

● Do you think it is important to make a place set aside for prayers 'special' to God? Give reasons for your answer.

● Think of your own daily programme, and try to work out what you would be doing at the Muslim prayer times.

THINGS TO DO

▶ Explain why prayer mats are used.

▶ What sorts of things are used to decorate prayer mats?

▶ Explain why prayers are not said at sunrise, sunset or noon.

▶ Design a prayer mat, or draw a poster showing a Muslim at prayer to illustrate the words 'Glory be to my great Lord'.

بِسْمِ اللهِ الرَّحْمٰنِ الرَّحِيْمِ
اَلْحَمْدُ لِلّٰهِ رَبِّ الْعٰلَمِيْنَ ۙ الرَّحْمٰنِ الرَّحِيْمِ ۙ مٰلِكِ يَوْمِ الدِّيْنِ ۙ
اِيَّاكَ نَعْبُدُ وَاِيَّاكَ نَسْتَعِيْنُ ۙ اِهْدِنَا الصِّرَاطَ الْمُسْتَقِيْمَ ۙ
صِرَاطَ الَّذِيْنَ اَنْعَمْتَ عَلَيْهِمْ ۙ غَيْرِ الْمَغْضُوْبِ عَلَيْهِمْ
وَلَا الضَّآلِّيْنَ ۙ

Bismillāhir raḥmānir raḥīm
Alḥamdu lillāhi rabbil 'ālamīn.
Arraḥmānir raḥīm.
Māliki yawmiddīn.
Iyyāka na 'budu wa iyyāka nasta'īn.
Ihdinaṣ ṣirāṭal Mustaqīm.
Ṣirāṭalladhīna an 'amta 'alaihim,
Ghairil maghdūbi 'alaihim wa lāddāllīn. (Āmīn).

(The Fatihah in Arabic)

'In the name of Allah, the Compassionate,
the Merciful.
All praise be to Allah,
the Lord of the worlds,
the Most Merciful, the Most Kind,
Master of the Day of Judgement.
You alone do we worship,
From You alone do we seek help.
Show us the [next step
along] the straight path
of those earning Your favour.
Keep us from the path of
those earning Your anger,
those who are going astray.'

(The Fatihah in English: surah l)

The **rak'ahs** are the sequence of movements, following a set pattern, that accompany salah. But the physical movements are not so important as the intention in the heart.

'Woe to those who pray, but are unmindful of their prayer, or pray only to be seen by people.'

(surah 107:4–6)

'When a person is drowsy during prayers, let him sleep until he knows what he recites.'

(Hadith)

Muslims may perform as many rak'ahs as they like, but the compulsory duties are:
- salat-ul-fajr – two rak'ahs
- salat-ul-zuhr – four rak'ahs
- salat-ul-asr – four rak'ahs
- salat-ul-maghrib – three rak'ahs
- salat-ul-isha – four rak'ahs

There are eight separate acts of devotion.

1 **Takbir** – shutting out the world and its distractions, delights and miseries. Muslims stand to attention, with their hands raised to the level of their shoulders, and acknowledge the majesty of God.

'Allahu Akbar' – *'Allah is Supreme'*

2 They place the right hand over the left on the chest, and say:

'Glory and praise to Thee, O God; blessed is Thy name and exalted is Thy majesty. There is no God other than Thee. I come, seeking shelter from Satan, the rejected one.'

Next, they recite Fatihah, the first surah of the Qur'an (the words given at the start of this unit). Now they may recite any other passage from the Qur'an, e.g.

'He is God, the One; He is the Eternal Absolute; none is born of Him, and neither is He born . There is none like Unto Him.'

(surah 112)

The Prophet recommended keeping passages short for public prayer, thinking of the difficulties faced by some of the congregation. He rebuked imams who demanded too much of people (see page 140).

3 **Ruku** – the bowing. Muslims bend their bodies forward, and place their hands on their knees. Their backs should be straight. This is to show that they respect as well as love God. They repeat three times:

'Glory be to my Great Lord,
and praise be to Him.'

4 **Qiyam** – they stand up again, and acknowledge their awareness of God with the words:

'God always hears those who praise Him.
O God, all praise be to Thee,
O God greater than all else.'

5 The humblest position is called **sujud** or **sajda**, when Muslims prostrate themselves on the ground, demonstrating that they love God more than they love themselves. They kneel, touching the ground with their forehead, nose, palms of both hands, knees and toes, and repeat three times:

'Glory to be my Lord, the Most High.
God is greater than all else.'

6 They kneel again, palms resting on the knees – a moment's rest before the next prostration. They may repeat three times:

'O my Master, forgive me.'

7 Sujud is repeated once again.

8 Muslims either repeat the rak'ah, or finish it. At the end of the sequence, they pray for the Prophet, for the faithful and the congregation, and make a plea for forgiveness of sins. The last action is to turn their heads to the right and left shoulders, to acknowledge the other worshippers and the guardian angels, with the words:

'Peace be with you, and the mercy of Allah.'

This final prayer is called the **salam**.

'The prayer said in Madinah is worth thousands of others, except that in Makkah, which is worth a hundred thousand. But worth more than all this is the prayer said in the house where no one sees but God, and which has no other object than to draw close to God.'

(Hadith)

FOR YOUR FOLDERS

▶ What is the significance of the physical activities during salah? Do you think these movements make any difference to the way a Muslim feels?

▶ Read the Hadith of the Prophet given on this page. Try to explain what you think is meant by the importance of personal prayer.

THINGS TO DO

▶ Copy out the following list of feelings, and tick which you think are expressed in Muslim prayer:

conceit

humility

pride

forgiveness

devotion

sense of togetherness

embarrassment

superiority

love

desire for forgiveness

desire to show off

putting God before self

Imam giving a sermon at Friday prayers

On Fridays Muslim men are expected to form a special congregation (**jamaah**) for the midday prayer. The word for Friday is **jumu'ah**, so sometimes these 'communal prayers' are called Salat-ul-Jumu'ah.

All adult male Muslims are expected to leave all worldly activities and attend. Women may come, but if they cannot get away from their household duties they are expected to pray at the same time, at home. In Muslim countries all shops and businesses close during the midday hour on Fridays.

> 'O ye who believe! When the call is heard for the prayer of the day of congregation, leave your trading and hasten to remember Allah!'
>
> (surah 62:9)

CONCENTRATION

When prayers are being performed, Muslims

- should not talk, or look around
- should not make any movement or noise that would draw attention to themselves, or distract others
- should not try to look too holy – which suggests superiority and foolish pride
- should concentrate on the prayer alone and let nothing else enter their minds.

If they make a major mistake it can be put right by adding extra prayers at the end.

KHUTBAH

Before the Friday prayer, the teacher or **imam** will give two short talks called the **khutbah**. These sermons are usually based on verses from the Qur'an, or traditions about Muhammad, or some subject of immediate interest to the people. Sometimes the sermons can be highly political, especially in times of persecution or suffering from tyranny.

There are no priests or paid religious leaders in Islam. The imam can be any Muslim of decent character who:

- has good knowledge of the faith
- is respected by his fellow Muslims
- has studied the Qur'an and Hadiths
- is known for his piety and common sense.

Some mosques do not have full-time imams, and their chosen leaders have full-time jobs outside the mosque.

The Friday prayer consists of only two rak'ahs after which people pray individually, then go back to work.

WOMEN

Women usually pray at home, but when they pray at the mosque they form rows behind the men. Some mosques have a room or balcony set aside for them, should they wish to use it.

They do not sit among the men for worship – not because they consider themselves in any way inferior, but out of modesty, and because their presence might distract the men from worshipping. Minds have to be free of desire for the opposite sex, or worries about family matters.

When you see the pictures of the prayer positions you will see why women are content to pray at the back!

Takbir – shutting out the world and concentrating on God

Reciting al-Fatihah

Ruku – bowing from the waist

Sujud – prostration before Allah

Kneeling with palms on knees

Salam – greeting the angels at the end of prayer

FOR YOUR FOLDERS

▶ Draw a series of pin-people showing the various prayer positions (use the information on pages 56–7 to help you).

▶ What are the qualities looked for when choosing an imam?

▶ What advantages or disadvantages do you think there could be in a community choosing its own religious leader or imam?

FOR DISCUSSION

▶ How important do you think it is for Muslims to meet together for communal worship, at least once a week?

▶ Why do Muslims believe that sitting and praying separately or at the back, does not indicate a female worshipper's inferiority?

29 DU'A (PERSONAL PRAYER)

Private du'a prayer

DU'A

People who love God and feel close to Him pray many other times during the day. They feel constantly aware of His presence. Although Muslims try to accept the tests of their life as being God's will, it is only human nature to speak to Him, lay before Him their worries and ask for help and guidance in times of suffering or anxiety or panic.

Personal supplications or requests, are called **du'a** prayers. These may be:

- private thanksgivings for some blessing received (e.g. recovery from sickness, birth of a child, release from worry)

- cries for help

- pleas for forgiveness

- general requests for God's guidance and blessing.

These are not part of the formal or set prayers, but may be offered at any time and be of any length.

SUBHAH

Sometimes Muslims hold a little string of 99 beads. This is called a **subhah**. After the rak'ahs, Muslims may remain to praise God using the beads as an aid. Others prefer to count using the finger joints of their right hand. They say 'Subhan-Allah' (Glory be to Allah), 'Alhamdu lillah' (Thanks be to Allah), and 'Allahu Akbar' (God is great) 33 times each, as they pass the beads.

Muslims often make God their first thought on waking, and the last before sleeping. They often think of Him throughout the day. This is also du'a.

Any prayer for yourself, for your family, for the solution to some problem, or for protection, is du'a.

Subhah or tasbih

▶ Write a few sentences to answer the following questions:

a Why might Muslims set aside a room (or part of one) in their homes to be used as a place of worship?

b What do you see as the advantages or disadvantages for them in this?

c What does having such a place in a Muslim's house say about that family's attitude to religion?

'O Allah, I have been unjust to myself and no one grants pardon for sins except You. Forgive me, therefore, in Your compassion, for surely You are the Forgiver, the Merciful.'

(du'a prayer)

'In the name of Allah, the Most Merciful, the Most Kind.
I seek refuge in the Lord of the Daybreak
from the evil of what He has created;
from the evil of the intense darkness;
from the evil of those who practise secret arts;
from the evil of the envious one.'

(surah 113)

But Muslims always remind themselves that God knows everything – all their sufferings and problems, and that they are always for a reason.

The best du'a prayer is not a cry to God for help, but to ask for strength and faith to endure the tests.

FOR YOUR FOLDERS

▶ Is it better for believers to worship God alone, in the secrecy of their hearts, or shoulder to shoulder with companions? Are both necessary? Give reasons for your answer.

▶ Copy out the words of one of the Muslim prayers.

▶ Du'a prayers are personal requests. Salah prayers are disciplined training in shutting out the world and its distractions. Which do you feel to be the most important sort of prayer, or do you think they are both equal? Give reasons.

Giving zakah at Regent's Park mosque

GIVING

All Muslims are expected to be charitable, which means 'generous and kind'. To a Muslim, the word 'charity' implies any good deed that is done purely for the sake of God – and not out of any selfish hope of getting some reward for it. Any act of giving done out of compassion, love or generosity (e.g. famine appeals) is called **sadaqah.**

Zakah, on the other hand, is a duty performed on a regular basis, and not regarded as a charity. The word 'zakah' means to purify or cleanse. It is a contribution paid once a year on savings at the rate of 2·5 per cent or one-fortieth in order to 'cleanse' your money and possessions from excessive desire for them, or greed. This rate applies to cash, bank savings and jewellery. There is a different rate for agricultural produce and livestock.

'Be steadfast in prayer, and regular in giving. Whatever good you send forth from your souls before you, you will find it [again] with God; for God sees well all that you do.'

(surah 2:110, 270 and other passages)

AIMS

The aim of paying zakah is to keep your wealth free of greed and selfishness. It is also a test of Muslim honesty and expenditure.

It tries to clean the heart of love of money and the desire to cling to it. Money is for the service of humanity, and for promoting good and justice in the world.

Zakah money may only be used for certain set purposes:

- to help the poor
- to release from debt
- to help needy travellers
- to free captives
- to win people over to the cause of Allah
- to pay those who collect it.

It is one of the basic principles of Muslim economy, based on social welfare and fair distribution of wealth. Making interest on money (called usury) is absolutely forbidden (see surah 2:275, 278, and other passages. See also pages 120–1).

'He is not a believer who eats his fill while his neighbour remains hungry by his side.'

(Hadith)

Zakah is usually paid in secret so that rich people receive no false praise or admiration, since they are doing no more than their duty; and poor people are not made ashamed in receiving (see surah 2:271). Giving openly is only encouraged when it is necessary to influence others to give.

What is given must not simply be things that are not wanted or not needed, or are second rate. When you give for God's sake, it must be nobly done.

'O believers! Don't cancel your charity by reminders of your generosity, or by holding it against them – like those who give their wealth only to be seen by others… They are like hard, barren rock on which is little soil. Heavy rain falls on it and leaves it just a bare stone.'

(surah 2:264)

RATES OF ZAKAH

(The table below is a simplified version.)

Wealth	Amount	Rate
Cash in hand or bank	Over value of 595g silver	2.5%
Gold and silver	85g gold, 595g silver	2.5%
Trading goods	Value of 595g silver	2.5%
Cows and buffaloes	30	1
Goats and sheep	40	1
Mining produce	Any	20%
Agricultural	Per harvest	10% from rain-watered land
		5% from irrigated land
Camels	Per 5	1 sheep or goat

GOD IS THE OWNER

Muslims may not pick and choose; they are obliged to help those who are poor and those who cannot earn a living, or earn such a low wage it does not cover basic needs. Muslims must remember they are all one family, and the poor have a claim upon the rich.

Muslims believe that:

- People do not own anything, but are loaned things in trust by God. So if anything is sacrificed for God, it is only being given back to its rightful owner.

- God chooses who to make rich or poor. The wealthy are obliged to give to the poor.

- Naked you came into the world and naked you leave it – so there is no point in clinging foolishly to possessions, or even worse, letting them become your masters.

- Only by giving something away for the sake of God will you receive its true value; this is not its earthly value, but is increased beyond measure.

TALKING POINTS

- The person who gives money away is richer than the person who keeps it.
- The most valuable possessions in life cannot be bought with money.
- Helping the poor should be left to the government.

THINGS TO DO

▶ Find a newspaper picture to illustrate the world's poverty. Use it to make a poster stating that we are all one family, and should look after each other.

▶ Make a list of things which are more valuable than money.

FOR YOUR FOLDERS

▶ In what ways does the practice of zakah help a Muslim to become detached from love of self and love of possession?

▶ Do you think zakah is a reasonable amount of a person's wealth for a Muslim to devote to God? Should more be demanded, or none at all? Give reasons for your answer.

QUICK QUIZ

▶ What is the difference between zakah and sadaqah?
▶ What does the word zakah actually mean?
▶ Who is the true owner of all wealth?
▶ What is the zakah rate for cash savings?
▶ What is the zakah rate for cows, sheep and camels?
▶ What is the zakah rate for coal or oil?

'O believers, you must fast so that you may learn self-restraint. Fasting is prescribed for you during a fixed number of days'

(surah 2:183–4)

Sawm, or fasting, is the deliberate control of the body by an act of will. During the 29 to 30 days of the Muslim month of **Ramadan** healthy adult Muslims will go without all the pleasures of the body during all the hours of daylight. The fast begins as the first light of dawn touches the horizon and ends with sunset. Hunger, comfort and sex are the three things which have to be brought under control.

Nothing must pass the lips (not even chewing-gum, a cigarette, or the smoke of someone else's cigarette!), and a real conscious effort must be made to make sure no evil deed or thought is committed. If the emotions of the heart or mind, or the behaviour of the Muslim are wrong, then the fast will lose its real significance.

'If you do not give up telling lies God will have no need of your giving up food and drink.'

'There are many who fast during the day and pray all night, but they gain nothing but hunger and sleeplessness.'

(Hadith)

AIMS OF SAWM

- to develop self-control and overcome selfishness, greed and laziness
- to restrain passion and appetite
- to prepare for any real sufferings that may be faced later
- to experience hunger, and thus develop sympathy for the poor
- to gain spiritual strength
- to experience companionship through shared 'ordeals'.

After a couple of hours the body is sure to feel uncomfortable, and starts complaining like a spoilt child for its usual supplies of food and drink. But Muslims allow the mind to take control. The body will not get its way. The path of obedience gradually becomes easier, and so does resisting temptation.

It is possible to cheat, but Muslims believe that God sees everything. Human beings might be deceived, but you can never deceive God. Therefore there is no point in fasting in order to show off – the fast is a matter between the individual and God alone.

THOSE EXCUSED FASTING

Muslims are excused if they would suffer real hardship. The following people do not have to fast:

- children under twelve
- pregnant and nursing mothers
- the aged
- those sick or on a journey, if it would cause real pain or suffering. It is obvious that a ten-mile journey on foot carrying baggage would be much harder than 1000 miles by aeroplane.

Whenever possible, the days of fasting missed should be made up later. Those excused fasting should provide food for needy people.

RAMADAN

Ramadan is the ninth month of the Muslim year, and it is regarded as a very special month, because it was during this time that the Prophet received his first message from God (see pages 8 and 76).

Since Muslim months are based on the moon, Ramadan falls eleven days earlier each year. When it falls in the blistering summer heat it is a real challenge to faith and devotion.

There is enormous excitement at the start of the fast, as Muslims await the announcement that the new moon has been sighted. Some make telephone calls to Makkah. In some countries the start of Ramadan is announced on the radio. Sometimes a cannon is fired, or there is some other public signal.

THE NIGHT MEALS

Even more exciting is the end of the fast each night. There is a wonderful feeling of joy and achievement after each day's successful discipline.

The food that breaks the fast after sunset is called **iftar.** It is sensible not to eat too much (Muhammad himself had only a couple of dates or a drink) otherwise you can feel sick.

More substantial meals follow, for at night wholesome meals are allowed. Often there are many friends and relatives to visit.

If the day's fast starts very early an extra meal called **suhur** can be squeezed in before first light.

Ramadan ends with the great feast of **Id-ul-Fitr** (see page 78).

Breaking the fast

INTERVIEW WITH A NEW MUSLIM CONVERT (A FIRST TIME FASTER)

Interviewer: How long did you fast for, Aishah?

Aishah: It seemed like a lifetime, but it was only for 30 days out of 365!

Interviewer: Thirty days sounds a lot. Did you really go without food and liquid all day?

Aishah: In fact, the hardest part for me was giving up my 11 a.m. coffee and cigarette! By 3 p.m. I was in agony, but by 6 p.m., when I had to feed my non-Muslim family, I was really past eating. I felt a bit sick.

Interviewer: Did you lose any weight?

Aishah: Yes, I lost five pounds! And yet each night I had an enormous meal with my Muslim friends. We couldn't move for half an hour afterwards! Another failing, I'm afraid – over-indulgence.

Interviewer: Did you feel all right?

Aishah: Yes and no. I got a bit bad-tempered, and sometimes I had to lie down in the afternoon. I wanted help with my jobs, and became very slow and sluggish. It made me realize how hard it is for Muslims who are out at work – no allowances are made! Actually, it was rather nice to go on the streets and see other Muslims, and know that we had a kind of secret, that passers-by had no idea what we were up to.

FOR YOUR FOLDERS

▶ In what ways do you think the experience of the Ramadan fast draws Muslims together?

▶ In what circumstances would a person's fast be of no value whatsoever?

THINGS TO DO

▶ Imagine you are a Muslim. Write a letter to a friend explaining how you keep Ramadan, and how it might affect your behaviour at work or at school.

▶ Try to fast for one day – but don't be silly about this. Drink a glass of milk if you feel faint. Keep a log book of your feelings and experiences as you go through the day. (Perhaps your class could do this together, or even make it a sponsored event.)

QUICK QUIZ

▶ What is meant by fasting?

▶ Which is the special Muslim month for fasting?

▶ Why is Ramadan harder if it comes in the summer?

▶ Which people are excused from fasting?

▶ What is the name of the meal that breaks the fast?

▶ What is the name of the feast that ends Ramadan?

The Ka'bah Mosque, Makkah

The dearest wish of any devout Muslim is to be able to perform the **Hajj**, or pilgrimage to Makkah. 'Hajj' means to 'set out with a definite purpose', and it is the duty of every Muslim who can afford it, and who is physically fit, to visit the Ka'bah and stand before God at **Mount Arafat**, once in their lifetime.

For Muslims who live near Makkah the journey can be made many times, but most live so far away and are so poor that it is virtually impossible. Some people save for a lifetime in order to be able to go. Sometimes a family or community will club together in order to be able to send one representative.

The true Hajj has to be made between 8 and 13 Dhul-Hijjah (the twelfth month). If a Muslim goes at any other time it is known as **Umrah**, or the lesser pilgrimage, and the significance is not the same.

All the pillars of Islam require a breaking-off of normal everyday life, but Hajj demands much more. It is a complete suspension of all worldly activities for a few days, when the pilgrim becomes just a naked soul, living and moving for God alone.

CONDITIONS

There are certain rules for pilgrims. They must be:

- Muslim. It is not a side-show for tourists, so non-Muslims are not allowed

- of sound mind, and able to understand the significance of the experience

- physically fit and able to take the strain and rigours of the journey

- in a position to provide for any dependants left behind

- able to pay for the Hajj without recourse to dishonest ways of raising the money.

Before modern transport it sometimes took months, perhaps years, of hard travel to get to Makkah and back. Nowadays many pilgrims fly in to the Hajj Terminal at Jeddah airport.

Pilgrims of every race and social class meet in equality before God. It is the climax of a Muslim's life. Rich, poor, employer or servant, all are united before Him who made them.

NIYYAH

If a Muslim cannot go on Hajj because of

● ill health
● lack of funds
● unavoidable circumstances

then it is the **niyyah,** or intention (see page 49), that counts.

Muslims can join the pilgrims in spirit and in prayer. They can, if they wish,

● pay for a substitute (who has already done his or her own Hajj) to go on their behalf
● give their Hajj savings to charity.

Any Muslim who does not offer a sacrificial animal should fast (see surah 2:196).

Nowadays over a million people gather on Hajj, and the Saudi Arabian Government allocates around 300 million dollars a year to the Ministry of Pilgrimage. The King Abdul Aziz Airport at Jeddah is the largest in the world, and the Hajj Terminal takes ten jumbo jets at a time.

Pilgrims are organized into groups under the leadership of people who know what to do and where to take them. Fitting so many into a mosque, and putting them in tents in a valley less than two kilometres wide, is no easy task!

People get split up, lost, or overcome with heat – yet despite every obstacle there is a wonderful feeling of being one great family. Inconveniences and difficulties are brushed aside by the emotion, joy and triumph of being a pilgrim.

FOR YOUR FOLDERS

▶ Why is the niyyah, or intention, to do Hajj as important as the pilgrimage itself? How could Muslims take part in Hajj, even if they could not go?

▶ In what ways is Hajj different from all other pillars?

▶ Explain why a Muslim might be forgiven for taking the title 'Hajji' or 'Hajjah' (a Muslim who has completed Hajj) with some pride.

▶ Make a list of the conditions necessary for pilgrims on Hajj. Explain why you think these conditions were made.

The camp site in the valley of Arafat

ADAM AND EVE

The symbolism of Hajj goes way back to the beginnings of the human story, to Adam, the first man, and after him to Ibrahim, the friend of God.

The story begins with a small mountain in the Plain of Arafat which is known as Jabal ar-Rahman, or the Mount of Mercy. It was here, according to tradition, that Adam and Eve were forgiven by God for their sins, and were brought back to His love and protection.

After they had given in to the devil's temptation they were banished from their lovely paradise and lost each other. They wandered the earth in confusion and terrible unhappiness.

God watched over them, waiting for them to turn back to Him and exchange their defiance for a desire for forgiveness. When at last they understood what separation from God was, they prayed to be restored to grace, and the Lord of Compassion was able to forgive them. Their dramatic reunion took place at the little mountain of Arafat. In gratitude, they built a simple shrine nearby, the first building on earth constructed for the worship of God.

For Muslims, to be on that mountain on 9 Dhul-Hijjah is the main part of the Hajj ritual. As for Adam and Eve, this 'meeting' between themselves and God, if done with spiritual awareness, brings total forgiveness of all past sins and gains the promise of paradise.

IBRAHIM

The second important moment celebrated by Hajj is the occasion when the loyalty of Ibrahim was put to the test.

Ibrahim had vowed to sacrifice everything in his life to God. He was a most humble and devout man, even though he was the wealthy owner of vast herds of sheep and goats.

He lived peacefully with his childless wife Sarah, and a second wife – an Egyptian woman called **Hajar** – who had given birth to his son **Isma'il**.

One day God decided to test Ibrahim's faith and loyalty. Ibrahim had a vivid dream in which he was asked to sacrifice that which he loved most, his only son Isma'il. When he awoke, in fearful agony of mind, he told his son the dream.

THE TEST

Isma'il was terrified, but replied bravely – 'O my father, do what you are commanded to do, and do not worry about me.'

Such was their obedience, that even though they did not know *why* God had ordered this, they accepted that if it was His will, it had to be done.

The family set out for **Mina**, the place of sacrifice. On the way the devil appeared in human form using various arguments to make Ibrahim change his mind and doubt whether the dream was genuine. Each argument was so reasonable that it made the sacrifice much harder to bear:

- Only the devil would ask Ibrahim to do such a wicked thing, not God. Ibrahim was being tricked by the evil power.

- Didn't Hajar love her son? Didn't Ibrahim love her, and wouldn't he do anything she asked? How could she allow him to take the foolish dream so seriously, and kill their only boy?

- Didn't Isma'il realize his father was mad? He was being cruel and unloving. Where were his feelings? Isma'il should run away and not get himself killed like a fool!

All three of them resisted these temptations. According to tradition, Ibrahim picked up stones and flung them at this stranger to drive him away.

THE SACRIFICE

They reached the appointed place. 'Put me face downwards,' begged Isma'il, not out of fear, but so that his father would not hesitate when he saw his face. Ibrahim lay him on the altar, and such was the boy's acceptance and courage that he did not need to be tied. Both had consented to the sacrifice.

But at the last moment God stopped Ibrahim, and the reward for his obedience was that his barren wife Sarah gave birth at last to a son of her own – Isaac.

Isma'il was the founder of the Arab tribes, and Isaac the founder of the Jews (see surah 37:100–113).

HAJAR'S THIRST

Because of Sarah's jealousy on behalf of her son, Ibrahim was told by God that he should separate from Hajar and Isma'il, and leave them to God's care beside the remains of the ancient shrine associated with Adam.

In this barren, waterless desert Hajar and Isma'il were tested again, for God seemed to have abandoned them, and they were dying of thirst. Hajar ran frantically between the tops of two hills, **Safa** and **Marwah**, to see if she could spot a passing camel train that would be carrying water – but there was none to be seen.

At last, when all hope had gone save her hope in God, the angel Jibril appeared and showed her a spring at the feet of her suffering child. This is the spring now known as the **Zamzam** well.

MAKKAH

Later the family was reunited, and Ibrahim and Isma'il built, out of rough stone laid dry, a square-walled sanctuary with no roof, the walls a little higher than a man. To lay the top layers, Ibrahim stood on a large rock, the **Maqam Ibrahim**. The building became known as the Ka'bah, or Cube, a very holy place quite unlike the grandiose ziggurats (temples) and pyramids of the surrounding nations.

For around 4000 years the Ka'bah has been reconstructed on that same foundation, and the faithful have gone there on pilgrimage.

> *'O our Lord, receive [this] from us…make us submissive to You, and of our seed a nation submissive to You…and our Lord, send among them a messenger, one who will tell them Your signs and teach them the Book and the Wisdom, and purify them.'*

(surah 2:127–9; see also surah 14:35–8)

A village of tents swiftly grew up around the water-supply in the desert, and eventually the town of Makkah grew up.

TALKING POINTS

● Should believers always have the right to know the reasons why God wants them to do certain things, or should they act out of trust? Why do they feel they can trust God?

● Is it impossible for a believer to live a life of submission to God without facing the tests and temptations of the devil?

FOR YOUR FOLDERS

▶ What do you think are the most important lessons to be drawn from the stories of:

a Adam and Eve
b the testing of Ibrahim and his family
c the sacrifice of Isma'il
d the testing of Hajar in the desert?

▶ In what ways does the Ka'bah symbolize for Muslims the idea of complete submission to God?

Hajj pilgrims in the Safa-Marwah walkway

IHRAM

On arriving at certain points outside Makkah, pilgrims must enter the sacred state known as **ihram.** They have to make a conscious effort to attain purity, as the pilgrims dedicate themselves to worship, prayer and denial of vanity.

All normal clothing must be put away. Male pilgrims put on just two sheets of unsewn white cloth, one wrapped round the waist, the other over the left shoulder. Women wear a plain undecorated ankle-length, long-sleeved garment, leaving only their hands and faces bare. For once, women can uncover their faces – even if they normally cover them – because no man should look at them with lust at this time.

These clothes symbolize three things: equality, single-mindedness and self-sacrifice. All pilgrims give up their personalities, so often expressed in dress, and are equal with their neighbours.

Ihram also reminds Muslims of death, when all 'disguises' of rank, wealth and appearance are left behind.

Other rules are:

- Do not do anything dishonest or arrogant, but behave like servants of Allah.
- Flirtatious thoughts of the opposite sex are forbidden; one may not get engaged to marry on Hajj; normal marital relations are set aside (any sexual act on Hajj would nullify it).
- Men must not wear jewellery or rings.
- No one may use perfume or scented soap – unscented soap is on sale for pilgrims.
- To express humility, men must not cover their heads (an ordeal in fierce heat – but they may carry an umbrella).
- To express confidence in the atmosphere of purity and that all lustful thoughts have been put aside, women may not cover their faces.
- To express non-interference with nature, no one must cut hair or finger nails.
- To express simplicity, everyone must go barefoot or in sandals that leave the toes and heels bare.
- To curb aggression and feel unity with God's creatures, no blood must be shed by killing animals except fleas, bedbugs, snakes and scorpions.
- To develop mercy, no hunting is allowed.

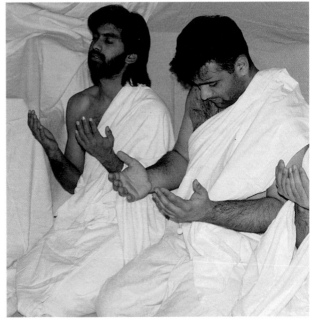

Pilgrims in state of ihram

- To feel love for nature, no plants may be uprooted or trees cut down.
- Muslims must strive to keep their minds at peace, and not lose their tempers, quarrel or get exasperated by difficulties.

*'Here I am, O God, here I am!
I am here, O Thou without equal,
here I am!
Thine is the kingdom,
the praise and the glory,
O Thou without equal, God Alone!'*

This is the prayer called the **talbiyah** which the pilgrims utter over and over again as they arrive in Makkah – the answer to the divine call to come. Some shout it joyfully, others are overcome with emotion and weep.

To stand in the midst of hundreds of thousands of people and feel that *you* are important to God, that God has seen *you* arrive, is a humbling experience, and can be quite shattering. It is no wonder that so many pilgrims shed tears.

'O God,
this sanctuary is Your sacred place,
and this city is Your city,
and this slave is Your slave.
I have come to You from a distant land,
carrying all my sins and misdeeds
as an afflicted person seeking Your help
and dreading Your punishment.
I beg You to accept me,
and grant me Your complete forgiveness,
and give me permission to enter
Your vast garden of delight. '

This is the prayer said as pilgrims enter Makkah.

THE CIRCLING

The first thing the pilgrims do on arrival in Makkah, no matter what time of day or night, is to hurry to the Ka'bah and encircle it seven times at a fast pace, running if possible, to symbolize love for God. This is called the **tawaf**.

As they arrive they call out *'Labbaika, Allahumma, Labbaika!'* which means 'At Your command, our Lord, at Your command!' – the cry of response to the call to come and dedicate their lives to God.

If the pilgrims can get near the Black Stone they will kiss it or touch it, but if it is impossible because of the vast numbers, they shout and raise their arms in salute each time they go past. An example of the prayers used is this one, used on the fourth round:

'O God who knows the innermost secrets of our
hearts, lead us out of the darkness into the light.'

The next event is the **sa'y**, the procession seven times between Safa and Marwah in memory of Hajar's search. It symbolizes patience and perseverance, and can be quite an ordeal in the summer heat. Special provisions are made for people in wheelchairs or on stretchers.

During the pilgrimage, women do not veil their faces, trusting in the purity of men's hearts

THINKING POINTS

- Why do you think pilgrims on Hajj – who must be very tired, uncomfortable, hot and hungry – are normally so happy and excited?

- Why do you think the ihram cloths later become treasured possessions

FOR YOUR FOLDERS

▶ Imagine you are a Muslim. Write a letter to a friend describing the things you must do or must not do while in the state of ihram. Explain what the experience of entering this state means to you.

▶ Write out the talbiyah prayer or the prayer of the pilgrims entering Makkah. You could do this as a decorated scroll or poster.

▶ Explain what is meant by 'tawaf' and 'sa'y'.

▶ Why do you think it is significant that Muslim women do not cover their faces during Hajj?

1 – The Great Mosque   4 – Muzdalifah
2 – The Ka'bah   5 – Plain of Arafat
3 – Mina   6 – The Mount of Mercy

The route of Hajj

BAITULLAH

The Ka'bah is known as **Baitullah**, the House of Allah. It is a plain cube-shaped building made of blocks, not very pretty or striking to look at. Yet Muslims claim it is on the site of the oldest shrine to God on earth, built originally by the first man, Adam. Later it was abandoned and broken down, but Ibrahim and Isma'il were shown the foundations and rebuilt it.

The plain dull exterior guarding a brilliant and exciting treasure within symbolizes the plain dull wrappings of the body hiding from the world the shining brilliance of the soul; and the fact that the most splendid being of all – God Himself – is invisible, and yet glorious to those who have 'eyes to see'.

When the Prophet captured Makkah he broke up the idols of 360 other 'gods' that had been placed there.

Nowadays only very rare visitors are allowed inside the Ka'bah to stand at the very centre and pray in all four directions, a unique experience. Inside is simply a room decorated with texts from the Qur'an.

AL-KISWAH

The Ka'bah is covered by a huge jet-black cloth known as the **kiswah**. There is a different one every year, because at the end of Hajj it is cut up into pieces and given to the pilgrims as mementoes of the greatest moment of their lives. The rim of gold lettering round the cloth is usually sewn by specially chosen men in a factory just outside Makkah.

THE BLACK STONE

This is an oval boulder about 18cm in diameter, set in the south-east corner of the Ka'bah, that marks the start of the walk encircling the shrine. It is encased in a silver frame. The pilgrims try to touch it or kiss it. Pre-Islamic traditions suggest:

● It was dug out of the earth by Isma'il at a place indicated by the angel Jibril.

● Jibril brought it from paradise and gave it to Adam.

● It was given to the descendants of Nuh (Noah) after the flood.

It certainly existed long before the Prophet's time, and was mentioned by the writer Maximus of Tyre in 2 CE.

It is probably a meteorite, and therefore a symbol of that which comes to earth from heaven.

MARWAH AND SAFA

These are two small hills, now enclosed under domes and joined by a walkway – the two hills between which Hajar frantically dashed when she tried to find water. Her actions symbolize the soul's desperate search for that which gives true life.

ZAMZAM

The angel showed Hajar a spring of water near the place where she had laid the dying Isma'il. A tradition suggests the water issued from the place where his feet had scoured the sand as he suffered his fever. Hajar called the well Zamzam, from the sound made by rushing water in the Babylonian language. It symbolizes the truth that when all seems lost, God is still present, with healing and life for the soul.

The Zamzam well is in the courtyard of the Great Mosque in Makkah. Pilgrims collect water from it to drink and take home. Many dip their white garments in it, and keep them to be used one day as the shrouds for their burial.

ARAFAT

This is the plain where the pilgrims erect a vast camp site. During Hajj the plain is dotted with little tents in neat rows and squares as far as the eye can see (see page 67). About two million people camp here.

Mount Arafat is the Mount of Mercy where God was said to have reunited Adam and Eve. The Stand before God here is the most important part of Hajj.

MUZDALIFAH

Pilgrims camp overnight at **Muzdalifah** on their journey between Arafat and Makkah. Here they pick up pebbles to hurl at the pillars of Mina.

MINA

Here are the pillars, or **Jamaras,** which represent the places where Ibrahim and his family resisted the temptations and stoned the devil. The Saudi Arabian Ministry of Pilgrimage has recently built a huge walkway to Mina.

THINGS TO DO

▶ Copy the diagram of the pilgrimage route. Explain what is significant, or what is done, at the following places:

Ka'bah shrine	Black Stone
Safa and Marwah	Zamzam
Mount Arafat	Muzdalifah
Mina	

Pilgrims stoning a Jamara pillar which represents Iblis (the devil)

The entrance to the Ka'bah temple, Makkah

The road to Mina

On 8 Dhul-Hijjah the pilgrims set off for Mina, and camp there for the rest of that day and night. On 9 Dhul-Hijjah they head for Mount Arafat – a good day's journey on foot. Many pilgrims nowadays take modern transport straight to Arafat and miss out Mina, because of the sheer numbers involved.

THE STAND

On the plain of Arafat, at the Mount of Mercy, the pilgrims make their stand before God, the **wuquf.** They stand from noon to sunset in the blistering heat, meditating and praying, and concentrating on God alone.

Latecomers rush to be in time, for if the stand is missed, the Hajj is not valid.

It is a time of great mystical and emotional power. To be there with a repentant heart wipes out all the sins of the past, and enables life to begin anew. There is a tremendous sense of release – being totally wrapped in love, totally 'washed', totally cleansed.

A stony climb leads to the top of Arafat, and from there a sermon is delivered to the people. Then they all spend the night in the open, in thankfulness and prayer. After this, Muslims may go home from the Hajj 'released', as sinless as the day they were born, and full of inner peace.

Muslims return to Mina via Muzdalifah, where they hold the night prayer and gather pebbles to 'stone the Devil'. The night of 10 Dhul-Hijjah is spent at Muzdalifah. As dawn approaches there is another mass standing before God, and the pilgrims depart for Mina just before dawn breaks.

COMMENT

'To have stood before God at Arafat is like having a baby. You have either had the experience or you have not. No one can truly explain how it feels – but those who know it, know. Perhaps those whose hearts God has seized can understand.'

(a woman pilgrim's comment)

TALKING POINT

- Pilgrims slip into Hajj like drops being merged into a vast ocean. In such a mass of people, why is Hajj such an intensely personal experience?

The 'stand' at Mount Arafat

THE UNFURLING

The remainder of the pilgrimage is called the unfurling.

- When the pilgrims arrive at Mina, they hurl pebbles at the pillars to symbolize their rejection of the Devil and all his works.

- Next, on 10 Dhul-Hijjah, the Feast of Sacrifice (Id-ul-Adha, see page 80) begins. The pilgrims all camp at Mina for two to three days of the feast. Every pilgrim must sacrifice an animal.

- The Saudi authorities organize the freezing and disposal of the carcases. Nowadays, with about two million pilgrims, it is impossible for all the meat to be eaten immediately, even if it is shared among the poor.

- After the sacrifice, the men have their heads shaved and the women cut off at least 2.5cm of their hair. At this point ihram ends.

- The pilgrims then return to Makkah for another encircling of the Ka'bah. The final events are enjoyed in the holiday spirit. Many go back to Mina for a period of rest and recovery.

- Finally they return to Makkah for the farewell. Some take water from Zamzam, and dip their white cloths in it to be used later as shrouds. They drink as much water as possible, believing it cures diseases, and they take as much as they can carry home to their families. Some are given pieces of the Black Cloth as souvenirs.

- They are at last entitled to take the name Hajji or Hajjah.

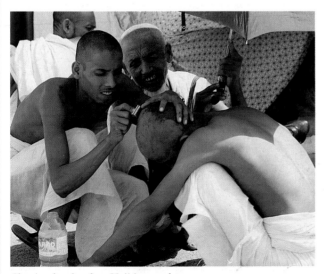

Shaving heads when Hajj is complete

MUSLIM TOURISM

After the Hajj, most pilgrims go to visit Madinah, to pay their respects at the Prophet's tomb. At Madinah there is the mosque that was the Prophet's home, and behind it the **hujurah** or chamber which was the room of his youngest and beloved wife Aishah. Here Muslims may see the graves of the Prophet himself, his companions Abu Bakr and Umar, and, according to some traditions, a place reserved for Isa after his second coming.

The energetic can visit Mount Nur, where the Prophet first saw the angel, and Mount Thawr where he sheltered from the Quraish. Other places of interest are the battle sites, and the Masjid at-Taqwa – the mosque built when the Prophet entered Madinah. This one is notable for having two mihrabs, one facing Jerusalem .

The cemetery of al-Baqee contains the graves of Uthman, Aishah and Hasan (Ali's son, see page 146), plus other celebrities. It is notable for the extreme simplicity of the tombs, which are simply mounds of small stones. There had been grander mausoleums in the past, but these were destroyed by the strict Islamic sect of Wahhabis during the reign of King Abd al-Aziz al-Saud, who wished to discourage hero-worship cults.

THINGS TO DO

▶ Imagine you have been all night in the vast crowd at wuquf. The dawn is breaking. Write a paragraph describing what you might feel.

FOR YOUR FOLDERS

▶ Explain how Hajj

a brings 'release' and inner peace

b builds up courage and trust in God

c draws all Muslims together whether on Hajj or not

d unites Muslims not only with each other but with their beloved prophets of the past.

FESTIVALS

The Muslim word for a festival is 'id' or 'eid', taken from an Arabic word meaning 'returning at regular intervals'. The regular cycle is important, for this gives a repeated opportunity to:

- praise and thank God for His blessings
- remember loved ones (including those in distant parts of the world, and those who have died)
- forgive enemies
- resume contact with people not seen for a long time.

The festivals are times for reducing tensions and establishing new and renewed relationships. The poor must be remembered, the rich must share, the lonely and the stranger must be made to feel at home, the orphan must feel loved and cared for, the lazy and forgetful must make an effort to make up for things they have not done, and the quarrelsome must make peace.

DATES

Months in the Islamic calendar are calculated according to the moon. Therefore each month has 29–30 days, and the Islamic year is shorter than the solar year by about eleven days. For this reason, feasts are not always on the same date each year. Instead Muslim festivals come eleven days earlier each year and thus move round the solar calendar.

Islam has only two chief festivals, **Id-ul-Adha**, the feast of sacrifice during Hajj, and **Id-ul-Fitr**, the breaking of the month-long fast of Ramadan (see page 64).

Muslims also keep six days as special occasions.

MAWLID AN-NABI

Mawlid an-Nabi is the birthday of the Prophet, probably originally 20 August, 570 CE. The day is celebrated by some Muslims with joyful processions and accounts of Muhammad's life, mission, character, sufferings and successes.

In some parts of the world the whole of the following month is marked by gatherings in remembrance of his life.

LAYLAT-UL-QADR

This is the Night of Power, when the Prophet received his first revelation of the Qur'an. Because the date is not certain, it is remembered throughout the last ten days of the Ramadan fast. It is often held on 27 Ramadan (see page 8).

Many Muslims stay up all night in prayer, or reciting the Qur'an. Some spend all the last ten nights of Ramadan in this way, remembering God's mercy and forgiveness.

LAYLAT-UL-MIRAJ

This commemorates the night the Prophet made the miraculous journey to Jerusalem and ascended through the heavens to the presence of God.

Muslims gather in remembrance that it was at the height of his persecution that the Prophet was given this special moment, one feature of which was the institution of the five daily prayers.

LAYLAT-UL-BARA'AT

This is the night of the full moon before the start of Ramadan. It was at this time that the Prophet used to begin his preparations for Ramadan by passing nights in prayer. Many Muslims celebrate this night by staying awake and reading the Qur'an.

Id prayer at Regent's Park mosque. There is no room left inside for all these worshippers

MUHARRAM

Muharram was declared the first month of the Muslim calendar by Khalifah Umar, the New Year's Day being celebrated after the sighting of the new moon. It commemorates the Hijrah, the departure of the Prophet to Madinah, the moment that marked the beginning of his successes and led to the spread of Islam. Muslims date their years from this event, so the year after the Hijrah is year 1 AH. The intention is for Muslims to 'migrate' from their past to their future, put old sins and failings behind them and make a fresh start with new year resolutions.

10 MUHARRAM OR ASHURA

This was a traditional day of fasting before the time of the Prophet. In the Jewish tradition it is the Day of Atonement when sacrifices are made for the sins of the people. In Muslim tradition it was also the day when Nuh left the Ark after the flood, and the day on which God saved Musa from Pharaoh. Fasting is not obligatory, but many Muslims fast anyway, and enjoy special meals at night.

It is a particularly important day for Shi'ite Muslims. It is a day of great sorrow and mourning, as it marks the day when the Prophet's grandson **Husayn** was martyred. Public grief is expressed dramatically with processions, plays and religious

Ashura celebrations on 7th Avenue, New York, USA. Shi'ites beat their chests as a sign of mourning

gatherings at which emotions are stirred until the tears flow. Sometimes the more fervent men even beat themselves with chains and cut their heads with swords – to share in some small way the sufferings of Husayn.

THINGS TO DO

▶ Calculate the date: to find the Muslim year (AH) you must take 622 (the year of Hijrah) from the year in the calendar we use and multiply it by $\frac{33}{32}$, e.g.

$$1902 = \tfrac{33}{32} \times (1902 - 622)$$
$$= \tfrac{33}{32} \times 1280$$
$$= 1320 \text{ AH}$$

What is the Muslim year for 1996?

FOR YOUR FOLDERS

▶ List the six special days, and state briefly what each one commemorates.

▶ In keeping the special days connected with the life of the Prophet are Muslims really remembering the Prophet or God? Give reasons for your answer.

TALKING POINT

● Would the Prophet have approved of too much celebration of these days? How do you think he would have liked people to honour his memory?

77

THE PREPARATION

Id-ul-Fitr is the feast that marks the end of the month-long Ramadan fast. It begins with great excitement. On the last evening of the fast, as the time draws near, most Muslims go out into the open to catch the moment the new moon appears in the sky when there is an outburst of rejoicing and goodwill. Preparations for the feast begin well in advance.

- Food is bought and carefully prepared beforehand (sometimes Muslim shops are so busy they stay open all night the few days before).
- Decorations may be bought and hung up.
- Cards are bought or made, and sent to relatives and friends.
- Gifts and sweets are prepared for the children.
- Houses may be painted or generally smartened up.
- Money is collected for the poor.

The Id day is the last day for sending **Zakat-ul-Fitr**, a special payment made during Ramadan, and post offices are often busy as people fulfil this part of their duty.

Dressed for Id

THE ANNOUNCEMENT

Originally Id-ul-Fitr was announced by the eagerly awaited call to prayer from the mosque, which appeared more moving and significant than normal. Nowadays the time is announced on radio and television. In the West (where skies are often too cloudy to see the moon!) mosques receive the news by radio, telex and telephone.

As soon as the signal comes, everyone rushes to congratulate and greet each other. There is much hugging and handshaking, and wishing of 'Id Mubarak' or 'Happy Id'. There is great holiday spirit – people are out on the streets in happy mood. Visitors call round on friends and congratulate each other on completing a successful fast.

In memory of Muhammad, and because it is sensible, the fast is usually broken with something very simple, like dates or a drink. One popular drink is 'qamar al-din' (moon of religion) which is made from apricots.

After this the family leaves the table to pray together, and then comes back to enjoy what is probably the most appreciated meal of the month!

ID DAY

On this day there is no work or school. In non-Muslim countries understanding employers make allowances for absence; in Muslim countries it is a three-day holiday.

THE ROUTINE

- a bath or shower
- putting on best clothes or new clothes
- quick breakfast
- huge special gathering in the largest mosque, or maybe a park or playing field, or even a car park – this congregation can consist of thousands of people!
- women and children are encouraged to come, but many mothers stay at home getting things ready
- everyone prays together, as one huge family. The sermon is usually about the importance of giving
- more greetings and embraces, then round to the houses of friends and family. The children are very excited because they know they will receive presents and pocket money. Whole convoys of cars may go back to one house. People come and go all day

- a splendid dinner – the first meal eaten at midday for over a month! It may be in many sittings, according to the number who arrive. Everyone pitches in and helps with supplies and cooking
- some visit the cemetery, to remember the loved ones who are divided from their families by death
- it is a day of joy and tears, forgiveness and love. The day ends with more visits to friends, as people are anxious to leave no one out, and the celebrations often go on late into the night.

QUICK QUIZ

▶ What is the Muslim word for festival?

▶ Id-ul-Fitr comes at the end of which month?

▶ What must be seen before Id can begin?

▶ What are sent to friends and relations?

▶ What money is paid now?

▶ How does the Id congregation differ from the usual ones?

THINGS TO DO

▶ Design and draw your own Id card.

▶ Make a diary or list of the preparations you would have to make in order to celebrate Id in your own house.

FOR YOUR FOLDERS

▶ In what ways does Id-ul-Fitr bring Muslims close together as

a   individual families, and

b   one complete family, the ummah (see page 82)?

▶ Why is Id-ul-Fitr especially enjoyed by children?

▶ Why is the fact that festivals must occur in a regular cycle important? What might the consequences be if the festival did not keep coming around each year?

Greeting each other with 'Id Mubarak' – the blessings of Id

Id card

The feast of **Id-ul-Adha** is not only the climax of the Hajj pilgrimage (see page 75), but is the major festival in the Islamic year and takes place in the Hajj month, two months after the close of Ramadan. It commemorates the triumph of Ibrahim's faith over the temptations of the devil, and his complete submission to the will of God. For those taking part, it symbolizes the submission of each individual Muslim, and renewal of total commitment to God.

Every Muslim takes part in this feast, not just those on Hajj. It is a family occasion, bearing in mind the whole family of Islam and not just your own relations. It is a serious occasion, and concentrates the mind on self-sacrifice, symbolized by the sacrificing of an animal.

In Muslim countries schools, businesses and shops are closed for four days. Town streets are deserted and family homes packed with visitors.

Everyone thinks about the pilgrims making their Hajj and joins with them in spirit, particularly any who have gone from their own family or community. In Muslim countries Hajj events are now followed on television.

On the day commemorating the story of Ibrahim's testing (see page 68) there is a sense of emotional release, and real sharing in the experiences of the pilgrims, many Muslims remembering their own journey, and others wishing they could have gone too.

The feast represents Muslims' readiness to sacrifice all feelings, personal wants and needs, even life itself if necessary, to the service of God.

'Neither the flesh of the animals of your sacrifice nor their blood reaches Allah – it is your righteousness that reaches Him.'

(surah 22:37)

PREPARATIONS

These begin well in advance. Gifts are bought, new clothing is prepared, food supplies are organized for the big day and an animal must be selected for the sacrifice and kept apart. These include sheep, goats, cows and camels, and they may be purchased two or three weeks before the feast day.

THE SACRIFICE

When possible, the animals are cared for at home. Muslims are not hard-hearted, and they often become fond of these animals. This is especially true of the children.

Facing the responsibility of slaughter for yourself, instead of leaving it to a butcher, makes you realize in a small way how hard it must have been for Ibrahim to pass his test when he thought he was going to have to sacrifice his own son. A mixture of tenderness, love, grief and above all duty is what the sacrifice is all about.

It is the duty of a Muslim man to know how to kill an animal quickly and kindly, and take this responsibility for himself.

Nowadays many families have their feast animals slaughtered at an abattoir, by a specially trained person. This is compulsory in Britain.

The atmosphere should be such that the animal is not frightened, and its throat must be cut with a very sharp knife across the jugular vein, so that it loses consciousness immediately. Prayers are said

Sacrificing a sheep at the slaughterhouse

Dressed for Id

FOR YOUR FOLDERS

▶ Explain how the feast of Id-ul-Adha is an integral part of the Hajj, and how it binds together all Muslims whether on Hajj or not. Explain what it celebrates, and the significance of the sacrifice.

▶ You might never have to take a life, or be called upon to sacrifice your own life. How could a Muslim show readiness to love and serve God in normal daily life? What other kinds of sacrifice might they have to make for God?

▶ Some people never stop and consider how they would react if they were called upon to face the final challenge. Are there any things or people you would be prepared to lay down your life for?

throughout the proceedings. Killing the animal in this way causes very little distress or pain, and the blood drains away easily.

In the West, a special licence is needed to kill an animal, and licence holders go to the slaughterhouse to sacrifice there on behalf of the community. There have been isolated incidents of Muslims killing goats at home (to the horror of their non-Muslim neighbours), but this has usually been done by recent immigrants unaware of the facilities available.

Meat killed in the correct way is called **halal,** or permitted. Other meat is **haram** or forbidden (see also page 90).

The meat is divided up for the poor, for friends and relatives, and for the family use. In many countries, Id-ul-Adha is sometimes the only time in the year that the poor get meat to eat.

Instead of meat, money can be donated to the poor.

FOR DISCUSSION

▶ Having to sacrifice an animal teaches compassion and responsibility.

▶ Id-ul-Adha is wasteful and cruel.

▶ You can't learn about duty and obedience unless faced with the hardships of performing them.

'This is My straight path, so follow it, and do not follow [other] paths which will separate you from this path.'

(surah 6:153)

'God does not accept belief if it is not expressed in deeds; and He does not accept your deeds unless they conform to your beliefs.'

(Hadith)

TAQWA

The moment a Muslim 'opens the eyes' and becomes conscious of God, the most important questions become 'What shall I do now? How shall I live?' Awareness of God, or consciousness of Him in your everyday life, is known as **taqwa** (see page 10).

Being in a state of taqwa is quite different from ordinary living. It alters Muslims' entire motivation for doing things, and stops them doing many things that would give a great deal of selfish pleasure. Being aware of the 'eyes of God' alters even the way they think. The objective of Shari'ah is to find the best possible way, to give guidance for the regulation of life in the best interests of humanity.

JUSTICE

Muslims believe that societies have made many attempts to establish justice and fair living without making their laws dependent on God's will, and without His divine help – and that none of these attempts has worked.

They believe that people must start by living the right sort of life themselves as individuals, but that true justice can never come about until the whole society follows the will of God.

Believers attempting to live holy lives should not shut themselves off from the world – that is seen almost as a form of selfishness. They are to live within the community, with all its problems, and try to make it a better place. They must find the **Shari'ah** which means the 'path', and follow it.

This Shari'ah is the code of behaviour for a Muslim, the law that determines the rightness (halal) or wrongness (haram) of any particular action.

It gives a criterion for judging all behaviour and conduct, and relationships with other individuals, with society as a whole, and with your own self.

THE PRINCIPLES BEHIND SHARI'AH

- God *does* exist, and so does life after death.
- There *will* come a time of judgement.
- God *is* aware of everything you do and think.
- The world is full of hardships and evils that should be put right, and not just ignored.

UMMAH

Muslims believe that we are all one family. There are no 'chosen races'. All people belong to God and are equal, whatever their colour, language or nationality. There should be no barriers of race, status or wealth, but a feeling of love and kinship between all people – helping each other out when in trouble, consoling each other when in grief, delighted when people are happy.

The word **ummah** describes this feeling of awareness, love and respect for others. The words used to translate it are usually 'brotherhood', 'family feeling' or 'kinship', but the word really implies the care and responsibility of motherhood.

FOLLOWING SHARI'AH

To follow Shari'ah means living a morally responsible life. All humans are to

'hold tight to the rope which God [stretches out for you] and do not be divided amongst yourselves. Remember with gratitude that God showed mercy to you and blessed you while you were still enemies. And He united your hearts together in love, so that by His grace you became brothers.'

(surah 3:103)

If humans live in this way, recognizing all people as one family, aware of their rights and defending them, grieving when they get hurt, being determined to bring about their good and not their harm, then they have already started living according to Shari'ah.

'What will teach you what the steep highway is? It is to ransom the captive, to feed the orphan or the poor man who lies in the dust.'

(surah 90:12–16)

'Muslims who live in the midst of society and bear with patience the afflictions that come to them, are better than those who shun society and cannot bear any wrong done to them.'

'Believers are like parts of a building; each part supports the others.'

'If any single part of the body aches, the whole body feels the effects and rushes to its relief.'

'Everyone of you is a shepherd, and will be questioned about the well-being of his flock.'

'He who has no compassion for our little ones, and does not acknowledge the honour due to our elders is not one of us.'

(Hadiths)

Muslims have no time for people who talk as if they are religious and make a show of it, but in their lives remain heartless, selfish, lazy or mean.

Morality is seen as the basis of self-confidence and strength. The ideals to be aimed at are:

- love of God
- humility
- modesty
- naturalness
- unselfishness.

Pride and arrogance are not acceptable, for no individual is superior to another except in amount of faith and performance of good deeds.

The essentials are kindness, gentleness, consideration for others, and the general promotion of the happiness and welfare of society.

THE FIVE SCHOOLS

In the ninth and tenth centuries CE, Muslim rulers encouraged the leading scholars to formulate and write down the Islamic Law in full detail.

There were five main **madhhabs**, or schools of law, named after their leading imams: Jafar al-Sadiq, Malik, Abu Hanifa, Shafi'i, and Ahmad ibn Hanbal.

Most Muslims today follow one of these schools.

CLOSED OR OPEN?

Muslims who feel that the 'old' scholars had covered everything necessary, say that the 'gate of knowledge is *closed*'.

Those who feel that the principle of constant reinterpretation to keep pace with modern problems is necessary, say that 'the gate should be left *open*'.

This is the main cause of division these days between 'modernist' and 'fundamentalist' Muslims (see pages 85 and 141).

THINKING POINTS

- Why do you think Muslims disapprove of men and women living religious lives separated from ordinary society?
- Why do you think that Muslims believe modesty and unselfishness to be qualities that God particularly requires?
- Do Muslims regard equality as the same thing as worth? Does being 'equal in the sight of God' mean something different from 'being equal'?

FOR YOUR FOLDERS

▶ What is meant by taqwa, and what do you think might be the effects of taqwa on a person's life?

▶ Why do Muslims believe that it is not possible to create a truly just society in purely human terms, with no reference to belief in Divine Justice?

▶ Explain why many Muslims feel it is important to 'keep the gate open.'

THINGS TO DO

▶ Conduct an interview, with a practising Muslim if possible, to discover what it is like living according to Shari'ah in your community.

The Qur'an is the basis of Shari'ah, and gives all the principles and commands to be accepted by Muslims without question.

Further guidance comes from the **Sunnah**, the example of Muhammad, who spent his entire life after the Night of Power in guiding and directing the people. Whatever he said, did or approved provided an example.

PROBLEMS

How can a law laid down fourteen centuries ago in the Middle East meet all the complex demands and pressures of modern technological civilization? How can a person know whether it is right or wrong to drink whisky, play transistors, go to discos, and so on? Why should any human being in this day and age bother to look for a source of guidance outside the human level? And why should God, if there is one, condescend to bother with such trivial matters?

Muslims think in a different way. No Muslim can accept the idea of a society without God; the Compassionate One *cannot* be unconcerned, uncaring, or unable to help humans in the task of living their lives.

FREEDOM

Muslims must *submit* to God, and that means they must not pick or choose which of the revealed laws they will or will not keep. How can they judge which ones are more important than others? Only God knows the full reasoning behind them.

Yet submission to God is the highest freedom, for it implies that a person can choose to *disobey* God, and many do.

However, in submitting to God alone, all slavery to other things is broken – a person is no longer a servant of any other person, set of ideas, or artificial objects or institutions. In submitting to God, a person becomes God's **khalifah**, or vice-regent, on earth (see page 33).

QIYAS

Working out Muslim principles by analogy is called **qiyas**. This means the right of any devout Muslim to use his or her reason and judgement to decide on a course of action most in keeping with the spirit of the Qur'an and Hadiths, where no specific guidance is given.

The decisions made by the leading scholars of old are known as **ijma**. The only ijma accepted as totally binding were those consensus opinions of the Prophet's actual Companions.

Later ijma based on human opinions can be accepted as guidelines – but it should always be possible to replace them by others. The exercise of any individual's opinion is called **ijtihad**.

Shi'ite imams (see page 147) known as **mujtahids** – 'living religious scholars', or **ayatollahs** – chief imams, the 'shadows of God', claim the right to exercise ijtihad freely, always basing their opinions on the Qur'an, Hadiths, and sunnah. However, they claim that this is only the right of the scholar and not of an untrained person. **Sufis**, on the other hand, feel that every devout individual has the right (see page 150).

PRINCIPLES

In making a decision, account must always be taken of:

- the opinions of respected people
- previous decisions
- justice and concern for the public good
- the acceptance of the masses.

The technique of working out Shari'ah law is called **fiqh**, from the word for 'intelligence' or 'knowledge'.

LIMITS

The principles behind the Shari'ah deter various pressure groups (even highly religious ones) from imposing on people burdens and duties which go beyond the spirit of Islam, and keep the opportunities for solving problems as wide as possible. Fanaticism is not encouraged. An over-zealous religious leader may not force anyone to do a sixth prayer during the day, or charge more than the usual amount of zakah. If he tried this, any Muslim would have the right to demand to see the basis for it in the Qur'an or Hadiths. The dictates of a narrow-minded tyrant would never be acceptable.

The job of the Shari'ah is to provide the rules of divine guidance in any new or changed situation, so that God's will may be done on earth as it is in heaven.

RULES OF BEHAVIOUR

These are divided into five categories:

- **fard** or **wajib** – things which *must* be done, e.g. prayer, fasting in Ramadan

- **mandub** or **mustahab** – recommended actions, e.g. unselfish hospitality, extra prayers, forgiveness

- **mubah** – actions to be decided by conscience, because there is no clear guidance

- **makruh** – actions not forbidden, but disapproved of, e.g. divorce, smoking

- **haram** – things *never* to be done, e.g. worshipping another besides God, adultery.

Most of modern life falls in the mubah section. Whatever is not actually forbidden is permitted, under the guidance of your conscience. If an action is harmful to yourself or anyone else, it cannot be recommended by a Muslim.

MODERNISM AND FUNDAMENTALISM

If qiyas and ijtihad are used properly, it remains always possible to offer fresh thinking on past decisions, and to keep pace with the ever-changing world.

Modernist Muslims feel that this is vital, and that the reason for the past stagnation of Islam was the over-emphasizing of and clinging to the decisions of the madhhab imams of the five classical schools (ninth to tenth centuries CE, see pages 83, 105), and the neglecting of today's great scholars and thinkers.

Other reformers are known as **fundamentalists** because they seek to keep nothing but the original teachings and reject all modern interpretations as 'innovations' (bida).

Fresh thinking on past decisions is always possible

THINKING POINTS

- What do you think Muslims consider to be the chief qualities that set the tone of a civilized society? Explain why the quiet acceptance of tyranny is not acceptable to a Muslim.

- Why do Muslims regard the details of seemingly small laws to be as important as the seemingly more serious laws?

QUICK QUIZ

- What is meant by the Sunnah?
- What is meant by ijtihad?
- Whose 'ijma' are regarded as binding?
- What is meant by fiqh?
- Give an example of something mandub.
- Give an example of something mubah.

FOR YOUR FOLDERS

- Explain what the five categories of behaviour are. Which ones are ordered in the Qur'an? Which is the largest area? How are the rules worked out to deal with that area?

- Why is submission to God seen by Muslims as the greatest of freedoms?

- Explain the importance of qiyas to a modernist Muslim, and why it might be resisted by a fundamentalist.

Islam lays great emphasis on showing consideration to others – to parents, wives and husbands, children, servants and employees, and animals. The kind of qualities encouraged are kindness, understanding, respect, restraint of anger, patience and modesty.

It is not enough just to avoid doing harm to others, or even to wish for others what you would wish for yourself. Muslims are requested by Allah to be actively hospitable and generous to the guest or the person who has sought help, eager to visit friends, to visit the sick or those in prison, to give support at funerals and to console the bereaved.

EATING TOGETHER

Islam recommends feasts from time to time, and also special meals to celebrate weddings, births, congratulations, and so forth. Eating together makes social ties stronger, and visitors are always offered hospitality. Hosts might feel offended if they are refused. Feasts and parties are also opportunities to give the less fortunate a treat, for feasts where none but wealthy friends are invited are disapproved of.

CLEANLINESS

Personal purity (**taharah**) is a very important aspect of Islam. Muslims bathe frequently (over and above the ritual wash before prayer), and pay particular attention to body odours – especially those of the mouth, feet, underarms and private parts.

Children are taught young how to use the toothstick (miswak – used in the Middle East) or toothbrush, and that they should keep their clothing clean and pure. Clothes should be free of drops of urine, dogs' saliva, street dirt or drops of blood. Muslims therefore steer clear of dogs and are very careful about personal hygiene after going to the toilet or during menstruation. They usually wash with water, and do not regard wiping with paper to be sufficient. Muslim toilets always have a water supply, even it is only a jug or bottle. Muslim first-time visitors to the UK are quite distressed when they find no access to water in most toilets.

The whole body is to be bathed after sexual intercourse (and it is more pleasant for one's partner to bathe before as well), and at the end of childbirth and menstruation. It is also recommended to bathe after contact with a dead body.

The Prophet recommended cutting the nails and keeping nails and fingers very clean, and shaving off all body hair (underarms and private parts).

Muslims are never ashamed to take off their socks in public – feet sometimes get washed five times a day! In Muslim houses, carpets are kept spotless, and ready for use in prayer – so Muslims usually take off their shoes when they enter a carpeted room. They prefer slip-on shoes or sandals.

TABLE MANNERS

Use of silver or gold tableware is forbidden as gross ostentation. Meals should always be simple and wholesome, and cooking vessels kept scrupulously clean. Plates and glasses are scrubbed and polished. Guests should be invited wherever possible – most food eaten by Muslims (frequently based on rice and curry or stew) will 'stretch' well for unexpected visitors. A good hostess is always prepared for the guest.

Hands should be washed both before and after the meal. Many Muslims choose to eat with the right hand and not with a knife and fork, as this was the Prophet's sunnah. Others do so because the family or group eating together is so large there is not enough cutlery available. Sometimes people share the same plate, or even glass – confident of each other's cleanliness.

On eating, Muslims bless the food saying 'Bismillah-ir-Rahman-ir-Rahim' ('In the name of Allah, the Compassionate, the Merciful').

Children should not start eating before parents, and hosts should not start before guests. No one should speak with their mouth full, or read while eating. Food should be taken from the nearest side offered, and not touched and then put down. It is impolite to complain or find fault. People should be aware of the comfort of others and not eat too fast, or too slowly.

Muslims try to finish the meal together, and leave the table together. Sometimes the hostess (and/or host) does not eat with the others but concentrates on serving everyone, and eats afterwards.

GREETINGS

Muslims greet each other with 'As-Salamu-Alaykum' ('Peace be with you'), to which the reply is 'Wa-Alaykum-as-Salam' ('And on you be peace').

Men frequently hold and kiss each other, but Muslim women are not expected to touch men who are not related to them, so Muslim men do not usually even offer to shake hands with them. They certainly should not embrace or try to kiss them.

Greeting one another at the mosque

AT WORK

At work Muslim women try to behave in such a way as to discourage male familiarity, and any sexual banter and remarks. They regard as their right the kind of equality many Western women have fought hard to achieve in male/female relationships at work.

VISITORS

When Muslims visit others unannounced, they should knock and wait for a reply. If they have knocked three times with no response, they should go away without taking offence, accepting that their visit was not convenient.

The Prophet disapproved strongly of people invading the privacy of others. He said once that people who peeped into the homes of others should have their eyes poked out!

However, it is recommended not to go more than three days without visiting a friend.

FOR DISCUSSION

▶ Should a Muslim mother with guests object to being treated 'like a servant'?

▶ Are people who frequently sit on the floor, eat with their hands, and walk about with no shoes on, dirty?

ISLAMIC MANNERS

Say 'As-Salamu-Alaykum' ('Peace be with you') when meeting a Muslim.

Say 'Wa-Alaykum-as-Salam' ('And on you be peace') in reply.

Say 'Insha Allah' ('If Allah wishes') when hoping to do something.

Say 'Subhanallah' ('Glory to God') to praise someone.

Say 'Ma sha Allah' ('As Allah wills') in appreciation of something.

Say 'Jazakallahu Khairan' ('May Allah give you the best reward') to thank someone.

Say 'Al-hamdu-li-Llah' ('Praise be to Allah') when you wish to give thanks.

Say 'Astaghfirullah' ('Oh Allah forgive me') to show sorrow for a bad action.

Say 'Yarhamukallah' ('May Allah bless you') when you hear someone sneeze.

Say 'Na'udhubillah' ('We seek refuge with Allah') to show your dislike.

FOR YOUR FOLDERS

▶ Explain what is meant by taharah. How does this concept affect Muslim life?

▶ Some people think Muslims are dirty (they might see drops of water splashed on the toilet seat) or frightened of dogs, or dirty to eat with their hands. How would a Muslim reply to these points?

▶ Imagine you are going to practise taharah for one day. Make a brief diary of events, from when you get up in the morning to when you go to bed.

THE RIGHT TO MODEST DRESS

'Say to believing men that they should lower their gaze and guard their modesty... and that believing women should lower their gaze and guard their modesty; that they should not display their ornaments except as is normal, that they should draw their veils over their bosoms and not display their beauty except to their close male relatives.'

(surah 24:30–1, the surah gives the precise list of these relatives)

Muslim women out on the street or at business will not try to draw attention to themselves, but will always behave modestly. If they catch a man's eye, they do not stare at him, but look away.

'Believing women should cast their outer garments over themselves [when out]; that is most convenient, that they should be recognized [as such] and not be molested.'

(surah 33:59)

The Shari'ah tries to maintain values in societies that are becoming increasingly corrupt. Millions of Muslim women do not go round wearing black tent-like veils, but simply dress modestly according to the customs of their particular country.

Some traditional costumes are not acceptable as Muslim because they are not modest – they are too attention-seeking, by being either too revealing or too colourful. Muslim dress is always modest.

Muslim women do not flaunt their attractions. They certainly should not wear clothes that are revealing, low-cut, short, transparent or tight. To dress in such a way is to be regarded as 'naked', and the only object in dressing like that must be to stir up the passions of men, which is not fair, kind or sensible.

Passions, if not under control, cause endless hurt and disturbance, therefore a woman who deliberately causes temptation is badly thought of. Muslims regard sex within marriage as healthy and wholesome, but not to be indulged in when it causes hurt to others or to self. They believe that sexual freedom harms individuals, parents, unwanted children, and the security of other families. Therefore behaviour and dress should be studied carefully.

Muslim women expect to be appreciated for their minds and characters, not just for their bodies. Modest dress does not degrade women, but it discourages lust in men.

Muslim women usually cover their heads, necks and throats with some kind of scarf or veil; they cover their arms to the wrists and their legs to the ankles. This is called wearing **hijab**. Hijab (more properly called **satr**) indicates modesty in dress and behaviour. Hijab does not prevent women from going out on business, or taking an active part in society. Westerners should remember that this was normal female dress in the West too until this century.

A Muslim woman's standards of behaviour and dress should never come from pressure by relatives, or the social norms of society, but because she herself has the desire to please Allah. In fact, many Muslim women wear hijab *in spite* of opposition from husbands, or secular governments, and can actually become victims of harassment, violence and abuse.

In practical terms, many women prefer the traditional long dress and head-veil because:

- it is easy and practical

- it covers up the less-than-perfect and disguises the results of increasing age, comfortable diets, etc.

- it is graceful and feminine without being 'sexy'.

PURDAH

Complete social separation of men from women, and dressing in such a way that the body and face are not 'visible' is called **purdah**.

Covering the face is a matter of local tradition in certain countries, and is not actually part of Islam. In certain parts of the world women hide their faces from strangers, yet are not Muslim. Elsewhere very devout Muslim women do not veil because this would be regarded as odd, or attention-seeking, which defeats the object.

However, where Muslim women are reluctant to talk to strangers, wearing a **chador** or burqa gives complete privacy. They can get on with their business without being disturbed, flirted with, or made the object of unwanted attention. Since they cannot be recognized, they can ignore people they do not wish to meet or spend time with on the streets.

Iranian woman in chador

Wearing hijab

MALE CLOTHING

Muslim men are expected to be modest too, and always to be clean and smart. Cleanliness is the most important aspect. When praying, men should at least be covered from naval to knees, even in very hot weather.

They may not wear silk (unless they have a skin condition which requires it), or gold jewellery. There are many cultural styles, but basically they should not be luxurious, flashy or ostentatious. Bare legs, chests and arms are disapproved of.

It is not compulsory to wear a turban, head-cloth or white lace cap.

> *'Modesty and faith are joined closely together; if either of them is lost, the other goes also.'*
> *'Every religion has a special character; the characteristic of Islam is modesty.'*

(Hadiths)

FOR DISCUSSION

▶ Has a female Western tourist the right to walk through Muslim streets in shorts and a sun-top, or a transparent blouse? What sort of reaction might she expect if she does so? What about male tourists in shorts and open shirts?

FOR YOUR FOLDERS

▶ People often think that veiled women are treated as inferior to men. What are the real aims of Muslim clothing?

▶ Should the Muslims who come to live in the West accept the West's standards and customs and give up their own?

▶ Make a list of what Muslim women regard as the advantages of hijab. Why would dressing like this not appeal to all women?

Muslim laws about food and drink are not a matter of likes and dislikes, but of discipline. Since Muslims believe that every thought and action must be dedicated to God, and His will accepted, so the basic need to eat must also be under discipline. The Qur'an ordered certain foods to be 'haram' or 'forbidden'. Any food not declared haram is quite lawful for the Muslim to eat, or 'halal'.
The unlawful foods include:

- any product made from a pig

- meat containing blood

- meat from an animal which 'dies of itself' due to disease or other natural causes

- any flesh-eating animal

- any animal which has been strangled, beaten to death, killed by a fall, gored by another animal, or partially eaten by another animal

- any animal sacrificed to idols.
  (see surah 5:3–4)

Muslims consider that eating certain things, such as blood or dead meat with congealed blood in it, would disgust any refined person. If an animal dies by one of the methods outlined above, it is presumed that its blood will have congealed, and its flesh will have become carrion. Muslims should not eat anything of that nature, or anything dedicated to superstition. A similar rule applied to Jews and to the early Christians (see Acts 15:29).

HALAL KILLING

Animals which do not eat other animals are lawful food, but they must be killed according to the halal (permitted) method. This means that they must have the jugular severed by a sharp knife, while the name of God is invoked.

Sometimes non-Muslims who are not used to animal slaughter think this method is barbaric and cruel (though they may not know how their own meat is killed!). Muslims regard their method as being the kindest there is, and refuse to eat meat killed any other way.

Muslims do not eat animals which have been killed by electrocution or shooting, which they regard as very cruel methods. (They also disapprove of factory farming and animal experimentation.)

Pronouncing the name of God is a rite to call attention to the fact that Muslims are not taking life thoughtlessly, but solemnly for food, with the permission of God, to whom the life is being returned.

The principle is of kindness to the animal. If one creature has to die to provide food for another, it should be killed as swiftly and painlessly as possible. It should not have to die in the terror of a slaughterhouse atmosphere, but be gently led away, not knowing its fate, and killed with compassion.

Most people do not like the thought of killing animals at all, and would not wish to have to do it themselves. Some argue that the halal method is cruel, and that it is kinder to stun the animal with an electric shock first. Muslims insist that when this is done it is not kinder at all. If a human patient had to be stunned like this, an anaesthetic would be given first! Passing a high-voltage electric current through an animal's brain so that it is unable to feel the knife is illogical.

THINKING POINT

- What is the intention behind halal killing? Why would a Muslim not be shocked by the thought of slaughtering a sheep in his or her own garden? Discuss the reasons why such an action gives offence in the West.

Halal butcher's shop

PERMITTED FOODS

Muslims are allowed to eat fish, poultry, all the meat of sheep, goats and camels, and game caught by hunting animals which are trained not to kill out of savagery or their own appetite, but for their trainer's needs. In this case, the name of God can be pronounced when the hawk or dog releases the quarry.

Chicken is one of the meats most frequently eaten. All fruit, grains and vegetables are permitted. In an emergency, if nothing else is available, anything edible becomes permitted.

'O ye who believe! Eat of the good things that We have provided for you, and be grateful to God if it is Him you worship. He has only forbidden you meat of an animal that dies of itself, and blood, and the flesh of pigs, and that on which any other name has been invoked besides that of God. But if one is forced because there is no other choice, then one can eat other food without being guilty.'

(surah 2:172–3, see also surahs 5:4 and 6:145)

The last words of the Qur'an revealed to the Prophet suggest that meat butchered by Jews or Christians is also permissible.

'This day are all things good and pure made lawful to you. The food of the People of the Book is lawful to you, and yours is lawful to them.'

(surah 5:6)

SOCIAL CONSEQUENCES IN NON-MUSLIM SOCIETY

These laws greatly affect the Muslim's ability to mix socially with non-Muslim neighbours, since nearly all meat in the West has been killed by electrocution or firing a bolt into an animal's brain, and is therefore forbidden to Muslims. They should not buy meat from a market unless it is known to be halal.

If they cannot get access to halal meat, they are obliged to follow a vegetarian diet, although they may not wish to be vegetarians.

Non-vegetarians may not realize that if Muslims are carrying out the ban on pork products and non-halal meat, it not only means that they cannot eat bacon, pork sausages, ham, tinned luncheon meat, or salami, but a whole range of other products is forbidden – certain bread, biscuits, soups, chocolate, ice-cream, fried breakfasts – in fact anything that contains animal fat as opposed to vegetable fat. Muslims have to examine every packet!

Many Muslims actually fear eating pork by accident, thinking it will make them ill. Non-Muslims might scoff at this, but it is becoming increasingly known that pork products are responsible for many allergy conditions.

The ban against pork products is shared by Jews, and Muslims think it should also be shared by Christians, who have apparently ignored completely the example of Isa (Jesus), who never ate pork himself and left instructions that the laws of God were not to be broken.

Many Muslim children do not eat school dinners because of the food restrictions.

FOR YOUR FOLDERS

▶ It is the duty of a Muslim wife to safeguard the purity of the home, and make sure all the food eaten is halal. Explain what is meant by halal. What laws regarding food and drink do Muslims have?

▶ What difficulties do you think a Muslim family might have in keeping the food laws?

▶ On what grounds do Muslims argue that halal killing is not cruel?

FOR DISCUSSION

▶ People shouldn't eat meat if they are not prepared to be responsible for the animal's slaughter in the kindest way.

'It is He who has made you custodians (khalifas), inheritors of the Earth.'

(surah 6:165)

'It is Allah who has subjected the sea to you... and He has subjected to you all that is in the Heavens and the Earth.'

(surah 45:12–13)

RESPONSIBILITY

Muslims believe that Allah has handed the planet over to humankind, for them to look after, cherish and protect it. Human beings are to be guardians, responsible for every part of it. They are certainly not to damage, pollute or destroy it. On the Day of Judgement, Muslims expect to be asked questions about their responsibility towards Allah's Earth and the creatures on it, and the natural resources (animal, vegetable and mineral) which Allah has given for them to use and not abuse.

Scientists have observed that human activity now affects the atmosphere and climate. Notable examples are the increase of the greenhouse effect caused by CFC gases which warm up the planet and destroy the protective ozone-layer, and 'seeding' clouds by dropping chemicals into them to produce rain. Muslim scientists consider that uncontrolled industrialization has been very wasteful with the Earth's resources. They also think that people who do not understand that they are Allah's guardians of the planet do not care about what is taken out of the Earth, how thoughtlessly it is used, and how waste products are disposed of or dumped. Money-making companies have disregarded the effect of their actions – as can be seen in the massive applications of herbicide and pesticides, or the polluting of the seas with poisons and chemical wastes.

If deliberate disruption is caused to the Earth's natural systems, the consequences are all too clear. Species of living things become extinct, deserts spread, the atmosphere is reduced, and millions are impoverished and suffer starvation.

Muslims regard this planet as a place created out of love, and therefore it should be sustained through love. The Muslim desires to live at peace with nature, and to bring about its wholeness.

◇

COMPASSION

'Once, during a severe famine, a student of religion saw a dog lying on the ground, so weak it could not even move. The student was moved to pity, and immediately sold his books and bought food to give to the dog. That very night, he had a striking dream. "You need not work so hard to acquire religious knowledge, my son. We have bestowed knowledge upon you." '

(Muslim story, the *Muslim Voice,* January 1990)

Islam teaches that mercy and compassion are to be shown to every living creature, for Allah loves everything that he has made. Therefore cruelty to animals is totally forbidden in Islam.

BLOOD SPORTS

The Prophet forbade any 'sport' which involved making animals fight each other – a common enough practice in his time. By the same principle, modern blood sports such as fox-hunting, badger-, bear- or dog-baiting, or fights to the death between cockerels, are condemned.

HUNTING

Islam teaches that no one should ever hunt just for sport. People may only take the life of animals for food or another useful purpose.

'If someone kills a sparrow for sport, the sparrow will cry out on the Day of Judgement, "O Lord! That person killed me for nothing! He did not kill me for any useful purpose!" '

(Hadith)

Where an animal or bird, such as a hawk, is a natural predator, it cannot be blamed for doing what comes naturally to it, since Allah has created the instinct in it – but deliberate cruelty is never to be encouraged. All hunting should be for food, and any animal used for hunting should be well trained, kept under control, and not clumsy or savage.

If a weapon is used when hunting an animal it should be of a type that would pierce the animal, such as a spear, sword or bullet. Weapons which are used to club or throttle animals are forbidden.

Clubbing a wounded animal or throwing stones at it is totally forbidden. The idea of people clubbing seal pups in order to get their fur for luxury garments is disgusting to a Muslim.

ANIMAL EXPERIMENTS AND VIVISECTION

It is common, in the world today, for all sorts of experiment to be tried out on animals, for a variety of reasons. Some of these are genuinely beneficial to humanity, and bring about progress in medicine and medical welfare. Others are for cosmetic purposes, or involve testing reactions to various substances, even to cigarettes.

According to the principle of compassion and kindness towards all Allah's creations, any experiment simply for the development of luxury goods is forbidden. Muslims should always find out if the things they buy have been produced using **halal** methods, without inflicting cruelty on any other living thing.

In the field of medical progress, if there were no possible alternative to an experiment on an animal, then Muslims might accept it. However, they would far prefer to look for some other method of investigation. Experiments on animals should never be attempted lightly, or without very good reason.

ANIMALS IN CONFINEMENT

Some animals are kept in appalling conditions – for example, in factory-farms or in zoos. It is against the spirit of Islam to keep any animal tied up, in dirty conditions, or confined in a small space, just for convenience. Muslims believe that people who treat animals and birds like this will be answerable for their actions on the Day of Judgement.

Killing for luxury goods is forbidden

SOME GREEN HADITHS OF THE PROPHET MUHAMMAD

'The Earth is green and beautiful, and Allah has appointed you his stewards over it.'

'The whole Earth has been created a place of worship, pure and clean.'

'If a Muslim plants a tree or sows a field and humans and beasts and birds eat from it, all of it is love on his part.'

FOR DISCUSSION

▶ Why do you think Muslims are so against factory farming?

▶ Why are Muslims sometimes in conflict with the fashion industry?

FOR YOUR FOLDERS

▶ In what ways are Muslims expected to take responsibility for the use, and not misuse, of the planet in everyday life?

▶ What would be the Muslim attitude to a company that was only interested in making profit, and not in safeguarding the planet?

▶ Why would Muslims disapprove of:
  - using aerosols containing CFC gases
  - buying products obtained from the killing of rare or endangered species of animals (e.g. fur, ivory)
  - the unnecessary waste of paper and packaging
  - using products which will not break down and rot naturally
  - using detergents that pollute water supplies.

SCHOOL

School problems fall into four main areas:

- immodest dress, especially in compulsory PE lessons
- not separating boys and girls after the age of ten
- sexual instruction in the classroom
- religious instruction that is either Christian or Jewish (i.e. Bible based), or Islam presented in an incorrect manner.

Muslims consider that:

- girls and boys should be educated separately as soon as their sexual urges begin, to protect them, and make them concentrate on lessons
- girls should not be forced to wear short skirts – the uniform should allow trousers for girls
- PE should be carried out in track suits
- communal showers are immodest and should not be forced on girls or boys
- sex education should not be taught by people who are not in agreement with Muslim morality.

RELIGIOUS EDUCATION

This can be a problem if it is concerned with Bible material only (since the Muslim interpretation of many passages is different, e.g. the sacrifice of Isma'il rather than Isaac), or if it teaches Islam with prejudice, or inaccurately.

Muslims do not mind knowing about other religions, but cannot agree with teachers who:

- believe nothing themselves
- regard Muslims as non-believers, and try to convert them to Christianity
- think all religions are equal.

Muslims are also expected to withdraw from school worship because they will not pray to Jesus (Isa) or 'in Jesus' name'; they must also be left out of preparations for Christmas and Easter.

PRAYER

Some employers are not sympathetic if workers want to break off for a few moments to pray. Often there is no private place for them to go, or facilities

Muslim children praying at Islamia School, Brent

to wash first.

Non-Muslims are surprised to see people washing their feet in a high sink, and some even think it is dirty – although the opposite is obviously the case.

Prayer times are flexible, and tend to follow the normal breaks of the day, so timing should not really be a problem, but it is not always easy to find somewhere quiet where you will not be laughed at. In Muslim countries, of course, people can set aside an area and pray anywhere, while life goes on around them, and no one thinks anything of it.

Muslim men require time off to go to the mosque for an hour or so during Friday lunchtime, the time taken depending on the distance from the mosque. It is expected that secondary school boys should go too, so they often miss some lessons before or after lunch.

RAMADAN

Non-Muslims who have not experienced fasting can have no idea of the effects it sometimes has on people. Some get bad-tempered, impatient, or light-headed and giggly; many feel sick or faint at certain times; most feel very tired and drained of energy in the afternoons until their bodies get used to the regime of no food or drink until evening. Some find it hard to eat at night, even when allowed, and become quite weak by the end of the 30 days (see page 65).

It becomes very difficult to do hard physical work. Teachers might tell pupils off for being sleepy or lazy, without realizing that a pupil is probably very hungry and may have been up until 3 a.m. with the family the previous night.

In a Muslim country, the whole system is sympathetic, with school and office hours re-arranged.

MEDICAL TREATMENT

It is not thought proper for a Muslim woman or girl to be examined by a male doctor, or a Muslim man or boy to be examined by a female doctor. This is not usually a problem in a group practice, where you can choose a doctor.

The only major problem comes when there is no choice of doctor in hospital, and when a Muslim dies in hospital.

Muslims find the 'red tape' difficult to put up with, and expect to be with their relatives when they die, and to take them away immediately for washing, prayers and burial.

DOGS

Many non-Muslims keep dogs in their houses, and are pleased if they paw or snuffle at guests as a sign of affection. Muslims do not dislike dogs, but they are regarded as ritually unclean animals, so if a dog touches them before prayers they have to change their clothes as well as doing the ritual wash. If a person walking a dog meets a Muslim friend, they should not be surprised if the Muslim backs away!

FOR YOUR FOLDERS

▶ How does Shari'ah make life complicated for Muslim girls in a Western school? Do you think Muslim girls should give up their customs and adopt Western ways, or should they have allowances made for them? Give reasons for your answer.

FOR DISCUSSION

▶ How far do you think it is true that living according to Shari'ah makes it impossible for Muslims to mix socially with a non-Muslim community?

THINGS TO DO

▶ Imagine you are a Muslim parent. Write a letter to the head teacher of your daughter's school explaining the problems she is facing because she is a Muslim, and why you take your point of view so seriously.

▶ Imagine you are a Muslim who has recently arrived in Britain. You are finding things difficult and strange – the weather, food, shops, the people on the streets, the mosque in a converted house. Write a letter back home describing some of your experiences and problems.

'The best of you are those who are kind to your family.' (Hadith)

THE BASIS OF SOCIETY

Muslims regard the family as the basis for the human race, culture, society and civilization. They accept it as an institution founded by God (see surah 4:1) and intended to give a secure atmosphere for the growth and progress of all its members.

Anything which weakens or disrupts it is therefore regarded as a serious matter. The home is considered to be far more important, sacred, creative and rewarding than any place 'outside'.

THE EXTENDED FAMILY

The family is a complex interwoven unit consisting of many people. It is not just a husband and wife plus their parents and children. It includes brothers and sisters, uncles and aunts, cousins. In the atmosphere of a loving, outgoing unit, it also includes friends and neighbours, and anyone who falls within the sphere of that love and who needs help (see surah 2:83).

'Those who show the most perfect faith are those who possess the best disposition and are kindest to their families.'

'May his nose be rubbed in dust who found his parents approaching old age and did not enter Paradise by serving them.'

(Hadiths)

RESPECT FOR SENIOR RELATIVES

Today's old people were yesterday's providers and heroes, and are therefore always to be respected. In Muslim families age comes first, and the grandparents take priority over the children, who are taught to be respectful and considerate.

As people become old they often become confused, or bad tempered, or suffer from diseases, aches and pains. It is human nature for them to think they are *always* in the right, and *always* superior to their children, even if the children are themselves in their sixties! Muslims behave towards their parents with tolerance and understanding. They know that there may come a time when the parents' judgement will be clouded, or they may not be able to cope.

'Your Lord orders that you... be kind to parents. If one or both of them attain old age with you, do not say one word of contempt to them, or repel them, but speak to them in terms of honour... and say, My Lord, bestow your mercy on them, as they cherished me when I was a child.'

(surah 17:23–4)

It is considered unthinkable for a Muslim to pass over the care of their parents to a stranger. Just as the mother expects to bring her own child into the world and nurse it until it reaches independence, so the Muslim 'child' expects to care for parents who are approaching the end of life, and to nurse them safely into the next life.

RECOMMENDED RULES OF CONDUCT TOWARDS CHILDREN

- Avoid over-confidence and false pride arising from your love for them, and be on your guard against misdeeds.

- Give them the best possible education, not just to be clever but also so that they may be able to earn a living.

- Help them to make happy marriages.

- Always deal with them justly and with love. Never be unfair.

- Don't be overprotective, or negligent.

- Don't put heavy burdens on them by trying to force them to do things beyond their capability, or by being disappointed with their achievements.

- Accept their gifts with appreciation.

- Train them in Muslim worship. They should begin learning prayer and fasting by the age of seven.

'He who has no compassion for our little ones, and does not acknowledge the honour due to our elders, is not one of us.'

(Hadith)

No one child in a family should be made the favourite, but all should be treated equally, and with fair discipline.

'Do not ask me to be a witness to injustice. Your children have the right to receive equal treatment, as you have the right that they should honour you.'

'Fear Allah, and treat your children with equal justice.'

(Hadiths)

MILK BROTHERS AND SISTERS

If a baby's mother dies, and the baby is given to another woman to breastfeed, that child would be regarded as brother or sister to the mother's own children, and future marriage between them would not be allowed.

ADOPTION

'I, and the one who raises an orphan, will be like these two in the Garden.'

(Hadith – an occasion when Muhammad pointed to his middle and index fingers)

The Qur'an teaches that any orphaned or abandoned children should be looked after as an act of compassion, and given shelter, food, clothing and anything else they need – but there is *no* legal adoption in Islam. It is forbidden for Muslims to adopt a child of whom they are not the natural parents, or to make a child from another person's family an equal son or daughter to family members.

No 'adopted' children should ever be misled about their true parentage, or allowed the rights of the children born into a family. Human words or contracts cannot make an adoptive parent's blood run in the veins of an adopted child, or produce family affection and loyalty, or bestow genetic characteristics.

FOR YOUR FOLDERS

▶ How do you think living in an 'extended' family would be different from the parents and children situation common in Britain? In what ways might it be an advantage in helping people to grow together in loyalty and love?

▶ How did the Prophet think compassion should be shown to

a one's own children   b orphans?

▶ In what ways can a Muslim honour the old people in the family?

THINKING POINT

- Can Muslims sometimes cope better with their old people because of their stronger, bigger families? Is the strain of lack of privacy due to possible overcrowding less than the strain of loneliness and depression?

Whispering the adhan in the ear of a new-born baby

The birth of every new baby should be an eagerly awaited event, and in Muslim families no babies should be born illegitimate or unwanted. Babies should not be regarded as 'accidents' or 'mistakes', but as 'gifts from God'. A large number of children is often regarded as a great blessing.

The new baby is welcomed into the **ummah** – the one big family of Islam – as soon as it is born. The head of the family takes the baby into his arms and whispers the call to prayer (the **adhan**) in the right ear and the command to rise and worship (the **iqamah**) in the left ear. Thus, the first word a baby ever hears is 'God'.

TAHNIK

Next comes the **tahnik**, when a tiny piece of sugar, chewed date or honey is rubbed onto the baby's gums by the oldest or most respected relative,

perhaps the grandfather or a much-loved elderly aunt. This is to encourage the baby to suckle, and it also symbolizes making the child 'sweet' – obedient and kind. Prayers for the baby and the family follow.

AQIQAH

Seven days after the birth comes **aqiqah**, when relatives and friends come to a feast and the baby is named.

The baby's head is shaved, and by tradition the same weight as the hair in gold or silver is set aside for the poor. Even if the baby is bald, a money donation is still given, and usually the amount is well above the weight of the hair.

Some Muslims offer a sacrifice, the pre-Islamic practice of thanksgiving. The meat is shared with family, visitors and the poor.

NAMES

The choice of name is important, and it is usually a family name or one of the names from the Prophet's family. Names declaring that the baby possesses certain excellent moral qualities are avoided, and names suggesting slavery to anyone other than God are forbidden. Some of the names most often chosen start with '**Abd**' which means 'slave', added to one of the names of God, e.g. Abdullah, Abdul Rahman, Abdul Karim (Servant of God, Slave of the Merciful, Slave of the Generous One).

The parent of a first-born child may then drop their own name and become known by the name of the child. So, if the child is called Husain ibn (son of) Dawud, the parents become Abu Husain (father of Husain) and Umm Husain (mother of Husain).

KHITAN

If the baby is a boy, he must then be circumcised. **Khitan,** or circumcision, is the practice of cutting the

Turkish boy, dressed for circumcision

foreskin from the penis – the sign and practice of all the prophets of Allah. This is sometimes done at the same time as aqiqah if the baby is well and there is no need for delay. If the ceremony is left until a late age it would subject the boy to a form of shamefulness in Muslim eyes, and the parents would be considered cruel and neglectful.

If the baby is not healthy circumcision can be left for a few months. In some places, however, it takes place when the boy is between seven and ten years old. In Turkey, the boy is dressed up like a little prince, and the circumcision takes place at a family party. This is not the recommended way in Islam and is an ordeal for the boy.

Circumcision of baby boys is not cruel. It is a healthy practice, particularly in hot areas of the world, and avoids discomfort and disease. It in no way prevents the boy from enjoying a sexual relationship later on.

BISMILLAH

Around the fourth birthday some Muslims have a ceremony known as **bismillah**, the occasion when the child learns the first lesson from the Qur'an by heart – 'In the name of God, the Compassionate, the Merciful'. The child has to repeat each word carefully and is taught how to pray. The education as a Muslim has begun.

QUICK QUIZ

▶ What is meant by ummah?

▶ What are the first words a Muslim baby should hear?

▶ What is the tahnik?

▶ What happens at aqiqah?

▶ What sort of name should not be given to a baby?

FOR DISCUSSION

▶ Why do you think Muslims regard it as important to start training children in the faith early?

▶ Why would a Muslim not want to have the name Abdul Muhammad or Abdul Hussein, but would be pleased to be called Abdullah or Abdul Rahman?

FOR YOUR FOLDERS

▶ Imagine that you are a guest in a Muslim home where a baby has just been born. Write to a friend describing what celebrations and customs took place during the first week of the baby's life.

THINGS TO DO

▶ Look at the photo of a Turkish boy. Explain why he is dressed like this, what will soon happen to him, and why.

▶ Explain why most Muslims have their boys circumcised shortly after birth.

Muslim bride

Bringing a new husband or wife into the family is a very serious business, and never to be taken lightly. Two completely separate family units will be joined by the marriage, with all its implications, unless the new partner happens to have been chosen from the same family.

It is quite normal in Islam for relatives outside the immediate family to marry, and thought preferable that the new husband or wife is someone whose character and background is well known and understood.

Muslims are urged to choose their partners very carefully, and to remain loyal to them for the rest of their lives, for in due course, if God wills, the girl will probably become a mother and the youth a father.

ARRANGED MARRIAGES

For this reason, Muslim marriages are often arranged for young couples by their parents. In the West, most young people think it is natural to fall in love, get engaged, and then married. Muslims sometimes regard 'being under the influence of love' as a dangerous and intoxicating state of mind that could easily cloud the judgement.

Parents will always seek to find good, compatible partners for their children, and they may not approve of an unwise romance.

However, marriages should always be with the consent of both partners, and they have the right to disagree with the parent's choice. A forced marriage is forbidden in Islam, and usually doomed to failure.

MAHR (DOWRY)

The **mahr** is the dowry paid by the husband to the wife. This does not have to be a large sum but it is carefully negotiated for it is the wife's right to keep it should she later be divorced. If the wife later seeks to divorce her husband against his will, she may do so only if the mahr is returned.

It is against the sunnah of the Prophet to demand high dowries, or not to give a dowry at all, or to pay it to the bride's father as compensation for the loss of his daughter's services in his household, although these may be practised by uneducated Muslims.

THE WEDDING – NIKAH

The actual ceremony is a simple affair, consisting of readings from the Qur'an, the exchange of vows in front of witnesses, and prayers. No special religious official is necessary, but often the imam is present for the happy occasion. The bride does not even have to go, as long as she sends her 'wali' or 'marriage-representative' and two witnesses of her agreement.

The signing of the **nikah** (wedding) contract may predate the couple living together or having sexual intimacy by days, months, or even years (e.g. as with the Prophet and his wife Aishah). Nikah is not considered to be a sacred contract, or 'made in heaven', but is a binding 'business' contract, giving both husband and wife rights and responsibilities.

As 'love' is not necessarily present at the time, a sensible bride includes in the contract certain conditions that could help her if she later wished to start divorce proceedings herself. For example, she could make it clear she did not give permission for a second wife.

WALIMAH

Special clothes are not necessary for nikah, but the bride would certainly dress up for the **walimah** or party to follow.

This usually consists of a meal, and takes place within three days of the couple living together.

Presents are given, usually money, Huge, expensive parties are the tradition in some societies but this has nothing to do with Islam. The Prophet actually disapproved of lavish show, especially when it caused difficulties for the bride or groom or their families.

It is considered very impolite for an invited person not to attend the walimah.

COUSIN MARRIAGES

Many Muslims seem to marry their cousins. In fact, Islam neither encourages nor refuses this practice. The Prophet's seventh wife, Zainab bint Jahsh, was his cousin, but he only married her when she was 39 after his foster-son Zaid divorced her. Cousin-marriage has caused considerable heartache in cultures where it is common as it inbreeds genetic disorders, and makes it very hard for a couple to divorce from a failed marriage if other close relatives will be offended.

MONEY MATTERS

The husband should, if he can afford it, provide his wife with a helper, since cooking and cleaning are not part of her obligations. She is the supervisor of the household. However, if he is not well-off, or the wife enjoys housework, it is counted as an act of charity on her part.

A woman's salary, if she goes out to work, is regarded as her own and not her husband's. Any property she may own before marriage remains hers, and she does not have to give it to her husband unless she wishes.

Even if he is poor, the husband is expected to provide for her. A woman does not have to take her husband's name, but may keep her own.

MIXED MARRIAGES

Muslim boys may marry Christians and Jews, but Muslim girls are not permitted to marry non-Muslims because in Islam the children have to take the religion of the father, and so would become non-Muslims. If a youth wishes to marry a Hindu, Sikh or Buddhist girl, it is only permitted if she converts to Islam.

THE RIGHT TO COMPATIBILITY IN MARRIAGE

'The Prophet said "A woman should only be married to a person who is good enough for her or compatible to her."'

(Hadith)

In Islam, the only compatibility that really matters is **piety**. The Prophet permitted marriages between people of vastly different social status and financial backgrounds, knowing it was not these factors which made for compatibility, but what they were like in their hearts.

The most important ingredients in a Muslim marriage are shared values and beliefs, so that even if the couple come from different cultures and backgrounds, they possess the same basic world view, attitudes and habits which will bind them together.

'Do not marry only for a person's looks; their beauty might become the cause of moral decline. Do not marry for wealth, since this may become the cause of disobedience. Marry rather on the grounds of religious devotion.'

(Hadith)

The aim in marriage is that the partner should also be one's 'best friend', the one who shares the concerns and responsibilities of life, who offers peace, comfort and rest, and who helps to bear difficulties which are too much to be faced alone.

FOR YOUR FOLDERS

▶ Why do Muslims consider marrying 'under the influence of love' to be a dangerous practice?

▶ What kind of qualities does a Muslim look for in a bride?

▶ Explain what is meant by mahr, nikah and walimah.

▶ In what ways should the principles of Muslim marriage be helpful to wives?

TALKING POINTS

● Is it better for a girl to choose her own husband, or does the arranged marriage system have any advantages for the young couple?

● How important do you think it is for a person to marry someone who shares the same religious beliefs?

Islam stresses the importance of motherhood

MOTHER

A household in which there is love, peace and security is considered to be valuable beyond price, and it does not come about by accident. It has to be worked for by all members, and requires a strong commitment to patience, forgiveness, tolerance, sense of duty and love.

All these things are regarded as vital, and the key person in the household who sets the tone and does most of the work is undoubtedly the mother.

To be a good mother is so important in Islam that she is considered to be the most precious treasure in the world. Her role is the decisive factor in the family.

When a woman becomes a mother, she takes on an enormous responsibility. In allowing her body to produce a new living being she should bear in mind the inalienable rights of every child:

- the right to life, and equal chances in life
- the right to legitimacy – which means that every child should have a legal father
- the right to a good and loving upbringing.

THE TEAM

A Muslim mother is expected to take responsibility for:

- food for the hungry
- refuge for the weary
- hospitality for the guest
- comfort for the distressed
- peace for the troubled
- hope for the insecure
- encouragement for the weak.

The father is expected to *provide* the means whereby all this can actually be achieved, to *protect* the home, and generally to make the mother's role possible.

The father is responsible for bringing in money, and therefore it is his duty, as far as possible, to be strong, respected and honourable. Just as the mother's role involves far more than cooking and cleaning, the father's involves leadership, responsibility and duty, and an involvement in the world of economics, business, trade and commerce.

PARTNERSHIP IN MARRIAGE

In Islam, marriage is a partnership. Muslim women accept only Allah as their master, and do not therefore consider themselves to be inferior to a husband. It is basic in Muslim society that the man is responsible for the family's welfare and business outside the home, but the woman has virtually absolute rights within it so long as her behaviour does not shame her provider.

No institution works well without a clear leader, and therefore there should be one in every family unit. Most Muslim women are quite happy for this leader to be the man they love. If the man is not worth respecting, divorce is a straightforward matter, and the woman may look for a better one. Sometimes the woman in a household is more intelligent or organized or practical than the man, so he will quite sensibly leave most matters to her – but in Islam he is still responsible for her.

THE HUSBAND'S RIGHTS

Husbands have the right:

- to a sexual relationship. Husbands and wives should not refuse each other. This goes with the obligation of the promise of no sex outside marriage.
- to discretion. The couple's sexual relationship, problems, and family matters are private.
- to obedience, except in matters where the husband is going against Islam. Wives may not mix freely with those the husband disapproves of, or go where he disapproves. Where a decision must be made, after consultation and consideration, it should be the husband's decision, for better or worse.
- to fidelity. Unfaithfulness of the wife is the only instance where a husband is allowed to chastise his wife physically, and then only as a last resort. If even that fails, the marriage has failed.

'The best of treasures is a good wife. She is pleasing in her husband's eyes, looks for ways to please him, and takes care of his possessions while he is away; the best of you are those who treat their wives best.'

(Hadith)

THE RIGHT TO BE PROTECTED

'Men are the protectors and maintainers of women, because Allah has given them more [strength]... therefore righteous women are devoutly obedient, and guard in [the husband's] absence what Allah would have them guard.'

(surah 4:34)

Although Islam accepts that women are equal to men, it does take account of the physical differences between the sexes, and it makes allowances, to protect women and make them comfortable.

A Muslim woman has the right to remain a virgin, unmolested by strangers or by any male member of her own family. She has the right to go to her marriage untouched by any man, and to give herself to her chosen partner for life. She has the right to be cared for in times of physical pain and discomfort, for example, during her monthly periods, throughout pregnancy and while rearing her children. She may be excused from fasting during Ramadan, if necessary.

Muslim women have the right to be provided for and should not be forced to work to earn money. However, there is no text which prohibits a woman from seeking work. The Prophet's wife Khadijah was herself a successful businesswoman, as was his cousin-wife Zainab.

A woman has the right to be looked after by her husband if she does not wish to go out to work. She also has the right to work without sexual harassment in her place of employment, and safeguards this right by dressing modestly.

The Prophet was never chauvinistic or selfish. He helped his wives in the home, repaired his own clothes and shoes, looked after his own bed, and so on. Where a Muslim man's wife goes out to work, it is good manners for him to help in the home and share the duties in the evenings, as the Prophet did.

POLYGAMY

'Marry women of your choice, two or three or four; but if you fear you will not be able to deal justly with them, then only one.'

(surah 4:3)

'You will never be able to be fair and just between women, even if it is your ardent desire.'

(surah 4:129)

Polygamy means having more than one wife. One could deduce from the second quote that the ideal Muslim family is, in fact, **monogamous**, but for a Muslim man to have more than one wife is neither prohibited nor unlawful. Islam did not introduce it. On the contrary, polygamy had been the normal practice in many ancient civilizations for centuries. Even in societies which only allowed one wife men very often had numerous mistresses.

Although the practice of men having more than one wife is referred to as polygamy, in fact it should properly be called **polygyny**. True polygamy (either sex having more than one spouse) is not allowed.

The Prophet Muhammad had twelve wives after the death of his beloved Khadijah; Allah then revealed that Muslim men are allowed four wives, but only on certain conditions:

● The first wife should give permission.

● Later wives must not be a cause of distress.

● All wives must be treated equally, i.e. given the same quality and amount of food, clothing, medication, leisure, living space, time, compassion and mercy (see page 19).

● Making love equally is not required, but sharing time equally is.

'The Prophet prayed "Oh Allah! This is my justice in what I could control: do not blame me for what You control and I do not control." '

(Hadith)

If a man taking a second wife commits any injustice, that marriage can be declared illegal and against the principles of Islam. The principle is one of compassion towards unprotected women – not male lust selfishly seeking to trade in an old wife for a younger model.

POLYANDRY

Islam is against a woman having more than one husband because a child has the right to know who its father is, and this would be impossible if the woman was married to more than one man.

SOCIAL REASONS FOR POLYGAMY

In any society where there is a greater number of women than men, strict monogamy means that many women would have no chance of marriage and could therefore be tempted into immoral relationships. A widow or divorcee whose prospects of marriage were small might prefer to be a second wife rather than face lifelong loneliness and struggle on her own. Nevertheless, a man should not cause his existing wife distress.

Wives could suddenly become mentally or physically ill. Muslims think it is not reasonable to expect a husband to control his instincts for the rest of his life, or to be forced to keep mistresses, or to divorce the unfortunate woman. A second wife, if he chose well, would be a second mother to his children, look after the household and, if necessary, help her husband to look after the first wife.

Some elderly wives are quite pleased for the husband to take on a younger wife, especially if she is a good worker and may have had modern training, for example as a nurse.

DISADVANTAGES OF POLYGAMY

There are four considerable disadvantages to polygamy. These are jealousy, inequality, disharmony and conflicts between the children of different wives. Each of these must be taken very seriously when considering a polygamous marriage.

'The rights of a woman are sacred; ensure that women are maintained in the rights assigned to them.'

(Hadith)

Demonstrating birth control in a women's health clinic, Cairo

EQUALITY

> *'All people are equal…as the teeth of a comb.*
> *No Arab can claim merit over a non-Arab,*
> *nor a white over a black person, nor a*
> *male over a female.'*

(Hadith)

In all the world's societies, women have struggled with the situation in which all power – in high office, at work, at home – has been in the hands of men, with women sometimes being treated as servants and the property of men.

One of the key teachings of Allah is that men and women are different, but are of equal spiritual worth. Every instruction given to Muslims in the Qur'an refers to both male and female believers. When the Prophet's wife Umm Salamah asked about this subject a special revelation was given, making it clear that 'Man' meant 'all humanity' and not just the male sex. Both sexes have been given the same religious duties and will be judged according to exactly the same criteria. Women should therefore live and work actively alongside men, and should try to gain all the knowledge and skills which they will need, to succeed.

> *'For Muslim men and women, for believing men*
> *and women… for men and women who are*
> *patient and constant, who humble themselves,*
> *who give in charity, who fast, who guard their*
> *chastity, who engage in the praise of Allah – for*
> *them Allah has prepared forgiveness and great*
> *reward.'*

(surah 33:35)

EMPOWERING WOMEN

Muslims believe that men are natural leaders, but some talented women prove to be able teachers, carers and administrators. Those Muslims who object to women taking positions of authority often do so by quoting the Prophet's single wry comment, that misfortunes will always arise when men are governed by women. It was not an order or ruling. Indeed, the Qur'an gives the clear example of Bilqis, Queen of Saba (Sheba), who was asked to become Muslim but not to give up her throne (surah 27:31, 42–4).

Three of the world's prime ministers are Muslim women – Benazir Bhutto of Pakistan, Khaleda Zia of Bangladesh, and Tanzu Ciller of Turkey.

Many modern female scholars of Islam work for the improvement of conditions of women in backward societies, and hope to encourage the correct application of Islamic Law in societies where it has been abused by uneducated or extremist Muslim men who have misunderstood the true principles of Islam (see page 141).

TALKING POINT

● What do you think 'equality in marriage' means? Does it matter if a wife wishes to 'disobey' her husband? In what sort of circumstances do you think a Muslim woman would definitely disobey her husband?

FOR YOUR FOLDERS

▶ Make a list of the conditions under which a Muslim man might take more than one wife into his household.

▶ How might a Muslim woman answer a critic who believed that in Islamic faith women are inferior to men?

'Either keep your wife honestly, or put her away from you with kindness. Do not force a woman to stay with you who wishes to leave. The man who does that only injures himself.'

(surah 2:231)

Although Islam upholds the permanence of marriage and the need for its continuance, it also recognizes that, human nature being what it is, not every marriage will be successful. Rather than condemn people to a life of misery, Islam makes provision for legal divorce, as a last resort – although it is highly discouraged.

'If a wife fears cruelty or desertion on her husband's part, there is no blame on them if they arrange an amicable settlement between themselves. Such a settlement is the best way.'

(surah 4:128)

'The most detestable act that God has permitted is divorce.'

(Hadith)

Muslims believe that divorce should always be the last resort, after all attempts to put things right have failed. The fact that Islamic divorce does not involve long formal procedures does not mean that it is taken lightly (although obviously, some people abuse the system).

◇

DIVORCE BY MUTUAL CONSENT

- **Mubara'ah** – The husband and wife can agree between themselves to terminate the marriage, and work out the financial arrangements to be made.

- **Khul** – If the wife has a genuine grievance against her husband, she can obtain a divorce from him by returning his marriage gift to her in return for the dissolution of the marriage. A husband seeking divorce may not *demand* his gifts back, unless he finds his wife guilty of clear immorality. In fact, the necessity for the husband to allow his wife to keep the dowry, and the influence of the extended family in trying to help or sort out difficulties, often discourages any husband who is inclined to divorce his wife casually.

CONDITIONS NECESSARY FOR THE DIVORCE TO BE VALID

- The partners must be sane, conscious and not under pressure from some outside party.
- The divorce must be clear to all.
- The partners must not be under the influence of alcohol or drugs, or so angry they do not appreciate what they are doing.

GROUNDS FOR A WIFE TO DIVORCE HER HUSBAND

- Inability or refusal of her husband to maintain her.
- Abuse or mistreatment.
- Impotence of her husband.
- Incurable, repulsive disease, or insanity of her husband.
- Extended absence, or desertion if the husband has not communicated.
- The husband's imprisonment.
- Deception at the completion of the contract, or concealment of important information concerning the marriage.

TALAQ AND IDDAH

Talaq is divorce requested by a husband. The intention to divorce has to be pronounced three times. The laws of Islam require a husband to be honourable and considerate. It is a gross abuse of Islam if he merely sends his wife notification of divorce, or does not tell her until the last moment. There should be a waiting period or **iddah**, before a divorce becomes final. This is usually three months, although it can be as long as nine months if the woman is pregnant, or as little as 31 days if the husband divorces the wife when he is certain she is not pregnant. During this period, the wife is entitled to continue living at the family home. She is also entitled to full maintenance and to be treated well. It is a time in which both parties are given the chance to think again.

If a reconciliation occurs, there is no need for remarriage if it is during the iddah. If the couple seek remarriage after the expiry of the waiting period, they may remarry, but with a new contract. Such remarriage is allowed a second and third time.

If a wife has been divorced and remarried to the same husband twice, they are not allowed to remarry a third time until after the woman has been properly married to some other person. Islam does not allow couples to 'cheat' by arranging such a marriage – and a quick divorce – falsely in order to remarry. It is considered good practice for there to be at least one month between divorces.

After the waiting time, no one is allowed to prevent the woman from marrying whoever she chooses – not her ex-husband, nor her father or guardian. In some societies, the woman's family might try to prevent her from remarrying a disappointing husband whom they felt she was well rid of, but this is not allowed in Islamic society.

'Do not prevent them from marrying their [former] husbands if they agree among themselves in an honourable manner.'

(surah 2:232)

A wife may divorce by talaq if it was agreed at the time of marriage and put into the contract. Many women are too shy or reluctant to include this safeguard, but it is their right in Islam.

LI'AN

This is divorce where the wife is accused of adultery. Four eye-witnesses are required to prove adultery by li'an. If no proof is forthcoming, the husband can swear four times he is telling the truth, and the wife is obliged to swear her innocence. Judgement is left to their Eternal Fate. The marriage is usually considered beyond reconciliation, and dissolved.

RELUCTANTLY ALLOWED

Divorce is **wajib** when the marriage has completely broken down; **makruh** when it is not essential and they could be reconciled; **mubah** when harm is expected through continuing the marriage; **mandub** when the wife is not fulfilling her obligations, and **haram** during the times of the wife's monthly periods (see page 85 for terms).

CUSTODY OF CHILDREN

Small children remain in the custody of the mother, unless she is obviously unfit to raise them and providing she has not remarried. Financial care of the children is the responsibility of the father, who must pay for their upkeep. In the case of children old enough to express themselves, their wishes should be taken into account.

In some societies, when the divorce is the fault of the husband, he is required to pay the woman's living expenses for one year.

THINKING POINT

- Why is it a serious matter for a woman to be divorced by her husband in a Muslim society?

FOR DISCUSSION

▶ Many Muslims think it is better for couples to stick together 'for better or worse', no matter what is going on. Why do you think so many Muslims are set against divorce?

FOR YOUR FOLDERS

▶ How do Islamic principles of marriage and divorce compare with those in the West, in your opinion? Give reasons for your answer.

▶ Why do you think Muslims regard children of broken marriages as the responsibility of the father?

'The final goal is to your Lord. It is He who causes both laughter and grief; it is He who causes people to die and to be born; it is He who caused male and female; it is He who will re-create us anew.'

(surah 53:42–7)

'When a person dies their deeds come to an end except in respect of three matters which are left behind: a continuing charity, knowledge which still brings benefit, and righteous offspring to pray for them.'

(Hadith)

Saying goodbye to a beloved member of the family causes deep sorrow and pain, and a terrible sensation of loss. It is natural for those left behind to wonder how on earth they will be able to continue without the loved one.

Yet Muslims, if they have lived their lives constantly according to Shari'ah, have been preparing for this day from the moment of birth, and hope to face the passing with calmness and acceptance.

Some people do not care whether there is life after death or not. Others do not believe in it at all. But Muslims are certain that all humans belong to God and will return to Him. They do not see death as the end of life, but the time when a person withdraws from the earthly family before going to be close to God.

The separation may seem long to those left behind, but a consoling feeling of closeness is renewed during prayer and at each family festival.

Muslims believe that not to care about life after death is unreasonable, since we are certain that all humans die.

'Does Man think that We shall not assemble his bones? Yes, surely, yes – We are able to restore even his finger-tips.'

(surah 75:3–4)

THE LAST WORD

When a Muslim knows death is approaching, friends and relatives are sent for and gather around the bed. The dying one asks for forgiveness and blessing from the loved ones and from God. Just as the first word heard by a Muslim is 'God', so it should also be the last word heard or uttered, if possible.

A Muslim headstone, Hull Cemetery

THE WAITING

Muslims believe that the soul waits in **barzakh** until the Day of Judgement (see page 42). Judgement Day, or the Day of Resurrection, may not come for centuries, but unlike Earth time this will pass in a flash – for those in barzakh are outside time.

At the Judgement Day God will deal with everyone, living and dead. It is sunnah for Muslims to be buried in the earth and not cremated.

THE FINAL SALAH

Grief is normal and expected, but shrieking and other excesses are regarded as lack of faith.

As soon as possible after death the body is given the final ritual washing and prayers. Western hospitals may be alarmed if relatives come and ask for the corpse of a newly-deceased, but Muslims believe it is not fitting to leave this last service to strangers.

The washing, which is a complete one, or **ghusl**, can either take place at the mosque, in a community facility, or at home. Afterwards, the corpse is anointed with scents or spices and wrapped in a shroud made of unsewn sheets of white cloth, three for a man and five for a woman.

Martyrs are buried unwashed, with their blood, preferably at the place where they fell.

No difference is made whether a person is rich or poor, of great importance or very humble. Muslims believe death has levelled them, they are the same. The shroud cloths may be the precious ones dipped in Zamzam water on Hajj.

The prayers are called **Salat-ul-Janaza** – the usual salah words but with no prostrations to earth. Some special words are added, including:

'O Allah, forgive us all, the living and the dead; those near at hand and those far away; keep those of us who remain here always true to Your will; keep those who are experiencing death steadfast in strong faith.'

THE FUNERAL

Funerals should be simple and inexpensive. Extravagance is forbidden, and since there is no class system for the dead, there are no special cemeteries for leaders.

Muslims prefer that coffins should not be used, except to comply with special regulations for health reasons. The body should be buried simply in the earth, not wasting precious wood, and should be carried to the cemetery rather than taken in a vehicle. Walking is considered more respectful than riding comfortably.

Muslims request burial with the face turned to the right, facing Makkah. It is therefore preferable if they can have their own cemeteries, or their own special plot, because if cemeteries are organized according to garden design or the customs of another religion, Muslims may not be able to have their graves facing in the right direction. Also, Muslims only allow one body per grave, and this sometimes causes a problem for local authorities.

As the body is lowered, they say:

'In the name of God we commit you to the earth, according to the Way of the Prophet of God.'

A little earth is then thrown down with the words:

'We created you from it, and We return you into it, and from it We will raise you a second time.'

(surah 20:55)

Money should not be spent on elaborate tombstones or memorials, but donations given to the poor.

Mourning should not last for more than three days, except for widows who may mourn for four months and ten days, and should not remarry during that period.

Some Muslims hold memorial gatherings known as rawdahs on the fortieth day, but these are disapproved of by other Muslims.

Any outstanding debts are paid off by the relatives, and the bereaved family is visited by countless well-wishers who help them over their grief by not abandoning them to loneliness. They often fill the house of the deceased for weeks, bringing their own cooked food so as not to be a burden, and do not withdraw until they are sure the bereaved person is ready to cope again.

'To God we belong and to Him we return.'

(surah 2:156)

FOR YOUR FOLDERS

▶ Give reasons why it is not thought to be a good thing for Muslims to show too much grief at a funeral, or to pay for an expensive tombstone. How are dead Muslims best honoured and remembered?

THINGS TO DO

▶ Imagine you are invited to the funeral of a Muslim boy. Give a brief outline of what happens from the moment of his death to his burial.

▶ Copy out one of the prayers or passages from the Qur'an or Hadiths. What does this passage reveal about the belief of Muslims about the after-life?

TALKING POINT

● In 1975 only 51 local authorities in Britain gave special burial plots to Muslims. Should Muslims accept local customs, and give up their own?

Praying in the desert sands

A **mosque** is a building set aside for worship. Its name in Arabic is **masjid,** which means 'a place where people prostrate themselves', in other words, where they bow and touch their heads to the earth before God.

Some mosques are very special buildings, like those at Makkah, Madinah, Jerusalem, Damascus, Cairo, Istanbul, Isfahan, Qom and Regent's Park in London.

At the other extreme are little rectangular areas marked out by roadside teashops, or in fields, or at railway stations, where you might find just a basic mat and something to indicate the direction of Makkah.

In Muslim countries, there are often arrows at railways stations, so that travellers know at once in which direction to pray.

In Britain, Muslims have taken over all sorts of buildings to use as mosques – old churches, houses, even a fire station. Anywhere will do, as long as it is clean.

As Muhammad said:

'Wherever the hour of prayer overtakes you, you shall perform it. That place is a mosque.'

(Hadith)

The place does not matter. The Qur'an states:

'Do you not see that God knows everything in the heavens and on earth. Three men cannot talk together in secret, but He is the fourth...Neither fewer than that or more, but He is with them, wherever they may be.'

(surah 58:7)

However, out of respect for God and for practical convenience, many Muslims keep a certain place in their houses, perhaps in a spare room, or part of a bedroom, so that there is always somewhere ready to set aside the thoughts and cares of the world and come before God in prayer.

The first mosque in Madinah was built around the Prophet's family house. This was a typical desert dwelling, consisting of several huts for the Prophet and his wives set around a square courtyard, surrounded by a mud-brick wall. Houses built like this can be seen all over the Middle East where there is mud available, hot sun to dry it, and no rain. The northern side had palm trees supporting a thatched roof to provide some shade. The first Muslims met together for prayer in the courtyard.

King Faisal Mosque, Islamabad, Pakistan

*The Badshahi Mosque,
Lahore, Pakistan*

*The Blue Mosque,
near Kuala Lumpur, Malaysia*

Jamia Mosque, Nairobi, Kenya

*Shir-Dah Madrasah and Mosque,
Samarkand, Uzbekistan*

FOR YOUR FOLDERS

▶ Is it important for a group of believers to have a special place where they can meet? What do you see as the advantages or disadvantages of such a place?

▶ Copy out surah 58:7. What does this teach about the presence of God?

FOR DISCUSSION

▶ God can be worshipped anywhere, and the most important place of worship is the heart.

▶ Splendid buildings should be disapproved of as a waste of money and effort.

Regent's Park Mosque, London

Inside Regent's Park Mosque

MIHRABS

The prayer leader usually stands in front of the **mihrab**, a special niche set in the wall that faces Makkah. Mihrabs are usually beautifully decorated with coloured tiles and texts from the Qur'an, and are sometimes known as the 'niche of lights', the symbol for divine presence in the heart.

Many are shell shaped, from the tradition that shells house a pearl, formed when they rise to the surface of water at night and open to receive a dewdrop. The shell symbolizes the 'ear of the heart' which absorbs the 'dewdrop of the divine word'. It is characteristic that the most sumptuous decoration is used to frame and venerate something which is not itself visible.

Mihrab, Cairo Mosque, Egypt

Before entering a mosque Muslims take off their shoes and perform the ritual washing. There will be a well, fountain or tap in the courtyard, or a special washroom in a modern building. It is normal for modern mosques to have separate facilities for women.

Shoes are left outside the prayer area on a rack. When there is a huge congregation they are carried in a bag to avoid a frantic scramble after the service.

Inside, visitors immediately feel a sense of peace, air and space. This is because the interior is not cluttered up with furniture. There are no seats to sit on, and no pictures or statues to decorate the building. Everyone is expected to sit or kneel on the floor, which is generally covered with carpets.

No one has a special place, as all are equal in God's sight. There is often a design on the carpet, or lines marked out, to help the believers form neat rows. Often, little individual mats are used, some with designs showing Makkah or the mosque at Madinah. All are placed pointing in the direction of Makkah.

In the roof there may be a dome. This gives a feeling of open space and represents the universe. It also permits the voice of the imam to be heard clearly by the worshippers. It encourages a powerful, calm atmosphere.

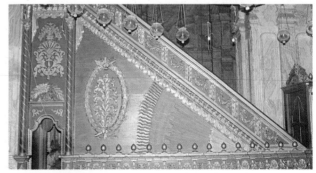

Minbar, Cairo, Egypt

NO PICTURES

There are no statues or pictures in case simple people begin to treat them as idols. Representations of God or spiritual beings are regarded as blasphemous and, in any case, misleading. Pictures of the Prophet could only be guesswork and would give a false impression.

Mosques are not dull places, however, as they can have rich carpets, often scarlet or green, brightly-patterned tiles, marble pillars, huge chandeliers, and intricate stonework and stained-glass windows.

To one side is the pulpit or **minbar**, from which sermons are given. It may be very ornate, or just a little platform at the top of a few stairs.

In modern mosques, men and women enter by separate doors and have separate rooms for worship.

At the men's entrance there is usually a notice-board for general business and a set of clocks giving the prayer times for the day. These will vary according to the seasons, or the country, depending on the times of dawn and dusk.

There is sometimes a room used as a mortuary, the place where bodies of dead Muslims are carefully washed and wrapped in shrouds before burial.

Decorative tile work, Isfahan, Iran

Outside the courtyard, dome and **minaret** are visible. In the East most courtyards are uncovered, because it seldom rains. The minaret is a tall tower from which the call to prayer is given. Some mosques have more than one minaret. The Blue Mosque in Istanbul is the only one in the world that has six. The **qiblah wall**, which marks the direction of Makkah, is often higher, or has a huge archway.

THINGS TO DO

▶ Imagine that you are interviewing a Muslim, Mr Qasim, at the mosque. These are the questions to put to him. Work out what his answers will be. (If you can speak to a Muslim you could conduct a real interview.)

a   What does the word qiblah mean, and what does it show?

b   What is a minaret used for?

c   Why do mosques need a water supply?

d   What do Muslims do when they enter a mosque?

e   Why are pictures or statues regarded as undesirable?

f   What do clocks in a mosque entrance show?

g   Why are there no chairs for worshippers?

h   Why are there lines on the carpet, or a pattern?

FOR YOUR FOLDERS

▶ Write to a friend giving a full description of the main features found at a mosque

a   outside, and
b   inside.

▶ How far do you think that the design of a mosque fulfils the practical purposes of Muslim worship?

Learning at the mosque school

USES

The Prophet did not separate religious life from his normal daily activities. In the open courtyard he entertained visitors, conducted business, and guided the day-to-day affairs of the community. It was the place where believers gathered for communal prayer and to hear his sermons, and it was also used for giving shelter to the poor, homeless and wayfarers, and for caring for the sick.

In the courtyard was a well, not only for washing before prayers, but for ordinary refreshment. Travellers could arrive there and have a cool drink and food. Visitors were allowed to rest in the corners, or even stay overnight.

It is important to realize that mosques today, no matter how grand the buildings, are still used to fulfil all these other functions.

The community function is particularly important in places where Muslims are in the minority – they need a place to meet and discuss their problems.

Mosques are also used:

- as schools – for learning Arabic and studying the Qur'an
- as law courts – for matters of Islamic law
- for functions such as birth, marriage and burial celebrations
- for parties, welcome home meetings, lectures, as a games room or reading room, for fund-raising activities.

BEHAVIOUR

People are expected to behave quietly and respectfully at all times, even if prayers are not taking place. Shoes are taken off and left outside or carried in a bag, and the feet carefully washed.

But people can relax there, and you can often see adult students (sometimes white-haired old men) reading and studying, or taking a peaceful nap, or maybe even playing table-tennis in a modern 'community room'.

SCHOOL

Most mosques have a **madrasah** or school, where young Muslims do their 'Islamiat' or Islamic studies. In Britain this usually takes place between 4 and 6 p.m., five nights a week, and some schools even demand weekend work.

Children in Muslim countries do not have to work so hard, because they can do Islamiat during the day as part of their normal lessons. Indeed, it is usually considered to be the most important part of their education.

Boys and girls usually start Islamic studies at the age of five. Girls generally finish at the age of twelve, and boys continue until they are fifteen. Good students can spend the rest of their lives continuing to learn, and become teachers themselves.

It is important to realize that most Muslims are *not* Arabs, and therefore Arabic, the language of Islam, is not their native language. If Muslims want

The mosque is used for social gatherings

to study the Qur'an properly they should attempt to learn Arabic. Good students learn a great deal of the Qur'an by heart. Some learn it all, and become a hafiz (see page 44).

There is an exam every year, and few children fail it. They all change classes after Ramadan. Most teachers are not specially trained, but are willing volunteers. They are allowed to use the cane, but almost never do in normal circumstances because the children learn from an early age to respect their elders and behave politely.

FOR YOUR FOLDERS

▶ What are the main social uses the mosque building provides a place for? How do these activities all serve to strengthen the community feeling of ummah?

▶ Explain the purpose of the madrasah. Why is studying Islamiat particularly hard for youngsters in

  a non-Arabic countries?
  b non-Muslim countries?

▶ Explain why it is important for a Muslim to

  a learn Arabic, and
  b learn as much of the Qur'an as possible by heart.

THINKING POINT

● Does the use of the mosque for purposes other than prayer prevent it from being a 'holy' place?

FOR DISCUSSION

▶ Why can no particular holy place claim that it alone contains the presence of God? Why do you think that some people believe certain places are helpful in bringing God close to them?

Faith in Allah is not simply a matter of beliefs about God and life after death. It also involves action (**amal**), the struggle to overcome selfish living and to mould the character according to the highest possible ideals.

Muslims are aware that God is not distant from us. They believe He is the supreme creator and sustainer of the universe, but that He is also our closest friend and helper.

> *'It was We who created Man, and We know what dark suggestions his soul makes to him* [i.e. our innermost desires and motives]: *for We are nearer to him than his jugular vein.'*
>
> (surah 50:16)

If you could imagine one gardener for the whole world, each of us is the equivalent of one tiny ant – yet Muslims believe God sees every one of us and knows us as individuals.

Muslims realize that:

> *'Allah does not look upon your bodies and appearances: He looks upon your hearts and deeds.'*
>
> (Hadith)

FAITH

Faith is the key virtue of a Muslim. This faith involves a deep love for God, and the desire to please Him. It means trusting in your relationship with Him, not only in your life of prayer, but in every moment of your conscious life.

> *'You should worship God as if you are seeing Him; for He sees you even if you do not see Him.'*
>
> (Hadith)

HONESTY

Honesty, truthfulness, sincerity and integrity are all fundamental aspects of being a Muslim. How can a person claim to love God, and then lie, cheat, break promises, and let others down? No one can trust the person who lies. A Muslim's sincerity and integrity should be beyond question, so that everyone knows they can be absolutely relied upon.

The Prophet said: *'Always speak the truth, even if it is bitter.'*

JUSTICE

Justice is closely linked with honesty and truth. Muslims have a strong desire to see fair play. Muslim justice is pure and uncorruptible; it is not influenced by personal relationships, or influence of wealth or status – for God sees all!

> *'O believers, be seekers after justice, witnesses for God, even though it be against yourselves or your parents and kinsmen; or whether [the person] be rich or poor; for God is the protector of both. So do not follow the base desires [of your hearts], lest you become "bent"; for if you distort or decline to do justice, truly God knows very well all that you do!'*
>
> (surah 4:135)

COMPASSION

Along with a strong sense of justice, a Muslim should also be merciful and compassionate. Compassion is the prime quality of Allah Himself, and every surah but one begins by naming Him as the Compassionate, the Merciful One.

People who are not compassionate are usually blind to the failings in themselves, or have lived a highly sheltered and protected life.

Honest Muslims know how often they have made mistakes, given in to temptation, shown weakness and folly, and been selfish, narrow-minded or unjust. On the Day of Judgement Muslims believe all faults will be revealed, but thankfully Allah has assured us that His mercy is greater than His anger.

Muslims believe that whenever we are genuinely sorry for our failings, they are immediately forgiven by God – even if the humans we have hurt and let down cannot forgive us quite so easily.

Allah asks Muslims to be more merciful than ordinary humans, to give that little bit extra.

> *'Be forgiving and control yourself in face of provocation; give justice to the person who was unfair and unjust to you; give to the one who did not help you when you were in need, and keep fellowship with the one who did not care about you.'*
>
> (Hadith)

Allah requests Muslims to show extra compassion to:

- parents
- children
- one's marriage partner
- orphans
- the sick, wounded and handicapped
- servants, helpers and employees
- animals.

'He who has no compassion for our little ones is not one of us.'

(Hadith)

GENEROSITY

True Muslims are generous and hospitable, never clinging to their own possessions but regarding every material blessing as an opportunity to share Allah's love with others. A truly virtuous person…

'gives food, for the love of Him, to the needy, the orphan, the prisoner of war [saying]: "We feed you only for the sake of Allah; we desire no repayment from you, and no thanks." '

(surah 76:7–10)

MODESTY

Muslims realize that all their gifts and talents are granted them by Allah, and so never show off. They are embarrassed by adulation and praise. They give of themselves quietly and humbly, seeking no return but God's pleasure.

They dress modestly and respect chastity and purity in sexual relationships. They do not seek to exploit or abuse, but protect and cherish.

'Modesty and faith are joined closely together; if either of them is lost, the other goes too.'

(Hadith)

TOLERANCE

Muslims should be gentle and tolerant of the rights of others.

'Let there be no coercion in religion.'

(surah 2:256)

PATIENCE, COURAGE AND FORTITUDE

When the tests of life come, as they inevitably will, Muslims remember their faith in God and face up to them with patience, courage and fortitude, the quality known as **sabr**. They do not run away from life, but they try to work out what it is God wishes them to do in each situation, and hold on to their faith while trouble lasts.

'Be firm and patient in pain (or suffering) and adversity, and throughout all periods of panic. Such are the people of truth, the God-fearing.'

(surah 2:177)

'Muslims who live in the midst of society and bear with patience the afflictions that come to them are better than those who shun society and cannot bear any wrong done to them.'

(Hadith)

FOR DISCUSSION

▶ If there is no God, and no life after death, virtuous living is a waste of time.

FOR YOUR FOLDERS

▶ In what ways could a person show courage and fortitude when faced with

  a divorced parents,
  b redundancy from work,
  c terminal illness (their own or another's)?

▶ Make a list of the Muslim virtues. Think of an example in your own life (or someone else's) when you put these virtues into practice.

▶ Is the self-sacrifice of virtuous living worth it? Give reasons for your answer.

The economic principles of Islam aim at building up a just society in which people behave responsibly and honestly, and are not just out to grab all they can for themselves.

Muslims bear in mind that whatever they do, it is known to God, and they will be held to account for it.

Muslims should be honest, decent, truthful, trustworthy and responsible. They should not waste money irresponsibly, or use it for any dishonest purpose. Extravagance and waste are strongly discouraged. Employed people have a duty to their employers, and also to the families they are supporting.

'Little but sufficient is better than the abundant and alluring.'

(Hadith)

THE IMPORTANCE OF WORK

It is considered very important that a person *does* work, and does not stay idle. Anyone who tries to avoid work for *whatever* reason (unless they are incapable through illness) is disapproved of – even if the purpose is devotion to religion. It is the duty of a Muslim man to earn sufficient money for his own and his family's needs, so that he is not a burden to anyone. Muslims consider it dishonourable to live off other people.

Some mosques support full-time **imams**, but whereas this is accepted, it is not really preferred. In a thriving Muslim community there should be many people to function as imams, and thus avoid dependence on one person. Any scholar of Islam should be able to contribute their knowledge without being paid.

Similarly, it is thought dishonourable for a Muslim to beg, except in cases of extreme necessity. Muslims are expected to safeguard their dignity, develop self-reliance and not to have to depend on others unless it is absolutely necessary.

'He who begs without need is like a person holding a burning coal in his hand.'

'It is better that a person should take a rope and bring a bundle of wood on his back to sell so that Allah may preserve his honour, than that he should beg from people.'

(Hadiths)

THE DIGNITY OF WORK

The Prophet taught that there is no room in Islam for snobbery. The man who acts as a simple porter has as much dignity as the manager of a great business concern. What counts is his dignity, his honesty, and his attitude to the work he is doing.

Since communities need rubbish collectors just as much as brain surgeons, nobody need regard any useful employment as being beneath them – Dawud was a metalworker, Nuh and Isa were carpenters, Musa was a shepherd and Muhammad was a market trader. Islam gave dignity to many professions which people had previously considered lowly and degrading.

Trading is regarded as acceptable employment, providing it is done honestly and does not exploit anyone. Muslims are not allowed to hoard substances at times of glut in order to make a large profit in times of shortage.

'He who brings goods for sale is blessed with good fortune, but he who keeps them until the price rises is accursed.'

(Hadith)

Any form of cheating or unfair trading is dishonourable. This includes lying about merchandise or tampering with weights and measures in order to cheat people. An honest broker is to be treasured and commended. The Prophet himself spent much time as an honest merchant, and recommended them highly.

'On the day of Resurrection Allah will not look at…the person who swears to the truth while lying about his merchandise.'

(Hadith)

COLLECTIVE OBLIGATIONS

Muslims have a duty to develop crafts and industries which are essential and beneficial to the community. Such professions are known as **fard kifiyah**, or collective obligations. Every Muslim community should try to include enough people engaged in essential sciences and industries to meet its needs. These areas include medicine, education, science and technology, politics, community welfare and leadership, and the clothing, utensil and agricultural industries.

If there is a shortage of personnel, the whole community is held at fault, for it has a duty to see to it that the needs of the people are met, and that nobody suffers.

Individual freedom may have to be sacrificed if it interferes with the good of the community – the people as a whole must come before any private interest or individual's profits!

FORBIDDEN WORK

Muslims are not permitted just to earn money in any way they can. Basically, the Islamic rule is that if someone's means of earning a living hurts another, or results in another's loss, it is **haram**. If it is fair and beneficial, then it is **halal**. Obviously, any form of making wealth that involves dishonesty, bribery, gambling, cheating, fraud, sexual degradation or any other means of making a profit by exploiting others, is forbidden to Muslims.

Forbidden professions include:

- any form of activity deriving money from prostitution, pornography, indecency
- any form of drama or dance entertainment that is deliberately erotic or suggestive
- drawing, painting or photography that is sexually provocative
- manufacturing intoxicants and drugs, or trading in them
- working in any organization supporting injustice
- working in a bar, off-licence, nightclub, dance hall, etc.
- being involved in armed forces fighting against Muslims
- trade in pork
- hoarding of foodstuffs and basic necessities in order to take advantage of hardship situations
- exploitation or artificial creation of shortages
- immoral practices
- gambling.

(See surahs 5:90–2, 2:275, 2:188, 4:2, 6:152, 7:85, 3:180, 9:34–5.)

'No body which has been nourished with what is unlawful will enter Paradise.'

'People make long prayers to Allah although their food and clothing are unlawfully acquired. How can the prayer of such people be accepted?'

(Hadiths)

DUTIES

- of employees – they should not cheat employers by dishonesty, theft, laziness or time-wasting
- of employers – they should not exploit their employees, or force them to work in unreasonable, unpleasant or dangerous conditions. People should not be made to work unreasonable hours, or to a state of exhaustion. They should be paid fairly and promptly.

'Give the worker his wages before his sweat dries.'

'An employer should not ask an employee to do anything beyond his/her capacity. If that which the employer demands is necessary, the master himself should lend a helping hand to the servant.'

(Hadiths)

FOR DISCUSSION

▶ Is it possible to maintain Muslim work ethics in a materialistic and consumer society?

▶ Find out about UK trade-union reforms. How far do you find Islamic principles to be in keeping with them?

THINGS TO DO

▶ Make a list of a dozen jobs traditionally done by (a) men, and (b) women. Put a tick against those jobs which you think would be acceptable to Muslims.

▶ Why are certain trades or professions forbidden to a Muslim? Give examples of forbidden work, and the specific reason why they are forbidden.

▶ How is a Muslim's honour affected by (a) unemployment, (b) begging, (c) dishonest marketing?

'It is not poverty that I fear for you, but that you might begin to desire the world as others before you desired it, and it might destroy you as it destroyed them.'

'Riches are sweet, and a source of blessing for him who acquires them by the way; but they are not blessed for him who seeks them out of greed. He is like one who eats but is not filled.'

(Hadiths)

Money plays an important role in the life of a nation. As a store of value it is the reserve of purchasing power and the medium of exchange. It is essential for a healthy economy and the provision of schools, hospitals, roads, rubbish collection, and so on. However, no Muslim could justify a wealthy person spending a fortune on themselves while the poor went without.

'He is not a believer who eats his fill while his neighbour remains hungry by his side.'

(Hadith)

Extravagance and waste are forbidden to Muslims, and thrift encouraged. At the same time, this does not imply that Muslims should not have any money at all, or not enjoy life. Muslims should always be grateful for God's blessings and use them responsibly.

'O believers! Make not unlawful the good things Allah has made lawful for you. But commit no excess, for Allah does not love those given to excess.'

(surah 5:90)

TIMES OF NEED

Although the Prophet disapproved of begging,

'for a person who suffers calamity and loses his property, it is permissible for him to ask until he is able to stand on his own feet.'

(Hadith)

Sometimes, inevitably, there do come times of great need. Disasters, national and private, occur. People need help with housing or business. They cannot be blamed if they are forced to ask for help from the government or from an individual. This is one vital reason why governments need to be thrifty – so that they might help others.

MODERATION

Islam attaches value to moderation, and not greed or ostentatious 'showing off'.

- Moderation in eating and drinking – no food, however little, should be wasted. Re-use leftovers, or feed to wildlife.
- Moderation in dress – Muslims should not spend too much money on elaborate clothes.
- Moderation in the household – furniture and ornaments should be moderately priced and not wastefully extravagant. Silver or gold should not be used for either furniture or utensils, or any other items.
- Moderation in building expenses – large sums should not be spent on lavish houses or palaces, or even mosques.
- Moderation at social functions – the ideal Muslim weddings or funerals are the least expensive. Coffins are thought to be a waste of wood, and fancy grave-memorials are disapproved of.
- Moderation in hospitality – although one should be generous to the guest, extravagance and 'showing off' is forbidden, and it is wrong to be so lavish that it is to the detriment of the family budget.

THE WARNING

The Prophet said:

'For every nation and Ummah there is a temptation or test, and the test for my Ummah is wealth.'

'If you possessed all the gold in the earth, you could not buy your place in the Hereafter with it.'

(Hadiths)

INTEREST – RIBA

One of the worst traps that can befall people on the poverty line is to get into debt. Moneylenders, so swift to offer help, extort crippling rates of interest (**riba**) from people who have only taken loans out of desperation.

A Muslim is forbidden to exploit any person in need by lending them money at interest (which has the cruel danger of getting the needy person deeper into debt). They are requested instead to help the poor out of charity – lending without interest.

Allah first laid down the law of not exploiting the poor through the Prophet Musa (Moses) – see Exodus 22:25, Leviticus 25:36, 37. Isa (Jesus) taught the same thing, 'lend without interest, not hoping for anything back' (Luke 6:34–5). This is exactly what Allah taught in the Qur'an.

'Give what is necessary to your family, the needy and the wayfarer, that is best for those who seek the Face of God, and they will prosper. That which you lay out for increase through the property of [other] people will have no increase with God!'

(surah 30:38–9)

'If the debtor is in difficulty, grant him time until it is easy for him to repay. If only you knew [it], your repayment would actually be greater if you cancelled the debt.'

(surah 2:280)

In the West, the system of banking and mortgages has ruined many people and runs on enormous vested interests. Many do not realize that a mortgage of, say, £40,000 means a repayment of around £120,000! Islam regards this as gross exploitation and deeply regrets any system that inflicts this kind of debt.

In Islam, providers of funds should only share the profits of other people's money or goods if they are also willing to share the losses.

TRADE DEALINGS

Honest trade is fine, but any exploitation in trade is also counted as a form of riba.

'Those who give of their goods by night and by day, in secret and in public, have their reward with their Lord; on them shall be no fear, nor shall they grieve. [But] those who eat usury [i.e. whose food is supplied by making profit from interest] will not stand, except as one whom the Evil One has touched and driven to madness. They say "usury is the same as trade"; but God has permitted trade and forbidden usury.'

(surah 2:274–5, see also 3:130, 4:161)

In Islam, to be honourable, money and goods should not be used to gain an unfair advantage over producers, traders or customers. Customers might also be guilty of riba. They could wait, for example, until merchandise lost value – fruit will only stay fresh for a limited time – and thereby force the merchant to agree to a lower price. Hoarding by the trader is also condemned.

Muslims believe that all productive resources should be brought into use as far as possible, including unemployed people, unused land, water and mineral resources. Governments commit riba when they deliberately create unemployment.

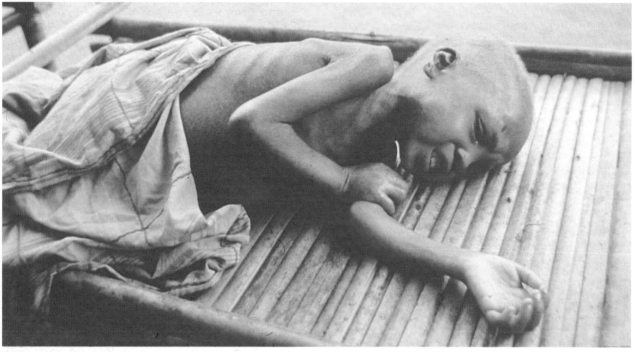

Famine in the Sahel

'If anyone supplies a need to any one of my people, desiring to please him by it, he has pleased me; and he who has pleased me has pleased Allah; and he who has pleased Allah will be brought to Paradise.'

(Hadith)

Muslims place care and compassion for others second only to love of Allah. In most cases it is by loving and caring for others that a person actually *shows* their love for God. Muslim parents often recite to their children some words of the Prophet to encourage giving:

'Every day two angels come down from Heaven, one of them says "O Allah! Compensate every person who gives in Your name." The other says "O Allah! Destroy every miser!" '

(Hadith)

ZAKAH AND SADAQAH

Muslims are expected to tax their income and wealth as a matter of duty, and to hand over a certain proportion on an annual basis to those who are less fortunate. This is not regarded as a matter of choice, but as a religious duty, the **zakah** (see page 62).

Acts of charity that are a matter of personal choice and not of duty are known as **sadaqah**. These acts can be small, individual examples of giving – usually prompted by compassion on hearing of the plight of someone unfortunate.

If a Muslim can see the distress of another and does nothing about it, he or she has departed from the spirit of Islam. Charity is so important that the Prophet said:

'An ignorant person who is generous is nearer to Allah than a person full of prayer who is miserly.'

(Hadith)

The *intention* is important. If a person gives openly in order to be admired by others, it actually shows a lack of faith in Allah – for the giver has forgotten that Allah knows every motive.

DON'T CAUSE EMBARRASSMENT

People are requested not to embarrass the needy.

'O believers! Do not cancel your generosity by reminders of your charity or by injury – like those who spend their substance in order to be seen by others, but believe neither in Allah nor the Last Day. They are like a hard barren rock on which is little soil; when heavy rain falls on it, it leaves just a bare stone.'

(surah 2:264)

The only time one should give publicly is when by doing so it will also encourage others to give.

THE RIGHT TO THE BASIC NECESSITIES OF LIFE

The Earth is a wealthy place, and there is enough for all. No human being should go in need while others are able to waste what they have. The needs of any suffering person must be attended to. The hungry should be fed, the naked clothed, and the wounded or diseased treated, whether they are Muslim or not, and whether they are friends or enemies.

There are many Islamic enterprises that organize charity on a large scale. The best known are:

Islamic Relief 517 Moseley Rd, Birmingham, B12 (0121 4403114). This is an international relief organization, which helps needy Muslims in the UK and abroad.

Muslim Aid PO Box 3, London, N7 8LR (0171 6094425). This does similar work to Islamic Relief.

The Red Crescent (the Muslim equivalent of the Red Cross) carries out acts of mercy ranging from medical care on the battlefield to famine relief.

Muslim Relief Fund at the Islamic Cultural Centre, 146, Park Rd, London, NW8 7RG (0171 7243363).

Smaller care organizations include:

Muslim Women's Helpline (0181 9086715 and 9048193). An organization which gives non-judgemental, caring emotional support to Muslim women and girls with various problems. (Service available Monday to Friday, 10 a.m.–4 p.m.)

Helpline (0181 4271751) offers advice on problems ranging from housing difficulties to racism; an offshoot of the paper *Muslim Voice*.

Appeals recently supported by these organizations have included the Somalia famine appeal, the Bangladesh flood disaster appeal, the Ethiopia famine appeal, the Kashmir war damage appeal, and they have also given support to people in Bosnia, Albania and Rwanda.

Raising money for Islamic Relief

FOR DISCUSSION

▶ 'Public giving is not as praiseworthy as private giving.' When might this be true, and when might it not be true?

FOR YOUR FOLDERS

▶ *'How can you call yourself a believer while your brother goes hungry?'*

(Hadith)

What do you think the Prophet meant by this?

▶ What is the difference between zakah and sadaqah? Make a list of possible acts of sadaqah a Muslim might do.

▶ Why do Muslims believe a generous but ignorant person is better in the eyes of God than a pious miser?

CAUSES OF CRIME

Muslims believe that there are four major causes of crime, all ultimately the work of humanity's enemy, the Devil, and his efforts to bring about its downfall:

- deprivation
- lack of moral awareness
- no belief in God and judgement in the afterlife
- the temptation and urge to sin.

THE NATURE OF PUNISHMENT

There are five main aspects of punishment:

- control – to remove the harmful person from society so that no more damage is done
- retribution – to have the satisfaction of seeing the offender get the punishment they deserve
- reform – to change the ways of the offender
- rehabilitation – to see the offender start a useful new life in society
- reconciliation – to see the society that has been hurt by the offender forgive them and receive them back.

JUSTICE – HUMAN, MUSLIM AND DIVINE

Muslims believe in strict justice, carried out according to the principles of honour, tempered with mercy. If someone has been wronged, then it is the duty of all Muslims to unite to put the wrong right. If they ignore the wrong done, they are themselves in the wrong, and have submitted to a tyrant. It is not considered right just to let it go, and ignore it.

If someone does wrong to themselves in private, then it is between them and their Creator. He may punish or He may forgive. If they do wrong publicly, upkeeping public morals may have to take precedence, so if Muslims admit to some wrong (even if it is done only to themselves), or boast of it, punishment may follow.

If someone has wronged another person, *their* demands of justice have to be satisfied first, before the wrongdoer can be forgiven. The wronged person could ask for compensation, or insist on punishment for the wrongdoer. It is accepted that Allah *always* forgives the truly penitent person; gaining forgiveness from another human being is harder!

If some wrong has been done against a Muslim. then it is always considered better in Islam to forgive and be charitable, as long as refusal to take revenge is consistent with honour. The first move should be to reason with the wrongdoer, in the hope that they will stop their offensive action and become a friend.

'The reward for an injury is an equal injury back; but if a person forgives instead, and is reconciled, that will earn reward from Allah.'

(surah 42:40)

NO ONE IS ABOVE THE LAW, OR UNPROTECTED BY IT

No citizen should ever be above the law, no matter how powerful, or beneath the protection of the law, no matter how humble. No one should ever be forced to act against the dictates of their own consciences.

No human being should ever be imprisoned unless they have been properly convicted of a crime by an unbiased court of law. No person should ever be threatened or punished or imprisoned because of the fault of others, or in order to intimidate others.

PUBLIC JUSTICE

Muslim justice should always be carried out publicly. This is not done for the sake of barbarity, or to please a blood-thirsty audience, but because it is important:

- that justice is seen to be done,
- that judges should not have the opportunity for corruption and brutality behind the scenes.

Muslims strongly disapprove of trials and punishments being carried out in secret, with the possibility of inhumane treatment and torture.

PUNISHMENTS

Some harsh punishments *are* laid down by Islam, and may be carried out in the stricter countries. These are generally for serious offences against another person's property, life or honour.

The devastating effects of alcohol on Western society have been well observed, and both drunkenness and theft are despised. People could be flogged for drinking alcohol, and hands are cut off for theft.

THEFT

'As to the thief, male or female, cut off their hands: a punishment by way of an example.'

(surah 5:41)

'A woman of a high and noble family was brought to the Prophet accused of theft, and they begged that she be spared the punishment. He said, "I swear by Him who holds my life in His hands, that even if my daughter Fatimah had committed this crime, I would have amputated her hand myself"'

(Hadith)

The Qur'an lays down a severe punishment for theft, but it is not true that Muslim countries are full of people who have lost hands! On the contrary, a true Muslim would not even consider committing theft, because of the belief that Allah sees everything. Only a fool would sacrifice nearness to Allah in the afterlife for the sake of a temporary temptation.

However, where theft has been committed, the circumstances leading up to it should be examined very carefully. If it can be proved that the thief stole out of dire need, because the family or individual was starving, and the state had not been able to fulfil its obligation as regards providing for them, then there would be no question of losing a hand. Hands are only amputated when there are two witnesses and when it can be proved that the person is a persistent thief, and there is no chance of reforming their character. Then and only then should it be done in Islam, to act as a deterrent.

Muslim scholars sometimes point out that Isa's (Jesus) teaching on the subject (*'If thy hand offend thee, cut it off! It is better to go through life maimed than with both hands to enter hell'* Mark 9:43) is supported by the Qur'an, and wonder by what standards Christian scholars pick and choose which of the commands they will keep.

What may seem barbaric in the West is taken as a point of honour by Muslims. They maintain the same justice for all, with no preferential treatment.

One story about Ali tells of his care and attention to a thief whose hand he had amputated, who later loved him so much he became one of his most devoted followers.

FINAL JUDGEMENT BEFORE ALLAH

'No bearer of burdens can be made to bear the burden of another.'

(surah 6:164)

'Let them bear, on the Day of Judgement, their own burden in full – and also [something] of the burdens of those without knowledge whom they misled!'

(surah 16:25)

Every Muslim believes that human judgements can be wrong, or influenced by bias or ignorance of circumstances – but Allah sees and hears everything, and no person can escape His true judgement on their life. On that Day, no one will be able to make excuses for another – all will stand alone, as individuals.

TALKING POINT

- Citizens in the West demand that Muslims living in their countries should obey the laws of the land, and indeed, they are obliged to do so. Should they therefore accept the same principle when living in Muslim countries, and accept Islamic law?

FOR YOUR FOLDERS

▶ What is the Qur'anic penalty for theft? Why would a true Muslim never be a thief in any circumstances? What are the only conditions for which a Muslim court should consider cutting off a hand?

▶ Why do Muslims believe in public execution of justice?

▶ *'If Allah were to punish people according to what they deserve, He would not leave on the surface of the [earth] a single living being; but He gives them a reprieve for a certain length of time.'*

(surah 35:45, 16:61)

What does this passage teach about Allah's attitude to justice and mercy?

'O Lord! I seek Thy protection against creeping sloth and cowardice and miserliness, and I seek Thy protection from oppressive debt and the tyranny of people.'

(Prayer of Muhammad)

Jihad, or 'striving', applies to any sort of activity made by a person because of love of Allah. The word comes from **juhd** which means *effort*, and the verb **jahida** means to be tired as result of making an effort.

THE GREAT JIHAD

For most Muslims, the concept is purely a personal one, and refers to the deliberate effort made by each of them to serve Allah to the best of their ability, by a life of devotion, self-sacrifice, and love and compassion for others.

It is jihad:

- whenever a Muslim is called upon to make an extra effort – for example, to get up before sunrise in order to pray

- when a Muslim tries to love and forgive someone who has hurt them or insulted them

- when a Muslim does not cling to personal possessions, but gives them up in the service of others.

PEACE

Millions of people, both soldiers and civilians, have died as the result of wars. Whole generations have been wiped out, and billions of pounds spent on warfare. Nobody in their right mind could possibly regard war as a good thing. No one could believe that it could be right to inflict suffering in order to take power, land, food or anything else, by force. When this is done, it is rightly regarded as tyranny.

When a tyrant is successful, even if there is no actual fighting, there is no peace, because:

- there is no security
- people feel dishonoured and ashamed in allowing the situation to continue
- people feel frustrated and helpless, and unable to do anything about it
- people feel ashamed because they think they have acted in a cowardly manner.

'If anyone walks with an oppressor to strengthen him, knowing that he is an oppressor, he has gone forth from Islam.'

(Hadith)

Islam is intended to be a religion of peace, goodwill, mutual understanding and good faith. But it will not acquiesce in wrongdoing, and warriors hold their lives cheap in defence of honour and justice.

The Muslim ideal is that of virtue combined with unselfish courage, obedience, discipline, duty and a constant striving by all the means in their power for the establishment of truth and righteousness.

They regard it as cowardice to ignore the challenge, flee the battlefield, or to fail to root out the tyranny.

Muslims are commended to exercise as much self-restraint as possible. Force is a dangerous weapon. It may have to be used for self-defence or self-preservation – but it should always be for a principle and not out of passion.

'If God did not check certain people by using others, surely many monasteries, churches, synagogues and mosques would all have been pulled down. God will aid those who fight for Him.'

(surah 22:40)

MILITARY JIHAD

'The Prophet was asked about people fighting because they are brave, or in honour of a certain loyalty, or to show off: which of them fights for the cause of Allah? He replied, "The person who struggles so that Allah's word is supreme is the one serving Allah's cause." '

(Hadith)

The word jihad is often used in speaking about a military situation, when Muslims are called upon to fight for the honour or preservation of their faith. Harb al-Muqadis, or Holy War, is the logical extension of fighting for their rights. Jihad does not mean forcing other people to accept Islamic beliefs, but striving to bring about a society in which Muslims are free to obey Allah's laws, leaving others free to worship or not as they wish.

It should be declared only:

- in *defence* of the cause of Allah, not for conquest

- to restore peace and freedom of worship

- to gain freedom from tyranny

- if led by a spiritual leader and fought until the enemy lays down arms.

Kurdish guerilla fighters

Women, children and the old and sick are not to be harmed, and trees and crops are not to be damaged.

Jihad does *not* include:

- wars of aggression or ambition
- border disputes or national or tribal squabbles
- the intent to conquer and suppress, colonize, exploit, etc.
- forcing people into accepting a faith they do not believe.

HUMANE TREATMENT OF ENEMIES

Fighting in a jihad is to be prolonged only so long as the tyrant continues to oppose. Once the enemy is defeated, the principle of mercy is to be applied instantly, and all hostilities should cease. The enemy should never be executed vindictively after their capitulation.

Wounded enemy soldiers are to be given exactly the same treatment as wounded members of one's own forces. The women and children of the enemy should never be molested or harmed. It would be a gross sin for a Muslim soldier to rape the women of the defeated enemy.

'Goodness and Evil cannot be equal. Repay [evil] with what is better, then he who was your enemy will become your intimate friend .'

(surah 41:34)

'If two sides among the believers quarrel, make peace between them. But if one trespasses beyond bounds against the other, then fight against the one that transgresses until it complies with the command of God; and if it complies, then make peace between them with justice, and be fair, for God loves those who are fair.'

(surah 49:9)

MARTYRS

Any person who is literally martyred in the cause of serving Allah is called **shahid**. Martyrdom for Allah is not the same thing as nationalism. Someone can lay down their life for their country without being religious at all – and this is *not* shahid.

For the true martyr for Allah, Muslims believe that the sacrifice of their life will earn them forgiveness for any wrongs they committed during their lifetimes, and they will go straight to Paradise.

THINKING POINT

- Just because there is no actual war does not mean that a country is 'at peace'. What things are necessary in a country before it can feel peace?

FOR YOUR FOLDERS

▶ Explain in your own words the meaning of these terms:
jihad   shahid   martyr   nationalism.

▶ What is the true meaning of jihad? Give some examples of things that are jihad in the everyday life of a Muslim.

▶ What are the rules that govern a military jihad?

Muslim students forced to shave beard and remove *hijab*

Two Muslim students, a boy and a girl, were forced to shave beard and remove *hijab* respectively by their head teacher. The incident took place at the beginning of the new academic year last month in Crawley, West Sussex. The Muslim community has condemned the decision as yet another example of discrimination against Muslims. "This discrimination is being targeted against Muslims only as they are not protected by law, unlike other faith groups, like Sikhs and Jews, who are protected under the Race Relations Act 1976," said Massoud Shadjareh, spokesman of the Human Rights Committee of the Muslim Parliament of Britain. Sikh boys in the school are allowed to wear beard and turban.

Mr. Rowe, spokesman of the education department of West Sussex council, explained the reason for the discrimination. "In relation to the beard the school does allow Sikhs to have a beard as it is a more clear cut case." He added that the Hazlewick Secondary School had a rule that no pupils are allowed to have a beard except on religious grounds. For Muslims, he said, there is "no clear cut case". Mr. Rowe is still investigating the matter. However, the education department has "no policy" on the matter. "It is up to the school's governors to decide," he said. The school's head teacher, Mr J Wilkinson, refused to comment on the matter. "It is an internal matter of the school," his secretary told the *Muslim News*.

From the Muslim News, *22 October 1993*

NOT ONE RACE

Islam teaches that devotion to Allah is the only true and acceptable loyalty, and that this should cut across all barriers of race and colour and class.

Islam started in Arabia, not far from the starting places of Judaism and Christianity. Like those two faiths, it has now become a worldwide religion with believers of every nationality.

In fact, the Prophet spoke out strongly against any nationalistic tendencies:

> *'Nationalism means helping your people in unjust causes.'*

(Hadith)

PREJUDICE

Some people are racist, others take a dislike to particular features. Many white western people do not accept black or brown people as equal to whites. They may not like coloured skin. They may not like certain cultural characteristics. They may not even like to see the sight of women dressing modestly, or wearing headscarves.

In the UK, there are laws protecting people from racial harassment, but not religious harassment. A white Muslim cannot get protection from the race laws.

Issues like hijab and beards for Muslim school pupils are complicated; these matters are sunnah (the example of the Prophet) but not compulsory – and millions of Muslims do not wear beards or hijab, and do not wish to be made to do so.

Most schools these days are very understanding about religious practices and allow girls to cover their heads and legs if they wish, so long as their clothing is neat and safe.

HISTORICAL 'HANG-UPS'

Some people regard Muslims as the 'enemy' because of the Crusades – the battles between Muslims and Christians over who should rule Jerusalem in the

Racism in society

Racism takes place not just because a person is of different colour, but it is due to ideological reasons, said Ibrahim Hewitt, a consultant on Islamic Education. He was speaking at the conference on 'Racism, its effects on society'.

"I have been laughed at, shouted at, and sneered at while wearing clothes which distinguish me as a Muslim," argued Hewitt, who is a 'white' Muslim. Therefore, he asked, "Is this racism, or religious abuse?" Ibrahim Hewitt believes it is because people feel superior on account of religion, culture, politics, colour and so on, that victimization takes place. Muslims are not a race and "yet we suffer from racism". Such racism exists in all areas of society. A Sikh, who is protected under the Race Relations Act 1976 "does not have to wear crash helmets or police helmets", and yet "when I went to the House of Commons I was ordered to remove my cap before I was allowed to enter the public gallery. Is that not racism?" he asked. Furthermore, the refusal of the British government to help the Bosnian Muslims (who are white) because they are *Muslims* is also racism due to ideological reasons, he argued. Muslims are refused funding for schools because they will be "ghetto schools for Asians (even though Muslim schools have pupils from different ethnic backgrounds)".

Moeen Yaseen, adviser of the Association of Muslim Schools, blamed Muslim leadership for neglecting to react to racism. The reason was that the older generation believe in the "myth of return". However, the new generation has "its roots here" and this "is our land". He added that the Muslim community should look at the issue of racism in a different way. He argued that poverty, unemployment, homelessness and other issues contributed to racial violence and not just colour.

Dr Cyriac Maprayil, director of Tower Hamlets Race Equality Council, agreed that the increase in racism was due to high unemployment and lack of resources for housing. He said the majority of people being attacked in Tower Hamlets were Muslims. However, he disagreed that Muslims are "doubly disadvantaged". "When the black people are attacked they are not being attacked because they are Christians or Muslims".

Chief Inspector Roger Kember, Community Affairs Branch, Scotland Yard, said racist attackers were "white, working class".

● Police are to be given greater powers to tackle racism. The move was announced by Home Office Minister, David McLean, in an amendment to the Criminal Justice and Public Order Bill on April 8. Police will be able to arrest people who "whip up racial hatred by putting out racist literature". However, the bill does not deal with material that incites religious hatred. "There is very little evidence to show that material being circulated is regarding religious hatred," the spokesman at the Home Office told the *Muslim News*.

From the Muslim News, *29 April 1994*

Middle Ages. Some are still resentful that the Muslims won. However, anyone who studies history will discover that Muslim chivalry was more than a match for the 'Christian', and most of the bloodthirsty massacring was done by the Christians. In any case, these wars are long over. It is usual, after a period of time, to have reconciliation.

RELIGIOUS 'HANG-UPS'

Others regard Muslims as the 'enemy' because they do not worship Jesus (Isa) as Son of God. However, Muslims *do* respect Isa as one of the greatest people who ever lived, a chosen miracle-working, virgin-born prophet – and they love him dearly (see also pages 36–7).

English and Malaysian Muslims praying together

FOR DISCUSSION

▶ Some people are prejudiced against Islam because of terrorist activity, hypocritical behaviour, noisy political rallies, and so on. Why is it unfair to judge these activities as examples of Islam?

THINGS TO DO

▶ Imagine you are a Muslim who has recently arrived in Britain. You may not be able to speak the language, and your skin is probably not white. Find out what is meant by 'racism' and see if you can collect any press cuttings illustrating this problem. How might racism affect an immigrant's chances of feeling at home?

▶ *'Whoever proclaims the cause of nationalism is not one of us; and whoever fights the cause of partisanship is not one of us; and whoever dies in the cause of nationalism is not one of us. Nationalism means helping your people in unjust causes.'*

(Hadith)

Why do you think Muhammad was so against nationalism?

'You shall not enter Paradise until you have faith, and you cannot have faith until you love one another. Have compassion on those who you can see, and He Whom you cannot see will have compassion on you.'

(Hadith)

True Muslims are under no illusions about their own greatness or importance – all praise is to Allah. They are humble about their talents and attainments, and aware of their own limitations. They are not self-seeking, trying to grasp fame or power; if those things come to them they try always to earn the pleasure and approval of Allah.

A strong sense of honour and self-respect is accompanied by modesty and self-control. A considerable amount of self-discipline is needed in order to live the Muslim life fully. Muslims are helped in their belief by the constant awareness of Allah as their only Master.

ANGER AND BITTERNESS

Self-control in governing one's temper is very strongly stressed, and Muslims are requested to be gentle, tolerant, understanding and compassionate when making allowances for others.

The Prophet said:

'Allah holds back His punishment from Him who holds back his anger.'

(Hadith)

Although it is obviously right to be angry about such things as corruption, tyranny, cruelty, waste, and so forth, for ordinary everyday dealings with the irritations of life the Prophet recommended that a person should not fall prey to hasty reactions. He advised people to calm down – sit down if you are standing when you become angry, and even go and lie down if you are already sitting. He taught that it is the gentle and compassionate reaction that turns away anger and brings profitable results.

When people have been hurt by life, it is important that they should not cling on to their anger and become bitter; this spoils their chances to put the upset behind them and become happy again. Bitterness and remorse lead to depression, and waste of life.

'Truly, anger spoils faith just as bitter aloes spoil honey!'

(Hadith)

PRIDE

Self-conceit, arrogance and pride are not compatible with the Muslim life. Strutting about thinking yourself a superior being, regarding other people as 'below' you, being loud and boastful, and contemptuous of others is all against the spirit of Islam.

'Don't turn your face away from people in scorn, and do not strut about in the earth exultantly; for God does not love the proud or boastful. Be modest in your walk, and lower your voice, for the harshest of sounds is the voice of the ass!'

(surah 31:19)

This does not mean that God has anything against donkeys, those patient and helpful workers, but refers instead to the kind of people who 'bray' about their achievements and triumphs.

ENVY

A Muslim is obliged to live in co-operation with others and not in competition. Muslims should be helpful, kind, just and compassionate to everyone, no matter what their race, colour, faith, culture or status.

Some people find it possible to control their prejudices against the first four of those things, but not the last. They are envious of other people's wealth, possessions, jobs, homes, cars and so forth. The Prophet never used the phrase 'keeping up with the Joneses', but this attitude was precisely what he disliked. He said:

'When you see someone who is wealthier than you, take a look at one who is less fortunate. That is more proper, so that you do not hold in contempt the favours Allah has shown towards you.'

'Beware of envy, for it eats up goodness as fire eats up fuel.'

(Hadiths)

GREED

Greed is an unpleasant aspect of envy – the desire to have more and more. The Prophet was against any form of greed, not only gluttony in eating, but greed for money, possessions, or anything else. It could be the desire to collect medals or sports awards, or collections of personal possessions. There is such a thing as 'humble pride and satisfaction' which is a gracious thankfulness for God's gifts. But greed usually implies personal conceit, lack of concern for others, grabbing and hoarding and preventing others from sharing and enjoying, as well as self-gratification.

Undisciplined desires and over-indulgence in physical appetites and luxuries are detestable to a Muslim. Material things should not be a preoccupation or goal in life.

BACK-BITING AND SUSPICION

A particularly unpleasant characteristic is being nasty about people behind their backs, either by speaking unpleasantly about them or by actually trying to bring them down – what we call 'stabbing people in the back'. Most of us would rather people spoke to our faces, and give us the chance to object and defend ourselves from false accusations. In Islam, this preference is an actual command of Allah.

'O believers! Avoid suspicion, for suspicion is a sin. And do not spy on one another or backbite each other.'

(surah 49:12)

AGGRESSION

'God will not show mercy to the one who does not show mercy to others.'

(Hadith)

The Prophet said: *'I swear by God that he does not believe!'* He was asked to whom he was referring. He said: *'The one from whose injurious conduct his neighbour is not safe.'*

Abuse and cruelty to any of God's creatures – human or animal – is abhorrent to Allah. Muslims should not be aggressive, or attempt to be domineering or hurtful to the thoughts and feelings of others. Bosses should not make their workers feel small; husbands and wives should not browbeat their spouses by aggression, dissatisfaction, criticism or constant nagging.

Revenge and blood feuds are serious sins; equal retaliation is seen as just – but even then, forgiveness is better!

◇

FOR DISCUSSION

▶ *'Goodness and evil cannot be equal. Repay evil with what is better, and then the one who was your enemy will become your intimate friend.'*

(surah 41:34)

Discuss how this command of Allah lies behind all the various prohibitions (things that are forbidden) mentioned in this unit.

◇

FOR YOUR FOLDERS

▶ In what ways could it be said that a person's worst enemy is themselves?

▶ What is meant by 'righteous anger'? How does other anger sour and spoil human life?

▶ Why does a Muslim regard pride and envy as incompatible with Islam? How far do you think a gentle and humble attitude encourages happiness and contentment?

Dishonesty is forbidden in Islam. It comes in many forms, and Muslims are requested by Allah (Who sees all that we do) to steer clear of them all.

LYING

Nobody likes or trusts the person who tells lies. It is one of those terrible failings that has a permanent effect – for once a person has been caught out lying, no one can ever be totally sure they will not do it again. The liar loses the trust and confidence of others.

The Prophet commented that even if a person prayed and fasted, lying rendered their religion null and void.

> *'If you do not give up telling lies, God will have no need for you giving up food and drink [in fasting].'*
>
> (Hadith)

SLANDER

Even worse than a person's lies to cover up faults or failings or when trying to get out of trouble, are the lies that hurt others or get them into trouble.

Slander or 'backbiting' (spoken accusations and lies against others) and libel (written ones) are especially unpleasant because it is difficult for the slandered person to fight back and put things right. Wealthy people could take the slanderer to court, but this is not so easy for the average person, and even when it is done, the evil thought still persists in people's minds. Once you have been accused of something, it is difficult to erase that thought.

Allah described backbiting as 'eating the flesh of your brother', and despised it (see surah 49:12).

The Prophet's wife Aishah was once accused of adultery, because she was a beautiful woman much younger than her husband, and had once been left behind by a camel caravan and returned home by a handsome young tribesman. She could not prove her innocence, and was helpless to stop what people were saying and thinking about her until Allah gave the Prophet a personal revelation on her behalf.

> *'Those who love to spread slander about the believers will have a painful punishment in this world and the next!'*
>
> (surah 24:14)

DISHONESTY AND THEFT

These things are regarded as completely dishonourable, and Muslims who devoutly believe that God sees and knows everything would not even consider them (see page 125).

FRAUD

By the same principles, fraud is forbidden to Muslims, whether on application forms, tax returns, or in any other way.

CHEATING

The Prophet, who worked many years as a trader, had particular contempt for the cheat, and admiration for the person who did not cheat even though he or she had the opportunity to do so.

> *'On the Day of Resurrection Allah will not look at…the person who swears [to the truth] while lying about his merchandise.'*
>
> (Hadith)

It is foolish to sell your Hereafter for the things of this world (see page 121).

> *'The truthful and trustworthy merchant is associated with the prophets, the upright, and the martyrs.'*
>
> (Hadith)

ABUSE

Foul language, obscenity and unpleasant name-calling are forbidden to Muslims.

GAMBLING

Gambling is not seen as 'harmless fun' but is discouraged by Allah because some people become so obsessed by it that it takes them over, and has an obvious bad effect on their family, finances and character. The whole idea of trying to 'get rich quick' by 'buying' a stroke of fortune is against the spirit of Islam.

> *'Humans shall have nothing but what they have struggled for.'*
>
> (surah 53:39)

'O believers! Intoxicants, gambling and [divination] with stones and arrows are abominations of Shaytan's doing; avoid them, that you may come to success. Be sure that Shaytan desires to sow enmity and hatred among you with intoxicants and gambling, and to lead you away from remembrance of God and prayer.'

(surah 5:93–4)

DIVINATION AND KUFR (UNBELIEF)

Kufr means lack of belief or trust in God. It often involves seeking hidden knowledge or trying to gain power through spirit forces or things other than God. Divination is the attempt to know the future by such things as astrology, horoscopes, crystal balls, spiritualism, magic and related matters.

The Prophet counted magic among the deadly sins that destroy individuals and nations. He said:

'Avoid the seven destroyers…shirk, magic, unlawful killing, usury, taking the property of orphans, fleeing from the battlefield, and slandering virtuous believing women who are indiscreet.'

(Hadith)

At the time of the Prophet there were plenty of soothsayers and diviners claiming to see into the future through contact with jinn (elemental spirits) or other secret sources – rather like psychics with crystal balls, or people playing ouija.

Such people can tamper with dangerous forces, raise false hopes, and even be involved in cursing others and wishing evil on them. The Prophet warned:

'Whoever curses a thing when it does not deserve it, the curse will rebound upon the curser.'

(Hadith)

The Qur'an makes it quite clear that divination is falsehood and deception.

'No one in the heavens and the earth knows the Unseen except Allah.'

(surah 27:65)

It is haram to consult with diviners concerning the secrets of the universe, or to seek the help of magic or those who practise it, even to cure illness or infertility, or to remove a difficulty.

Muslims believe charms and incantations are mere ignorance and error, even little Qur'ans on chains, or lockets containing verses. The Prophet once saw a man wearing a brass bracelet and asked what it was for. The man said it was to protect him from weakness. The Prophet said:

'This only increases your weakness. Throw it away, for if you die wearing it, you will never attain success.'

(Hadith Ahmad, Ibn Majah)

It cannot be Islam to imagine that any object, charm or incantation could have more power than Allah.

FOR DISCUSSION

▶ Gambling, astrology and lucky charms are just harmless fun.

▶ It is OK to lie if it prevents upsetting people.

▶ Raffles and lotteries to raise money for good causes are not the same as gambling.

FOR YOUR FOLDERS

▶ Make a list of the ways in which lying, cheating, gambling and divination could hurt others.

▶ How far is it possible to forgive and forget the person who lies or cheats?

▶ Muslims regard lying, cheating and 'magic' as not only foolish but also indications of disbelief in God (kufr). Can you explain why this is so?

DEATH

Muslims believe that every life has an allotted length. No human being knows when their life will be required by Allah and taken back. Therefore it is the duty of all Muslims to live every day as if it was their last – in readiness for the moment when they will face Allah and answer to Him for what they have done with their lives.

> 'The knowledge of [the Final Hour] is with my Lord, none but He can reveal when it will occur…All of a sudden it will come to you.'
>
> (surah 7:187)

Many people desperately try to put off their deaths and pray for Allah to grant them some miracle that will keep them alive – but nature runs its course and miracles are not often granted. On the other hand, many people long to die, because they are very unhappy or in great pain, but Allah wants them to go on living.

> 'When their time expires, they will not be able to delay [the reckoning] for a single hour, just as they cannot bring it forward [by a single hour].'
>
> (surah 16:61)

No true Muslim should fear death, or consider it to be the end of everything, as Muslims believe in the afterlife. This should be a time of great joy and reward for all their efforts on Earth.

> 'Do you think that We shall not reassemble your bones? Yes, surely, yes – We are able to restore even your individual fingerprints!'
>
> (surah 75:3–4)

SUICIDE

Muslims believe that every soul has been created by Allah, and is owned by Him. In other words, no person owns their own soul, or is allowed to damage or attempt to kill the body in which it lives. For Muslims to kill themselves is just as much against Allah's laws as killing other people unlawfully.

> 'None of you should wish for death for any calamity that befalls you, but should say: "O Allah! Cause me to live, so long as life is better for me, and cause me to die when death is better for me." '
>
> (Hadith)

Life may be full of hardships and terrible sufferings, but Muslims are taught to accept these as times of testing, and to face them with patience and humility. Not even the very worst things that could happen in life should make a person commit suicide out of despair. To do so, fully aware of the suffering it will cause others, is a terrible sin. However, nearly all people who commit suicide do it as the result of mental illness, or when the balance of their mind is disturbed. In these cases such people are not counted as responsible for their actions.

> 'There are three whose actions are not recorded; a sleeper till he wakes, a disturbed person until he is restored to reason, and a child.'
>
> (Hadith)

EUTHANASIA

Sometimes life seems such a burden for someone that people think it would be better to end it, in as kind a way as possible. **Euthanasia** means a gentle and easy death, and is sometimes called mercy killing. It is usually thought of as being 'put to sleep' painlessly.

Muslims reject the idea of euthanasia, because the reason for any suffering will be known to Allah. 'Mercy killing' does not always give the affected person any choice.

Muslims regard every soul as being perfect, even though the body it is in may be damaged for some reason. They also believe that Allah has decided how long anyone is to live so it is not the personal choice of the individual. It is Allah alone who knows the reasons for our sufferings and our tests. This may seem very unfair when nobody knows the reasons – but Muslims believe that all will be revealed in due course, and that Allah is *never* unfair.

CAPITAL PUNISHMENT

> 'Do not take life except for just cause. If anyone is wrongfully killed, We have given his heir the right [to demand retribution or to forgive]; but let him not exceed bounds in the matter of taking life, for he is bound [by the law].'
>
> (surah 17:33)

In Islam, there are two crimes which are considered **just cause** for giving the death penalty:

- murder
- openly attacking Islam in such a manner as to threaten it, having previously been a believing Muslim.

In the case of murder, the Prophet accepted the justice of taking a life for a life, although nobody is allowed to take the law into their own hands and seek revenge. The execution of a murderer should only be carried out after a proper legal trial.

One of Muhammad's sayings also suggests that the death penalty could be given for an ex-Muslim actively turning and attacking Islam, but it is not true that Muslims are condemned to death if they simply forsake the faith.

ABORTION

'Slay not your children…the killing of them is a great sin.'

(surah 17:31)

Abortion is only lawful in Islam where the life of the mother is at stake. The principle is that the actual life of the mother is more important than the possible life of the baby. The mother is alive and has duties and responsibilities, whereas the foetus has not yet formed any personality. Abortion is *only* performed as the lesser of two evils.

Some women argue that it is a woman's right to decide what she does with her own body. They insist that she has the right to choose whether or not to give birth to a child. Muslims maintain that this means conveniently forgetting that what the mother does will affect another person's body – her child's.

The Qur'an reminds these mothers that on Judgement Day the infants will want to know why they were killed.

'When the souls are sorted out; when the female [infant] buried alive is asked for what crime she was killed;…when the World on High is unveiled…[then] shall each soul know what it has put forward.'

(surah 81:7–9,11,14)

Islam does permit some birth control, however, provided that special circumstances justify it. However, a man may not practise birth control without discussing it with his wife, and vice versa. Some Muslim scholars believe that the breath of life or **spirit** does not enter the body until the end of the fourth month of pregnancy, and therefore abortion in the early days is not forbidden and can be seen as a form of birth control.

'The creation of each one of you is brought together in your mother's belly for 40 days in the form of a seed, then you are a clot of blood for a like period, then a morsel of flesh for a like period, then there is sent to you an angel who blows the breath of life into you.'

(Hadith)

So, if the soul enters the foetus after 120 days, an abortion, if it is absolutely necessary, should clearly be done before that time. After the fourth month abortion is unlawful.

Other Muslim scholars maintain that no one really knows what the soul or spirit is, and that when the Prophet was asked to define it he was told by Allah to reply that knowledge of the soul belongs to Allah alone. Therefore the foetus represents a potential life from the moment of conception, and should be protected and given all the rights of human life.

FOR YOUR FOLDERS

▶ Good Muslims live with a constant awareness of death. Why would Muslims say this is not a morbid preoccupation?

Why should good Muslims live every day as if it were their last?

▶ Explain what is meant by suicide, euthanasia and abortion.

Why are suicide and euthanasia regarded as crimes in Islam?

▶ What are the grounds for abortion in Islam?

Explain the time limit suggested.

FOR DISCUSSION

▶ If human life spans are fixed by Allah, how could this influence a person's attitude to battle, illness and disaster?

Sex is a very important aspect of human behaviour. All humans have three parts to their personality – spiritual, intellectual and physical – and have urges to satisfy the needs of all three. Islam teaches that they should be satisfied according to the commands laid down by Allah, in a wholesome and pure manner, without excess, and without causing suffering.

> 'When a husband and wife share intimacy it is rewarded, and a blessing from Allah; just as they would be punished if they engaged in illicit sex.'
>
> (Hadith)

Muslims do *not* believe that sex:

- is unclean
- is contrary to goodness, spirituality and faith in Allah
- should be resisted or suppressed.

Neither do they believe that sexual pleasures should be pursued regardless of moral considerations, since this only leads to preoccupation with sex and the development of sex as a business. Muslims maintain that both of these extremes go against human nature, which requires that sexual desires are satisfied, but that the individual and the family are protected from dangerous consequences.

PERMISSIVENESS

Muslims believe that permissiveness leads to the breakdown of society, to selfishness, rape, lying and deception, lack of responsibility, drug addiction, theft and even murder. If Muslims are listening to Allah they should be able to resist temptation, and know right from wrong.

SEX BEFORE MARRIAGE

> 'Let no man be in privacy with a woman who is not lawful unto him, or Shaytan will be the third.'
>
> (Hadith)

Islam prohibits any type of privacy between couples who are not married to each other. Muslims do not believe that sexual freedom before a commitment to marriage contributes anything to the future stability of that marriage. The assumption that the couple will have 'tried each other out' and so will 'know' each other is nonsense to Muslims. In societies where sexual freedom is tolerated, many marriages go wrong, and divorce is at a very high level. Muslims would not welcome marriage to a partner who had experienced many previous 'trial encounters', because they might quite easily seek other 'trials' even after the marriage.

However, it is not true that Muslim couples are prevented from seeing each other before marriage. The Prophet actually commanded that bridegrooms *should* go and see the prospective brides, so that feelings of love, companionship and closeness would develop. He also said that they should not be left on their own, but be **chaperoned**.

COURTSHIP

Courtship is only the first step towards marriage, and it *may not* always end in marriage – therefore the woman's reputation and chastity have to be protected. It is quite possible for an unscrupulous man to take advantage of a girl for his own satisfaction, and then abandon her without marrying her – perhaps even leaving her pregnant.

ADULTERY

Muslims regard the stealing of another person's wife or husband as the most dishonourable and shameful thing a person can do.

Adultery, giving in to having a sexual relationship with someone other than husband or wife, is the most dangerous threat of all to a family, and most people find it almost impossible to forgive because the hurt and betrayal is too great. Once discovered, trust has gone.

Therefore Muslim men are forbidden to tempt married women, and a wife should never willingly betray her husband's trust.

When sex outside marriage is discovered it is despised, and the penalty according to the Qur'an should be a flogging of 100 lashes for the unmarried and sometimes adulterers are even put to death. Death, however, is a penalty which goes beyond the statement in the Qur'an, although some Muslims justify it from Hadith.

Non-Muslims may disagree with such severe punishment for adultery, but Muslims cannot understand why other cultures make divorce laws so difficult and traumatic. For them divorce (although disapproved of) should be quick, dignified and simple, and adultery therefore shows a lack of self-control and a breaking of the family honour.

'Have nothing to do with adultery, for it is a shameful [thing] and an evil, opening the way [to other evils].'

(surah 17:32)

'The man and woman guilty of adultery or fornication, flog each of them with a hundred stripes; do not be moved by pity…and do not let any person guilty of these sins marry any but others similarly guilty…unless they repent and change their ways.'

(surah 24:2–5)

HOMOSEXUALITY

Islam prohibits all illicit relationships and sexual deviations. Homosexuality is not regarded as a normal variation on the way things are, but is considered to be against the laws of nature.

There is nothing new about homosexuality. But, the nephew of Ibrahim, lived among a community of people addicted to it.

'Of all the creatures in the world, will you approach males and abandon those whom Allah created for you as mates?'

(surah 26:165–166)

Homosexuality is regarded by Muslims at best as sickness, and at worst as a depraved practice which makes people slaves to their desire for sex when the opposite sex is not available to them, or when they fear or feel distaste for the opposite sex.

'If two men are guilty of lewdness, punish them both. If they repent and change [their ways] leave them alone…Allah accepts the repentance of those who do evil in ignorance and repent soon afterwards…of no effect is the repentance of those who continue to do evil.'

(surah 4:16–18)

In Islam, the only permissable form of sexual activity is that which takes place within a marriage. Therefore, it can be argued *on these grounds* alone that homosexuality is unacceptable.

The Prophet declared that neither sex should ever imitate the other in their way of speaking, walking, dressing or moving. Such behaviour constitutes a rebellion against the natural order of things.

'Three persons shall not enter Paradise – the one who is disobedient to parents, the pimp, and the woman who imitates men.'

(Hadith)

FOR DISCUSSION

▶ Western society and the Western world have become obsessed with sex.

▶ Many people would be much happier and more contented with life if sex was *not* stressed all the time.

▶ Girls need protecting from predatory men and boys (predatory – hunting, looking for 'prey').

FOR YOUR FOLDERS

▶ Why do Muslims think it is best if sexual activity only takes place in a marriage?

▶ Why do you think Muslims are against sexual permissiveness?

▶ What is the Muslim attitude to homosexuality?

▶ Why are the penalties for adultery so severe in Islam?

'Intoxicants are the key to all evils. A man was brought and asked either to tear the Holy Qur'an, or kill a child, or bow in worship to an idol, or drink a cup, or sleep with a woman. He thought the less sinful thing was to drink the cup, so he drank it. Then he slept with the woman, killed the child, tore the Holy Qur'an and bowed in worship to the idol.'

(A story of Uthman bin Affan)

Alcohol is strictly forbidden to the Muslim. This applies not only to wine – which existed at the time of Muhammad – but to any form of alcoholic liquor. There is one major reason for this. Alcohol causes people to lose control over their own minds and bodies.

The word **khamr** means *intoxicant* or *poison*, and was defined by the Khalifah Umar as 'that which befogs the mind.'

ISLAMIC PROHIBITION

At the time of the Prophet, many people drank a great deal of alcohol. It was perhaps even more widespread than it is today! The teaching of Allah in the Qur'an took human weakness into account, and the prohibition of alcohol was given gently, in stages (surahs 16:67, 2:219).

There is also the request that Muslims should not have their minds intoxicated when they come to prayer.

'O you who believe! Do not come to prayer with a befogged mind, but come when you can fully understand all that you are saying.'

(surah 4:43)

Since prayers were said five times during the day, this would mean that those praying were already virtually willing to give it up! Finally came the complete prohibition (surah 5:93–94).

As the news of this latest revelation spread through Madinah, the effect was dramatic. People poured away the drinks in their hands, and smashed their wine containers, pouring the liquid out on to the sand.

Muslims believe that Shaytan, or the devil, uses all sorts of devious tricks to combat belief in Allah, and alcohol is one of his greatest successes. It is a powerfully addictive drug. Even when people know perfectly well what the harmful results can be, most of them still carry on drinking until disaster strikes. It is even sometimes used as a 'medicine' given to

someone who is upset, shocked, bereaved, hurt or in distress. The media often present taking alcohol as a pleasant social habit – the expression of hospitality.

'Alcohol is not a medicine but a disease.'

(Hadith)

The only time a Muslim would be allowed to take medicine which contained alcohol would be if there was no alternative medication available. Since the principle of Shari'ah is always to promote welfare, in the conditions described, it would be allowed.

KEEPING A BARRIER

True Muslims will keep a barrier between themselves and any contact with alcohol. They regard even being in the presence of alcohol to be a danger. Some Muslims have now accommodated themselves to living in communities that accept alcohol. They will sit in pubs, or mix socially in houses where people are drinking, even though they themselves will have a fruit juice.

People who offer a drink to a Muslim may not realize that it is forbidden for them even to:

- trade in alcohol
- own or work in a place which sells it
- sell grapes to someone who they know will make wine with them
- give alcohol as a gift, even to a non-Muslim, on the principle that they should not give or receive anything that is not pure.

'Allah has cursed khamr, those who produce it, those for whom it is produced, those who drink it, those who serve it, those who carry it, those it is carried to, those who sell it and those who buy it.'

(Hadith)

DRUGS

Drugs such as marijuana (hashish), cocaine, opium, crack, smack, ecstasy and nicotine are powerful intoxicants which affect the human mind, and are therefore also khamr.

'Sinful people smoke hashish because they find it produces rapture and delight, an effect similar to drunkenness...it produces dullness and

TOBACCO

lethargy…it disturbs the mind and temperament, excites sexual desire, and leads to shameless promiscuity.'

(Shaikh Ibn Taymiyyah)

Drugs are often used by people as a means of avoiding the pains and distresses of their lives. They can escape to an exciting world of fantasy and bring on a 'high', a feeling of well-being and euphoria. The problem is that 'fantasy' experiences may be dangerous, and the good feelings are artificial, not real. All these things are against the spirit of Islam.

DISASTROUS EFFECTS OF DRUGS

Muslims are against drugs for many reasons. Firstly, they are forbidden in the Qur'an. Also, they damage people by harming their minds, their general health, affecting their ability to work, and they can cause mental breakdown, despair, suicide, and bankruptcy. They damage family life by causing harmful behaviour such as neglect and cruelty, and this can bring shame and dishonour on partners or parents. They damage other people by causing accidents. Innocent people may be hurt, immoral behaviour may be encouraged and hospital beds may be filled unnecessarily.

The general principle against drug use is based on the acceptance that Muslims are not the owners of their own bodies, but Allah is. Any substances which are harmful or injurious to the body, or might even cause death, are haram.

The penalty for taking drugs in an Islamic country where they are forbidden is the same as for drinking alcohol, a flogging.

MAKING DRUGS LEGAL

'Do not be cast into ruin by your own hands.'

(surah 2:195)

'Do not harm yourselves or others.'

(Hadith)

Nowadays there are frequently attempts to make drug-taking legal, in the hope that this will reduce the black market value of the drug. This would force big drug dealers out of business because they would no longer make an enormous profit. However, Muslims believe that more and more people would become addicted, thus giving the dealers an ever growing market. It would certainly put a bigger burden on society, because of the greater need for

rehabilitation centres, increase in crime, family break-ups, and so on.

SMOKING

Although there is no mention of smoking in the Qur'an (which was given before the discovery of tobacco), if Islamic principles are applied, the use of tobacco is makruh, and should probably be considered haram.

Until quite recently, tobacco advertisements implied that smoking helped concentration and creativity. The image they set was that an 'elegant' cigarette was a mark of sophistication, or that smoking was a 'manly' social activity. The truth is that if people are hooked on tobacco, they begin to lose concentration and suffer as their need for the drug builds up. *Then* a smoke calms them down. It should be obvious that this dependence is harmful. Muslims believe that people should give up smoking if at all possible, and allow their bodies to be restored to health.

FOR YOUR FOLDERS

▶ *'Every intoxicant is khamr, and every khamr is haram.'*

(Hadith)

What is meant by 'khamr' and 'haram'?

▶ Muslims know that it is hard to give up harmful habits. Why do they think people should be made to realize the serious consequences of their habits?

▶ Why do Muslims think it is wrong for people to 'drink themselves to death'? What other people, besides the drinkers, are affected by their habit? Why do Muslims feel they have the right to try to stop them drinking?

▶ What is meant by the barrier against alcohol, in Islam? How might this barrier affect a Muslim in the UK?

▶ In some countries where tobacco is grown, the local people go hungry while the landlords grow rich on this export crop. What do you think Muslim opinion would be on this practice?

MODERATION

Muslims are intended to be the:

'Middle Ummah, the best Ummah that has ever been brought forth for humanity, encouraging what is right and forbidding what is wrong, and believing in God.'

(surah 3:110)

The 'middle' way of the Prophet was a way of moderation, neither too casual nor too extremist about any aspect of life or belief. He said:

'Allah has laid down certain obligations upon you, so do not neglect them; He has defined certain limits, so do not go beyond them; He has prohibited certain things, so do not do them; and He has kept silent concerning other things out of mercy for you, and not because He forgot to mention them – so do not ask questions (or cause divisions) because of those matters.'

(Hadith)

Nothing is prohibited in Islam except what Allah Himself prohibited. No human authority, no matter how learned or devout or powerful, has the right to prohibit things allowed by Allah, or to stand in judgement over people who are acting according to their consciences.

ZEALOTRY

The Prophet was well aware of the fact that, human nature being what it is, some people would be far more pious and devoted to God than others. However, he also knew that certain people had the wrong motives for wishing to be thought holy. True humble believers do not make a pointed show of their devotions, but 'zealots' have a very different attitude. They go beyond the bounds of what is required, and their type of faith becomes oppressive and offputting.

The Prophet took a stern view of believers who were so 'holy' that they made difficulties for others. He called them 'zealots', and regarded them as trouble-makers.

The trouble with zealots is that they tend to look down on other people and regard them as inferior believers, especially if they are not agreeing with them or following their example. The sin of the zealot is *excess.*

'O believers! Do not make unlawful those good things which Allah has made lawful for you, and commit no excess. God loves not those given to excess.'

(surah 5:90)

SHIRK

Muslims believe Christians have committed excess in religious terms by elevating the status of the Prophet (and human) Jesus (Isa) to being part of a Trinitarian Godhead. (See page 36.)

'O People of the Book! Do not exceed the bounds in your religion, transgressing beyond the truth!'

(surah 5:80)

In Islam, it is wrong to 'idolize' any human being, no matter how meritorious. (It would certainly be wrong to idolize a pop-star or sportsperson – especially when you probably had no idea whatsoever of the quality of their private life!)

EXTREMISM

Muslim extremism never regards the Prophet as in any way divine, but it over-emphasizes particular personal devotions or practices to the extent that other Muslims feel uncomfortable or inferior.

For example, a Muslim might wish to practise prayer and recitation of the Qur'an as much as possible. However, the Prophet's attitude was that one could do as one chose in private and in one's own time, but *public* prayers should be reasonably brief – out of consideration for people in the congregation who were uncomfortable through sickness or old age, for people who were looking after fidgeting babies and infants, or for those who had business to attend to (see page 57).

He once discovered that a friend of his had avoided going to the mosque because the imam there was too lengthy and over-zealous. He reprimanded the imam!

Another example is that a Muslim might wish to spend as much time as possible at the mosque. The Prophet said this was *not* commendable if it meant neglecting the rights of the wife, family and friends. Some Muslim women suffer terrible loneliness when their menfolk spend all evening, every evening down at the mosque. The Prophet said: *'Do not make your houses graves!'* (i.e. places where they could not pray).

A further example is that a of a very pious woman who fasted so frequently that it deprived her husband of his rights to have intimacy with her during the day (fasting includes no sex – see page 64). The Prophet requested that she should only fast with his permission.

The 'good points' earned for their love of Allah were cancelled by the 'bad points' earned for their neglect of the rights of others.

FUNDAMENTALISM

In Islam, a fundamentalist is not necessarily the same thing as an extremist, although the two could coincide. Fundamentalists wish to promote the original teachings of Islam, without any later additions or innovations. Unfortunately, this noble intent depends on the interpretation of what the original teachings were, and is not cut-and-dried as regards some Hadiths.

To a certain extent, fundamentalism was accidentally caused during the years when Western powers conquered and dominated Muslim lands. Muslims felt weak and inferior, and traditional Muslim education was largely set aside in favour of a Western system. This prevented many scholars (**alim**) coming through to an advanced knowledge of Islam, and this resulted in a generation of Muslims largely without the skills to apply **ijtihad** in all its fullness. Without an adequate comprehensive background knowledge of Hadiths, some Muslims have the tendency to pick up unsound teachings and give misleading interpretations that can be the very opposite of true Islam.

NO FORCE

No person should ever try to *force* another to believe or do anything in Islam. It is not necessary.

> '*The Truth stands out clear from error.*'
>
> (surah 2:256)

Muslim duty is simply to remind and warn.

> '*Remind them, for you are a reminder; but you are not a warder over them.*'
>
> (surah 88:21–2)

COVERING FAULTS

A true Muslim should not always be on the lookout for things that others do wrong. The real spirit of Islam is to 'cover' faults with tact and gentleness.

> '*Kind words and the covering of faults are better than charity followed by injury.*'
>
> (surah 2:263)

> '*It is part of the mercy of Allah that you deal gently with people. If you are severe or hard-hearted they will break away from you, so pass over [their faults] and ask for [God's] forgiveness for them.*'
>
> (surah 3:159)

HYPOCRISY

Muslims must practise what they preach. There is nothing more worthy of contempt than people claiming certain things about their beliefs and lifestyles when they are really living a lie.

FOR DISCUSSION

▶ Muslims who are 'too holy' drive more people away from God than they bring to Him.

▶ Extremists care more about themselves than they do about God.

FOR YOUR FOLDERS

▶ Explain what is meant by zealotry, extremism, and fundamentalism.

▶ Explain what is meant by (a) hypocrisy and (b) covering faults. Imagine that your mother or teacher tells you to do something but you do it wrong. How would you like them to behave towards you when they find out?

▶ The Prophet said

'*Seek knowledge from the cradle to the grave.*'

(Hadith)

How might the integration of Islamic studies into the education system provide an answer to fundamentalism?

THE SUCCESSORS

During the first 30 years after the Prophet's death Muslims were governed by four **khalifahs** who were outstanding men chosen by the community for their closeness to the Prophet and their good characters. They were unselfish, tolerant and well-versed in the Qur'an, and had been the Prophet's dearest friends. They had learned from him all his ways and attitudes.

The word **khalifah** means 'successor'. These first four khalifahs were known as the 'Rashidun' or 'rightly-guided' or 'orthodox'.

WAY OF LIFE

Instead of living like princes (as you might expect, for they had access to enormous wealth), they lived very simple lives as the Prophet had done, in close touch with the people.

They ate little and were famous for the ragged state of their hand-patched garments, and their refusal to take any luxuries for themselves. (Their definition of a 'luxury' was anything that they did not actually need.)

They were just and kind, and totally dedicated to serving their people. They were the most important people in the Muslim state, but were horrified if anyone started to think of them as kings – they were simply servants. Only God was King.

DUTIES

- No khalifah was to make a law against the law of God, and if he did, he was not to be obeyed.
- Justice was to be done and oppression put down.
- No one was to live in hunger, or without shelter, education or someone to care for them.
- Good was to prosper and evil to be weakened.

ABU BAKR

Abu Bakr was the first male adult to have believed in the message delivered through the Prophet. He was the father of the Prophet's youngest wife Aishah.

He was not an impressive man to look at, but he was highly respected for his gentleness, wisdom, piety and humility.

Although many Muslims favoured the election of the Prophet's son-in-law Ali, Abu Bakr was the senior male Muslim and his supporters won the day. Ali, a man of exceptional piety and humility, stood aside, although his wife Fatimah, the Prophet's daughter, felt deeply hurt.

When Abu Bakr became khalifah, he was already about 60 years old, and in fact he ruled for only two years, 632–4 CE. He was known as As-Siddiq (the witness to the truth) and Amirul Muminin (ruler of the believers).

On his deathbed, he did not give the community the chance to elect the next khalifah, but nominated Umar. Ali and his supporters considered this to be wrong, but Ali refused to bear a grudge and accepted the authority of the Prophet's friend.

SAYINGS OF ABU BAKR

- 'O People. I have been chosen by you as your leader, although I am no better than any of you. If I do well, give me your support. If I do wrong, set me right!'
- 'Always fear Allah; He knows what is in men's heart.'
- 'Be kind to those who are under your care and treat them well.'
- 'Give brief orders; speeches that are too long are likely to be forgotten.'
- 'Improve your own conduct before asking others to improve theirs.'
- 'Honour the envoy of the enemy.'
- 'Always speak the truth, so that you get the right advice.'
- 'Be sincere to all with whom you deal.'

UMAR

Umar was a bald giant of a man, who became one of Muhammad's chief advisers. He was khalifah from 634–44 CE.

During his reign Muslim warriors captured Syria and Palestine. In Jerusalem, the Christian ruler, Sophronius, declared that he would surrender to none other than Umar himself. So in 637 the khalifah, wearing his famous shabby patched cloak, set out for the city with one servant and a camel, which he and the servant took turns to ride. When they arrived at Jerusalem it was the servant who was riding while the khalifah walked. Umar discovered that the site of the old Jewish temple was a dilapidated ruin, and had been used as a rubbish dump for centuries. He began to clear the debris with his own hands, and the people joined in and laboured until the 'holy rock' was uncovered.

A simple wooden mosque was constructed nearby, on the site of King Solomon's palace, which was said to have been the spot from which the Prophet ascended to heaven on his Night Journey.

The most important Christian shrine in Jerusalem was the burial place of Jesus (Isa). Umar happened to be there one day when the call to prayer sounded. He immediately hurried to say his prayers elsewhere, so that the Christians could keep their shrine. Had he not done so, it would automatically have become a mosque.

This is the contract Umar made with the Christians of Jerusalem:

> '…Their churches shall not be taken away, nor shall they be pulled down, nor shall any damage be done to them…They shall not be forced to give up their beliefs, nor shall they be persecuted for them. Whatever is written here is under the covenant of God, and the responsibility of His messenger, of the khalifahs and of the believers; it shall hold good so long as they pay the tax for their defence that has been imposed upon them.'

DEATH OF UMAR

In 644 CE Umar listened to the complaint of Firuz, a Persian slave, but gave judgement against his case. Firuz took revenge; he waited until the dawn prayer, and when Umar was kneeling he stabbed him six times. Umar died three days later, having appointed a six-man committee to elect his successor.

SAYINGS OF UMAR

- 'Do not be misled by a person's reputation.'
- 'Don't judge a person by his outward actions but by his truthfulness and wisdom.'
- 'Don't leave your task until tomorrow.'
- 'He who has no idea of evil can easily fall into its trap.'
- 'Judge a man's intelligence by the questions he asks.'
- 'It is easier not to commit sins than to be sorry for them afterwards.'
- 'Be grateful when you are shown your faults.'

The Dome of the Rock, Jerusalem

FOR YOUR FOLDER

▶ What were the qualities expected of a person chosen to be a khalifah?

▶ Choose three of the sayings of Abu Bakr and write them out as a scroll or a poster. What do these three sayings tell you about the character of the Prophet's successor?

▶ How was Umar's modesty and simplicity revealed by

  a his mode of dress
  b the way he treated his servants
  c his sayings?

▶ What did Umar's activities in Jerusalem reveal about

  a his character and leadership
  b the Muslim attitude to Christians

71 UTHMAN AND ALI

UTHMAN

The six-man committee appointed by Umar to choose the next khalifah included Ali and Uthman.

Uthman was a rich merchant from the powerful **Ummayyad** family of the Quraish; the only member of the Ummayyads to become a Muslim during the time of the Prophet's persecution. He had been married to two of the Prophet's daughters, first Ruqaiyyah, and after her death to her sister Umm Kulthum.

The khalifate was offered to Ali first, on the condition that he accepted not only the Qur'an and Sunnah, but also all the recorded judgements of the previous khalifahs. Ali rejected the second part. He had publicly criticized some of their judgements, and being a man of integrity, he refused to compromise his principles at this stage.

The khalifate was then offered on the same conditions to Uthman, and he accepted them – and thus became the leader.

Uthman was a simple and kind-hearted man, but his administration was not so disciplined as that of Umar, and he tended to appoint his friends and relatives to key positions. Many of the faithful felt that the Ummayyads were trying to take over, and resented this.

When he was 80 years old, many Muslims – particularly the supporters of Ali – felt that he should abdicate, but he refused to do so. He had angered the Egyptians because he had replaced a perfectly capable governor there with his own cousin, who set harsher taxes.

A party of 500 Egyptians went to petition him and demanded his resignation but Uthman rejected all advice and preached a public sermon against them. Soon afterwards, while he was at prayer, a group of these Egyptians killed him – the second khalifah to die in this manner. He had ruled from 644–56 CE.

His wife, Nailah, sent word (plus her fingers which were cut off as she tried to protect him) to his cousin Muawiya, whom he had made governor of Syria.

ALI AND HIS FAMILY

At last, 24 years after the Prophet's death, the khalifate passed to Ali – the idealist who had previously let the opportunity go because of one unacceptable condition. He ruled from 656–61. He had been the first male convert to Islam, and was famous for his extreme piety and faithful transmission of the Prophet's sayings. His supporters thought of him as the 'Conscience of Islam'.

ALI'S CONVERSION

Ali discovered the Prophet and his wife kneeling in prayer one day, and seeing no one, asked to whom they were prostrating themselves.

The Prophet explained about Allah and the revelations he had received. Ali was excited, but thought he ought to consult his father about it. However, the next morning he came rushing to the Prophet to declare his belief: 'Allah created me without consulting my father. Why then should I consult him in order to worship Allah?'

THE DINNER

When the Prophet first commenced his public ministry, he invited his kinsmen to a dinner, and tried to persuade them to believe. They were all embarrassed and would not support him. Only Ali, then aged ten years old, stood up and said: 'I am the youngest of you; I may be a boy and my feet may not be strong enough, but O Muhammad, I shall be your helper. Whoever opposes you, I shall fight him as my mortal enemy.'

The elders laughed at him, but Ali was to become known as Asadullah – the Lion of God.

HIS MARRIAGE

Fatimah was the youngest daughter of the Prophet, and Ali loved her. He married her after the Battle of Badr. She herself took part in the Battle of Uhud, nursing the wounded soldiers (including her own father). She was said to have been very like her mother in looks, but like her father in habits, manners and conversation. She used to sit beside him at meetings, and was highly respected for her kindness, politeness, grace and dignity.

She and Ali had three children. Sadly, she died a few months after her father, at the age of 30. It was said she was the embodiment of perfect womanhood and her outstretched hand became a common symbol for good fortune and divine protection.

THE CONTEST

Ali's appointment as khalifah was opposed by Uthman's cousin Muawiya, who was supported by the Prophet's surviving wife, Aishah.

Ali had condemned the murder of Uthman, but had understood the reasons for it and had not tried to track down or punish his killers. Muawiya and

144

Aishah demanded that Uthman's murder be avenged.

The assassins claimed that since Uthman had not ruled according to Qur'an and sunnah, he had ceased to be Islamic and should therefore be removed. (Throughout later centuries, including our own, Islamic revolutionaries have acted according to the same principle – for example in the murder of President Sadat of Egypt – or the overthrow of the Shah of Iran.)

A battle was fought in 657 CE, known as the Battle of the Camel, in which Aishah was taken captive, but was treated with great respect and returned safely to her friends.

In the next encounter, the Battle of Siffin, Muawiya forced the end of the fighting by having pages of the Qur'an fixed to his troops' lances, and Ali accepted arbitration. Representatives from both sides agreed to depose both of them and hold new elections, but somehow Muawiya's side tricked Ali's followers, and he was announced as khalifah. Ali's supporters promptly declared allegiance to Ali again, and as a result, Ali was virtually recognized as khalifah of the East, with Muawiya as khalifah of the North and West. One group of Muslims (later known as Kharijites) were so outraged by the whole business that they decided to end the 'impurity' and conflict by killing both of them and starting again.

SAYINGS OF ALI

- 'One who knows himself knows his creator.'
- 'If you love Allah, tear out your heart's love of the world.'
- 'One who is proud of worldly possessions in this brief existence is ignorant.'
- 'Learned men live after death; ignorant men are dead although alive.'
- 'A sign of a stupid man is his frequent change of opinions.'
- 'A hypocrite's tongue is clean, but there is sickness in his heart.'
- 'Better alone than in bad company.'

THE DEATH OF ALI

Ali was given many premonitions of his fate, including even the name of the man destined to kill him. Despite this, he refused to hide or run away. The last two khalifahs had been struck down while at prayer. Sure enough, Ali was also mortally wounded while in the mosque at Kufa. He did not die for three days, during which time he protected and fed his assassin, ordered that he should be spared if Ali should live, and killed with one stroke if Ali died. The man's family was not to be molested.

Ali's last words, before entering Paradise, were 'O God, most fortunate am I!'

QUICK QUIZ

▶ Who was the third khalifah?

▶ Which clan did he belong to?

▶ Who was his cousin, who later opposed Ali?

▶ What was Ali's nickname, and its meaning?

▶ How did Muawiya stop the Battle of Siffin?

▶ How did Uthman and Ali die?

FOR YOUR FOLDERS

▶ Why did many Muslims feel uneasy about the appointment of Uthman as khalifah? How did he come to be assassinated? Why did the Kharijites later oppose even Ali?

▶ What do the stories of Ali's conversion and defence of the Prophet, and the battles for succession, tell us about the character of Ali?

▶ How was the kindness and courage of Ali revealed even on his deathbed?

THINGS TO DO

▶ Choose four of the sayings of Ali and write them out carefully, explaining in your own words what each means.

THE SPLIT

Some people felt right from the beginning that Ali should have been the Prophet's successor. They were not content to see power going into the hands of the old chief family of Makkah which had so recently persecuted them and had always been jealous of the power of the Prophet. They claimed that the Prophet had always trained Ali to take over. Ali deputized for the Prophet in his lifetime and was the father of the Prophet's grandsons. They claimed that those who had elected Abu Bakr had done so while Ali was burying the Prophet's corpse with the family. Those who supported Abu Bakr insisted *he* was the Prophet's choice, and was the senior male Muslim leader.

However, the supporters of Ali still felt the khalifate should have stayed in the line of the Prophet and Khadijah, and now that Fatimah and Ali were dead, they insisted the next leader should be Ali's son Hasan.

Muawiya would not agree, and in the end Hasan came to an understanding that the khalifate would revert to his family only after Muawiya's death. However, when Hasan died (some claim he was poisoned) Muawiya made his own son **Yazid** the heir.

'ROYAL FAMILY' OR DEMOCRATIC LEADER?

Those who supported the Prophet's descendants became known as the **Shiat Ali** or Party of Ali. They are now called **Shi'ites.** They refused to accept the first three khalifahs and claimed Ali was really the first, followed by the Prophet's grandsons Hasan and Husayn.

Sunnah is the Arabic word for 'custom' or 'authority', and **Sunni** Muslims regard themselves as the true followers of the Sunnah or Way of the Prophet. They insist that the Prophet had intended elections so that the *best* man would succeed, and not to start a family line of rulers, like kings.

Sunnis are the major branch of Islam. In fact, around 90 per cent of all Muslims are Sunni. They base the standards of their faith on the Qur'an plus the Hadiths of the Prophet and the laws based upon them. They tend to regard the Shi'ite claim that leadership should be exclusive to the family of the Prophet and not a democratic election based on a majority vote with distaste and impatience.

The Shi'ites, on the other hand, are a smaller group – around 10 per cent of modern Muslims but with a tendency to devotion that borders on fanaticism. Some accuse Sunni Muslims of being in need of drastic reform. The number of Shi'ite Muslims is increasing as people in many developing countries are reacting against the decadence of the modern world.

Shi'ism is the state religion of Iran, and is rapidly increasing in strength in Pakistan, Iraq, India, the Yemen and the Lebanon.

THE MARTYRDOM OF HUSAYN

Husayn refused to acknowledge the corrupt Yazid as khalifah so warfare became inevitable. In 681 CE, Husayn and his courageous sister Zainab, and about 70 loyal supporters were surrounded by Yazid's vast army at Karbala. They were in sight of the river Euphrates, but Yazid's army tormented them by denying them any access to the water and watched them die of thirst.

For eight days they tried to negotiate the unconditional surrender of Husayn and Zainab, but they refused to give way. Let these so-called Muslims kill the Prophet's family if they dared. Husayn had already foreseen his martyrdom in a vision.

On 10 Muharram, Husayn put on the famous cloak of his grandfather the Prophet, and they went out to die. When Husayn held out his baby son Abdullah for mercy, an arrow fired through the baby's neck and pinned him to Husayn's arm.

At the end, the body of Husayn, riddled with arrows, was trampled in the mud. His head was hacked off and taken to Damascus, but Yazid did eventually return it for burial.

Yazid allowed safe passage to Madinah for Zainab, plus Husayn's son Ali Zain al Abidin whom the troops had left for dead on the battlefield. Zainab nursed him back to health and became the leader of the Shi'ites until he recovered. Also saved was Husayn's four-year-old grandson Muhammad al Baqir.

The shrine where Husayn was buried, at Karbala, became a holy place that rivalled Makkah. Shi'ites hold a ten day festival there every year, in remembrance of his martyrdom. During the festival the people weep for the seeming triumph of tyranny and evil (symbolized by the corrupt, cynical Yazid) over the good (symbolized by the piety and refusal to compromise of Husayn). They pledge themselves to keep up the fight to defend their faith and principles.

The main feature of the festival, which takes place in the month of Muharram, is a series of processions and passion plays commemorating the terrible deaths of Husayn and his family. There are daily gatherings, or rawdahs, in which emotions are stirred up until everyone weeps and dedicates their lives anew.

Sometimes the men in the processions gash themselves with knives and beat their backs with chains, in memory of the martyr's wounds.

TWELVERS AND SEVENERS

The title Imam, which generally means a leader in the act of worship, took on a new significance amongst the Shi'ites. They used this title in preference to khalifah for the descendants of the Prophet who guided their movement.

The Shi'ites later divided into two major branches, according to whether they believed in twelve or seven imams. In each group, it is claimed that the last of their imams mysteriously disappeared without dying, and now follows the course of history in a mystical way. They believe that the Hidden Imam is forever present in the world, although unseen, appearing to the faithful in their times of need, and sending out his light to convert all humankind. He appears to people in prayer, and strengthens the faithful in times of persecution. He will eventually reappear to establish righteous rule and bring about the end of the world.

The Hidden Imam is also known as the Mahdi, and some Shi'ites believe that the final Imam will be Isa (Jesus) returned to earth.

EXTREMISM

The Shi'ite movement is marked by a sense of persecution and emotional devotion to its leaders,

sometimes resulting in a fervour so extreme that many non-believers would describe it as a fanaticism. Shi'ism has tended to develop into secretive sects, which particularly attract rebellious or extremist young people who protest against any form of social injustice, and against those they regard as corrupt rulers.

They believe that they should challenge, with warfare if necessary, any form of government that has become unjust and oppressive, even if the chances of overturning it are slender. They feel it is better to fight and die in the cause of justice than to surrender and retreat.

SHI'ITE ISLAMIC GOVERNMENT

In the absence of the Imam, no government is accepted as valid. Shi'ites, and many Sunnis also, are dedicated to creating pure Islamic states where the government is based on the laws of Islam and the ruler is God alone.

QUICK QUIZ

▶ What is a Sunni Muslim?
▶ What is a Shi'ite Muslim?
▶ What percentage of Muslims are Sunni?
▶ What are the two chief branches of Shi'ism?
▶ What is meant by Mahdi?
▶ Which countries have the most Shi'ites?
▶ Who was Husayn?
▶ Where is Husayn buried?

FOR YOUR FOLDERS

▶ Strict Sunni Muslims often accuse the Shi'ites of 'adding' to Islam, and paying too much reverence to the family of Muhammad. Give a brief outline of the beliefs that might be considered 'innovations'.

▶ Why do you think the Shi'ite movement has become so closely linked with martyrdom and fanatical behaviour?

Shi'ite warriors for Allah

FIQH AND TASAWWUF

There are two aspects to the complete Muslim religious life – **fiqh** (meaning 'intelligence' or 'knowledge') which deals with a Muslim's observable conduct and the fulfilling of duties, and **tasawwuf** which is concerned with the spirit behind the actions.

Tasawwuf or Sufism is Islamic mysticism. Most Muslims are naturally aware of the spiritual aspects of Islam, and apply both fiqh and tasawwuf to their devotional lives.

For example, when considering salah the matters of fiqh are:

- the correct ablution
- facing the correct qiblah
- the times the prayers are said
- the number of rak'ahs performed
- the correct way of performing the rak'ahs.

The matters of tasawwuf are:

- the intention
- depth of concentration
- awareness and love of God
- purification of the soul
- feeling of genuine communion with God
- the effect of the prayers on morals and manners.

Fiqh governs the carrying out of commands to the minutest detail – the obedience of the body; tasawwuf is the measure of the spirit of obedience, sincerity and love.

> 'A worshipper devoid of spirit, although correct in procedure, is like a handsome man lacking in character; a worshipper full of spirit but defective in performance is like a noble man deformed in appearance.'
>
> (Muslim saying)

Sufism (tasawwuf) means being particularly aware of God's loving presence in an acute way that draws you away from normal life. Forgetfulness of self is known as **fana** or extinction. The seeker passes from conscious thought and arrives (arrival – **baqa**) at a state of union with God. More and more time is spent in prayer and contemplation, not always because the person wants to do this, but because the sensation of God's presence is so powerful and all-consuming that the person experiencing it can think of nothing else, and is sometimes even 'lost' in a trance-like state. This kind of experience is the beginning of **mysticism.**

Muslims who are drawn to like minded groups of people, following a religious leader or shaikh, are often known as Sufis. They might be either Sunni or Shi'ite. They do not regard themselves as separate from other Muslim believers, and usually worship in the same mosques.

MYSTICISM

Although it is not easy to speak in simple terms of what mysticism is about, basically the person who has been granted this kind of personal experience of God is so overcome by it, so thrilled and excited, that the rest of life becomes of little importance when compared to this moment of truth. The mystic yearns to experience this closeness with God over again.

Sometimes people might only have one such experience in a lifetime, maybe only lasting a few seconds, or more rarely, several minutes or hours. Sometimes people develop techniques for making it happen again. Others seem to be specially blessed, and have mystical revelations occurring to them spontaneously, throughout their lives.

AIMS AND GOALS

Sufis want to:

- abandon the desire for worldly wealth and luxury
- search for an inner, spiritual life
- achieve communion with God, with direct emotional experience
- become so close to God that human consciousness becomes totally lost and absorbed in consciousness of God
- overcome the appetites and desires of the human body with its concern for self.

LOVE

> 'Love is the bond that binds hearts, the basis upon which to build. If love is the foundation, your building will withstand all earthquakes and storms; and you may build it as high and wide as you please without it being in danger. Therefore, our Way is the Way of Love. Leave what is keeping you from following that Path and turn to follow it with perseverance, follow this path all the way to your destination.'
>
> (Shaikh Nazim)

'Go sweep the chamber of your heart. Make it ready to be the dwelling-place of the Beloved. When you depart out, He will enter it. In you, empty of yourself, He will display all His beauty.'

(Shabistari)

TOLERANCE

'O Marvel! a garden amidst the flames. My heart has become capable of every form: it is a pasture for gazelles and a monastery for Christian monks, and a temple for idols and the pilgrim's Ka'bah, and the tables of the Tawrah and the book of the Qur'an. I follow the religion of Love: whatever way Love's camels take, that is my religion and my faith.'

(Ibn Arabi)

Sufis are tolerant of other religions, since God can be 'seen' in so many ways. The truth is what counts, and inner peace and freedom. Particular religious rules and regulations are considered to be aids for the unenlightened. Enlightened people realize that all religious paths are attempts to find God – though all might not be of equal value.

This tendency to regard the rules which had been set for the masses as being of little importance inevitably led to suspicion on the part of the orthodox Muslim leaders.

The attitude of the saintly woman Rabia to the Ka'bah in Makkah reveals the typical Sufi attitude:

'I see only bricks, and a house of stone. It is only You, O God, that I desire.'

(Rabia)

The true Ka'bah was felt to be the residence of God in your heart – a concept many orthodox Muslims would agree with.

One great teacher, al-Hallaj, was crucified for claiming that he had become one with God. This was regarded as blasphemy – whereas the true Sufi found annihilation of self in closeness to God to be the greatest expression of humility.

TARIQAHS

The science of self which each group of mystics developed was called a **tariqah** ('Way' or 'path'). All Sufis claim a chain or linkage of revelation (called

the '**silsilah**') which goes back to the Companions and the Prophet himself. There are two kinds of membership: the initiates (or inner circle) and the associates (who attended group activities occasionally). Any initiate on a particular path is known as a **murid**, a disciple who owes absolute allegiance to his or her particular **shaikh** or leader. This close relationship with the shaikh is a vital part of Sufism, and a dying shaikh usually elects his successor (if a suitable person is available), to whom obedience and loyalty is transferred.

The three best-known tariqahs that claim their descent from the Prophet's son-in-law Ali (and are therefore Shi'ite in philosophy) are the **Qadiriyya**, **Chishtiyya** and **Suhrawardiyya**. The **Naqshbandiyya** are the only surviving group to claim their descent from Abu Bakr.

TALKING POINTS

- Mystical experience is no more than wishful thinking. It is all in the mind – and a peculiar mind at that!
- If all religions are not ultimately the same, then how can God truly exist?

FOR YOUR FOLDERS

▶ Explain what is meant by fiqh, tasawwuf, tolerance, tariqah, silsilah, shaikh.

▶ Why is LOVE the most basic quality of a Sufi? How far do you think it is true to say that 'love alters everything'?

▶ How is mysticism supposed to alter a person's life and consciousness? Why is it important for a mystic to be 'emptied of self'?

▶ Do you think it is true that closeness to God is the most valuable experience there is? Give reasons for your answer.

THE IMPORTANT ROLE OF SUFISM

Once the Islamic law-codes began to be structured, formalized and centralized, many so-called Muslim kings and rulers held power even though their human and spiritual qualities were generally low; many were not true followers of the Way laid down by the Prophet. The greater the emphasis placed by these rulers and their adopted scholars on outer conformity, the more the needs of inner qualities were emphasized by the Sufis in order to balance the outer orthodox rituals.

Many people consider that Sufism saved Islam from being over-influenced by 'legalism', for there is always the temptation for Muslims without understanding to concentrate on mere observance of rules and rituals, as if that was sufficient for salvation. Sufis fought to keep the love of God and the Prophet alive. Their humility, sincerity and devotion, character and conduct had a great impact on those who observed them.

However, Sufis have frequently been misunderstood. They have been persecuted by tyrannical rulers, and the power-mongering religious scholars who felt that their religious authority and position in society were being challenged and undermined by the popularity of the Sufis. For these reasons they have sometimes gone 'underground' in order to safeguard and continue their teaching discreetly.

The Sufi masters produced works of poetic literature which have inspired thousands. They also kept alive the spirit of theology, philosophy and Islamic ethics, and helped to preserve Islam in times of persecution by filling the hearts of believers and enthusing their spirits. They were and are the champions against materialism, and still play an important part wherever rule-keeping rather than movement of the spirit threatens to take over the Ummah.

AL-GHAZZALI

What orthodox Muslims most feared was that Sufis who practised communion with God might be falling into the sin of shirk. Al-Ghazzali (1058–1111 CE), one of the greatest and most respected scholars of Islam, reassured them that this was not so, but that it was a continuation of the ancient stream of mystical understanding experienced by the prophets. His teachings revived Islam, and safeguarded Sufism from non-Islamic beliefs and practices.

JALAL UD-DIN RUMI

One famous Sufi mystic was the Mawlana, Jalal ud-Din Rumi (1207–73 CE), who founded the order of whirling dervishes in Konya, Turkey. Son of an eminent theologian, he began experiencing visions at the age of six. His doctrines arose from three things – suffering, love and acceptance.

Acceptance of God's will, whatever it might be, was the highest form of sacrifice of self, the highest proof of love. Love was what mattered – not knowledge, greatness or striving. To achieve love meant understanding unity, God's light shining into all the dark places of the Earth and making them one.

For a little while the Mawlana found another mystic who completely understood his teachings. They experienced great joy, but when they parted he knew the terrible pain of grief and loneliness.

There is mystery over who his beloved guest really was, but the experience represented, for him, the awareness of the soul's separation from the Beloved, who is God.

Communion with God was that sense of breathtaking joy, of coming home, of being released from fear, of being transported from loneliness to overwhelming love.

> 'God speaks to everyone…He speaks to the ears of the heart, but it is not every heart which hears Him. His voice is louder than the thunder, and His light is clearer than the sun – if only one could see and hear. In order to do that, one must remove this solid wall, this barrier – the Self.'

> 'When you see with the eyes of your head you are no different from an animal. When you see with your heart's eyes all space opens up for you.'

> 'Sitting under a tree, clothed in rags you are wealthier than the richest – those who own the earth, and yet are in need.'

> 'There are many roads to the Ka'bah…but lovers know that the true Holy Mosque is Union with God.'

(Rumi)

DERVISHES

The word 'dervish' or 'darwish' means the 'sill of the door'. It is a word much misunderstood in the West where it is usually thought to mean a mad, ragged savage. Some dervishes may well be ragged, for they renounce everything other than the clothes they stand up in, but they are in fact held in very high esteem. They are Sufi mystics who practise particular exercises (or **dhikrs),** which bring them to 'the sill of the door'. Beyond that door lies enlightenment.

Some live in communities, others as solitary hermits cared for by communities. Dervishes believe that humanity is in a state of 'sleep', trapped by its own ignorance, dominated by what is called the 'lower soul'. The dervish seeks to be 'loosened from the Earth's glue', to come close to God. Freed from all worldly cares and anxieties, they are to become channels for God's light.

They are not impressed by cleverness or academic learning. Personal experience is what counts, and the most simple of souls could be the richest in this respect. They are also critical of 'empty' learning, clever knowledge for its own sake that cannot be put to practical use.

'A donkey may be loaded with books, but that does not make him intelligent. How does he know whether he is carrying books, or wood for the fire?'

'You belong to the world of dimension, but you come from the world of non-dimension. Close the first shop and open the second.'

(Rumi)

DHIKR

Opening the second shop is not an easy task. It requires a devotion, an effort of will, and a certain frame of mind. The dhikrs are the various practices by which it might be achieved. These include:

- concentration on God in an intense way (fikr)

- chanting or repeating religious phrases, to wipe the mind clean of attachment to material things

- contemplation of certain symbols

- breathing exercises

- the whirling dance, or **sama,** to bring about a feeling of loss of self and absorption into God.

'When the soul is attuned to God, every action becomes music. When the soul dances, every movement of life becomes a miracle.'

(Rumi)

FEMALE MYSTICS

Equality of female mystical experience is taken for granted in Sufism. Two famous mystics were **Rabia al-Adawiyya** of Basrah (d.801) and **Sayyida Nafisah** (d.824) the great-grand-daughter of the Prophet's grandson Hasan. Both were famous for their scholarship and their expressions of love for Allah.

'Would that You might be sweet to me even if life is bitter, pleased with me, even if all else is angry. Would that what is between You and me might flourish even if what is between me and all else is desolate. If I secure Your love, then all else is insignificant and all on earth nought but earth.'

'O God, if I have worshipped You for fear of hell, burn me in hell. If I have worshipped You for hope of Paradise, exclude me from it. But if I worship You for Your own sake then do not keep me from Your everlasting Beauty.'

(Rabia)

FOR YOUR FOLDERS

▶ Explain what is meant by persecution, legalism, dervish, dhikr, 'empty' learning.

▶ Why do 'orthodox' Muslims, and many Muslim leaders misunderstand or even persecute Sufis?

▶ Read carefully the mystical teachings in the sayings of the Sufis given here. Choose three of them, and see if you can explain what they mean.

FOR DISCUSSION

▶ Deliberate attempts to expand mystical consciousness are dangerous and might be misleading.

The 'Naqsh' of the Naqshbandi order

ORDERS

Three active Sufi orders in the UK British community are the Naqshbandis, the Chishti and the Murabitun.

NAQSHBANDIS

The Naqshbandi Sufi order is the largest and most widespread in the world. It adheres strictly to the shari'ah and claims its transmission through Abu Bakr al-Siddiq, the first khalifah. Shaikh Nazim is the fortieth in this line.

He has been visiting Britain every Ramadan since 1974. Lectures by the Shaikh take place in south London at the Peckham mosque. Formerly a church, the mosque is now owned and maintained by the local Turkish community. Every Ramadan it becomes very international, with Britons, Germans, Malays, Americans, Arabs, and Spaniards all seeking spiritual advancement and peace.

THE JOURNEY

'When you go on a pilgrimage you need to find out where to go and how to get there. Then you think about what to take and what you need as regards food and baggage.

To the Sufi, Allah is the goal of the pilgrimage, the Shari'ah is the food and luggage, and the tariqah is the way. All tariqahs are ways that take people to the Divine Presence.'

(Shaikh Nazim)

WHAT IS THE SUFI WAY?

Without ways nobody can reach from one place to another. Everyone has a particular destination. Every prophet and religion came with outer laws and inner ways to show people how to reach their destinations. The inner way is most important. This is the Sufi Way. When the inner life is all right, the outer life will be all right. So many people take care over the outer life, but their inner life remains untouched. The

Shaikh Nazim Adil al-Haqqani, Khalifah of the Naqshbandi Sufis

major obstacle to progress on the way is the human ego. Changing the ego's characteristics is very difficult. Like water, the ego always wants to run downhill; it never likes to go up. You must use power to get the water up from the valley to the mountain. The main goal of the Sufi Way is the changing of bad character into good character.

HEART

'It is more important to conquer hearts than to conquer the whole world. When hearts are conquered, they come to surrender. Today we are in need of conquerors of hearts, and not doctors of Law.'

(Shaikh Nazim)

LOSS OF SELF

'When a person comes near to Allah, Allah's greatness makes him disappear. When you look at the sun, you are not able to see anything else.'

(Shaikh Nazim)

DROPS AND OCEANS

'As long as a drop is falling from the heavens it may be called a drop; but when it falls into the ocean it is no more a drop, it is an ocean.'

(Shaikh Nazim)

MURABITUN

Shaikh Abd-al-Qadir is a Scottish convert to Islam who became a Darqawiyyah Sufi leader. His own spiritual guide was Shaikh Ibn al-Habib of Morocco.

He founded a Sufi community in London in the early 70s, then moved to Norwich in 1976. The Murabitun take their name from the Muslims who once ruled Spain and whose custom it was to build 'ribats' (fortresses). These were retreats into study, training and spiritual striving from which the disciples re-emerged into the wider community as teachers and trainers themselves. The Murabitun ribats in the UK are not physical buildings but a spiritual concept, the 'retreat into fellowship' of Sufi brothers and sisters in mutual support, awareness and spiritual striving for enlightenment. The Murabitun are not separated from other Muslims, but meet at the local mosque.

THE CHISHTI

The Chishti are the only sect that seeks ecstatic inspiration through music. Religious songs are called **sama**, and Chishtis acknowledge that certain music can touch the soul in a way nothing else can. Imam Chishti was quick to warn that not all music was acceptable, and even religious music had to be free from the desire to 'make a show' or distract from God.

Unlawful music includes:

- anything leading to sensuality or immoral desires
- anything connected to 'looseness' or drunkenness
- anything habit-forming
- anything inciting fervour for causes other than Allah (e.g. national songs).

FOR DISCUSSION

▶ Is it true that 'conquerors of hearts' are more important than 'doctors of Law'?

▶ How much of Western music would be totally unacceptable to a Muslim?

FOR YOUR FOLDERS

▶ Name three Sufi orders that have attracted many British converts. Why do you think Sufism has a special appeal to converts coming from a Christian background?

▶ Look through the last two units and make brief notes on: Jalal ud-Din Rumi, Rabia, and Shaikh Nazim. What can you tell about these three Sufis from their sayings quoted here?

'He is not of us who fights the cause of nationalism; he is not of us who dies in the cause of nationalism. Nationalism means helping your people in unjust causes.'

(Hadith)

Although there are many Muslim countries, there are not yet any perfect Islamic states based on Muhammad's model at Madinah. A Muslim state is one in which the majority of the population is Muslim and which has many Muslim features.

Muslims hope that all citizens of an Islamic state should enjoy freedom of belief, thought, conscience and speech. They should be free to develop their full potential, both in earnings and household. They should enjoy the right to support or oppose any government policy they think right or wrong.

An Islamic state is duty bound to implement the laws of the Qur'an and sunnah.

FEAR OF TERRORISM

Deep convictions lead to roused passions, desperate actions, unjustifiable 'accidents', indiscriminate violence, and wrong decisions – all in the name of principles, whether these be the cause of nationalism or God! And for these principles, many fervent Muslims are quite prepared to kill or to die.

Enthusiastic 'modernist' Muslims cannot accept:

- atheism or materialism
- departing from the revelations of the Qur'an
- corruption
- capitalism
- communism
- tyranny
- hypocrisy.

Their leaders may well be feared by politicians struggling to keep the peace or building up national economies, but they are generally admired as heroes by the deprived and downtrodden masses who have:

- observed the luxurious living, and perhaps corruption, of certain leaders
- not benefited from the booming economies of 'Muslim oil'
- 'benefited' in ways they repudiate as evil, i.e. being provided with alcohol, pornographic films, banks that take interest, etc.

Less militant Muslims wish to see peace and progress, and a building up of their nation's welfare not ruined by continuous war and insecurity, and are therefore opposed to the more extreme movements. Some are quite happy to adapt to

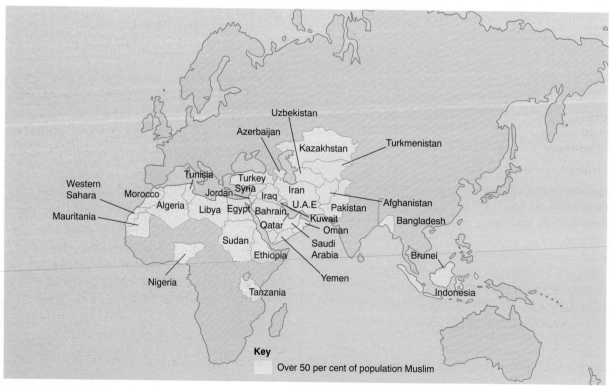

Key

Over 50 per cent of population Muslim

Countries with a Muslim majority

Western ways, and accept as much as seems good to them.

The mixture of longing for purity, plus spiritual awareness, has led to Islamic reform movements in many countries – Iran, Yemen, Algeria, Morocco, the Sudan, Libya, Syria and Indonesia. They are usually represented as rebellions or terrorist unrest.

Muslims form over half the population of some 46 countries, and make up over 80 per cent of the population in 32 countries.

The number of Muslims is growing rapidly, especially in the Far East, Africa and the old USSR (where about 50 per cent of the people are now Muslim).

The whole political and religious scene in the Middle East is confusing to Europeans, as they observe many instances of Muslim fighting Muslim.

The key movements in the Muslim world are for:

- socialism – to improve the welfare of the people, and to remove religion from politics
- Pan-Arabism – the desire for all Arabic-speaking peoples to unite.
- Pan-Islam – the desire for all Islamic peoples to unite.

(The word 'pan' means 'all'.) Pan-Arabism and Pan-Islam are similar, but with important differences.

Both are against any atheist political system, and nationalism, which they insist divides people instead of bringing them together.

Pan-Arabism aims to see a new empire of unified states, on the same lines as the United States of America (USA). It wants a Union of Arabic Republics.

Although all Muslims try to learn Arabic, millions of them are not Arab and want a different kind of unity. Pan-Arabism implies a 'land bloc', whereas Pan-Islam implies a 'mind and heart bloc'.

Pan-Islam is the movement for:

- true Islamic government under God
- a new rightly-guided khalifah (preferably a descendant of Muhammad)
- unity of all Islamic sects, especially Sunni and Shi'ite
- the reform of society
- the reform of Islamic higher education
- peace and justice for all
- freedom from tyranny (especially Western corruption, atheism and Zionism).

The campaign against atheism may well sweep Islam through the old USSR and China. It may also take firm hold in the more southern countries of Africa and in the 'atheist' West.

Intellectuals have already brought Islam into the universities, and immigrant populations have provided the framework, although many are reluctant to convert non-Muslims to Islam. Islam is now the fastest-growing religion in the UK and the USA.

No one is converted to Islam 'by the sword'; but millions are becoming aware in their hearts that God exists, and that the day has arrived when individuals from every country in the world can say 'I am Muslim, and I belong to the Ummah'.

FOR DISCUSSION

▶ *'The most excellent jihad is to speak the truth in the face of a tyrannical ruler.'*

(Hadith)

▶ Being wrong when you think you are right is the chief danger of fighting for your beliefs.

FOR YOUR FOLDERS

▶ 'Religion and politics are two separate things. Religious leaders should not get involved in politics.' How far do you think a Muslim would agree or disagree with this statement? Give reasons for your answer.

▶ Make a list of the chief aims of Pan-Islam, and explain briefly how it differs from Pan-Arabism.

▶ Why do many socialists and communists regard Islam as a serious threat? Although Islam approves of many aspects of socialism, it can never accept communism. Can you explain why?

GLOSSARY

Abd servant
Adhan (Hassan, Azan) the call to prayer
AH after the Hijrah (Hegira)
Akhirah belief in life after death
Alim (pl. **Ulama**) scholar
Allah God
Allahu Akbar 'God is great'
Amal putting faith into action
Angel messenger from God, visible under certain conditions
Ansars citizens of Madinah who helped the Muslims
Aqiqah party for a new baby
Arabesque decorative flourish in writing or art
Arkan a pillar of the faith
Ayah a verse of the Qur'an
Ayatollah a leading scholar in Iran

Baitullah House of God, the Ka'bah
Baqa arrival at awareness of God
Barzakh place of waiting, after death
Bedouin wandering tribespeople
Bismillah 'In the name of God'

Caliph see **Khalifah**
Calligraphy decorative writing
Chador black cloak sometimes worn by Iranian women
CE Common Era

Dhikr means of attaining mystic state
Din the Faith, religion
Du'a personal prayer or supplication

Fard (or **wajib**) things which must be done
Fatihah the first surah in the Qur'an
Fiqh technique of working out Shari'ah law

Ghusl complete bath for ritual cleansing

Hadiths sayings and traditions of Muhammad
Hadith Qudsi sayings of God not found in the Qur'an
Hafiz (pl. **huffaz**) someone who has learned the Qur'an by heart
Hajj pilgrimage to Makkah
Halal allowed
Hanif a devout person
Haram forbidden
Harem 'forbidden' rooms, private part of a house
Hijab the veilings of women in Islam (see also **Purdah**)

Hijrah the migration from Makkah to Madinah
Hujurah Muhammad's burial place in Aishah's room

Ibadah worship, being a servant of God
Id-ul-Adha (Eid-ul-Adha) feast of sacrifice that ends the Hajj
Id-ul-Fitr (Eid-ul-Fitr) feast to break the Ramadan fast
Iftar breakfast
Ihram state of religious 'separation' or purity
Ihsan realization of existence of God
Ijma scholarly agreement to form a decision
Ijtihad use of reason to decide correct action
Imam a teacher
Iman faith or belief
Injil the revelation given to Isa (Jesus)
Iqamah the invitation to worship
Iqra! Recite! – the command to Muhammad
Islam submission to God

Jamaah congregation or communal prayer
Jamara pillar representing Ibrahim's temptations
Jahannam hell
Jihad striving, holy war in defence of God's will
Jinn elemental spirit
Jumu'ah Friday (day of Jamaah prayers)

Ka'bah the 'Cube', shrine of God in Makkah
Kafir an unbeliever
Kalimah 'the word', declaration of faith
Khalifah deputy for God
Khilafah stewardship
Khitan circumcision
Khul divorce sought by a wife
Khutbah sermon
Kiswah the black cloth covering the Ka'bah
Kitab book
Kufr unbelief
Kursi 'seat', the stand for the Qur'an

Laylat-ul-Miraj the Night of the Ascent to Heaven
Laylat-ul-Qadr the Night of Power (when Muhammad received his first revelation)

Madhhab school of law
Madrasah school
Mahr bride's dowry
Makruh action disapproved of but not forbidden
Mandub recommended actions
Masjid a place of sujud (bowing down)
Mawlid an-Nabi birthday of the Prophet Muhammad

Mihrab   niche indicating the direction of Makkah
Minaret   tower from which the call to prayer is given
Minbar   pulpit for giving Friday sermons
Mosque   place for communal prayer and activities
Mu'adhin (Muezzin)   the person who calls to prayer
Mubah   actions decided by conscience
Mubara'ah   divorce by mutual consent
Muhajirun   the Muslims who left Makkah
Muharram   New Year
Mujtahid   Shi'ite imam
Mullah   a teacher
Murid   a Sufi initiate
Mystic   someone who knows God through intuition

Nabi   a prophet
Nafs   instinct to do either good or evil
Nazala   'sent down', revealed by God
Niyyah   intention

Pbuh   'Peace be upon him' (said of the prophets)
Purdah   Urdu word often used to describe complete seclusion. (Women cover their face and hands when in public.) (see also **Hijab**)

Qiblah   the direction of Makkah
Qiyam   standing during prayer
Qiyas   reasoning by analogy
Quraish   the leading tribe in and around Makkah
Qur'an   the Revealed Book

Rabb   Master, i.e. God
Rak'ah   a sequence of movements in ritual prayer
Ramadan   the month of fasting
Rasul   a prophet
Riba   making interest on money
Risalah   prophecy
Ruh   the human soul
Ruku   bowing during ritual prayer

Sabr   patience
Sadaqah   charity, acts of voluntary giving
Sahifa   the revelation given to Ibrahim (Abraham)
Salah   ritual prayer five times daily
Salam   peace, also end of salah prayer
Salat-ul-Janaza   funeral prayers
Sama   sacred dance used in Sufi mysticism
Sawm (Siyam)   fasting from sunrise to sunset
Sa'y (Saai)   Hajj procession from Safah to Marwah
Shahadah   declaration of faith
Shahid   someone who dies for the faith, a martyr

Shaikh   a tribal or spiritual leader
Shari'ah   the way of life followed by Muslims
Shi'ite   (Shiat Ali) sect of Muslims who insist on a descendant of Muhammad as khalifah
Shirk   sin of associating anything with God
Silsilah   chain of tradition
Subha   string of prayer beads
Sufi   a mystic
Suhur   early meal before fasting begins
Sujud (Sajda)   kneeling before God in prayer
Sunnah   the way or example set by the Prophet Muhammad
Sunni   Muslim who follows the orthodox way
Surah   a chapter in the Qur'an

Taharah   purity, cleanliness
Tahnik   ceremony of 'sweetness'
Talaq   divorce procedure
Takbir   shutting out all distractions before prayer
Talbiyah   Hajj prayer
Taqwa   consciousness or awareness of God
Tasawwuf   spirituality
Tasbih   see **Subha**
Tawaf   circling Ka'bah seven times on Hajj
Tawhid   the doctrine of the one-ness of God
Tawrah   the revelation given to Musa (Moses)
Tayammum   symbolic washing done without water
Tughyan   arrogance, taking powers for oneself

Ulama   scholars
Ummah   the 'family' of Islam
Umm-ul-Kitab   the 'mother of books', the Qur'an
Umrah   pilgrimage to Makkah not in the Hajj month

Wahy   insight, understanding revelation
Wajib   see **Fard**
Walima   a feast or wedding party
Wudu (Wuzu)   ritual washing before prayer
Wuquf   time of 'standing' before God during Hajj

Zabur   the revelation given to Dawud (David)
Zakah   giving of one-fortieth of savings for God's service
Zakat-ul-Fitr   special payment in Ramadan
Zulm   tyranny

PLACES

Al-Aqsa mosque in Jerusalem, traditionally place from where Muhammad ascended to heaven

Al-Badr site of Muhammad's first battle against the Makkans

Al-Quds the 'Holy', Jerusalem

Arafat Mount of Mercy, where Adam and Eve met after God forgave their sin

Madinah (Madinat an-Nabi) the city of the Prophet, formerly Yathrib

Maqam Ibrahim place where Ibrahim prayed beside Ka'bah

Makkah city of Ka'bah shrine, Muhammad's birthplace

Mina place of stoning the Devil on Hajj

Mount Nur (Mount Hira) Hill of Light. Place where Muhammad received his first revelation

Mount Thawr place where Muhammad sheltered in a cave during Hijrah

Mount Uhud site of second battle against Makkans

Muzdalifah where pilgrims on Hajj camp, and collect pebbles to stone the Devil

Safah and Marwah places where Hajar searched for water

Taif mountain oasis where Muhammad was rejected

Yathrib original name of Madinah

Zamzam well by Ka'bah, revealed to Ibrahim's wife, Hajar

PEOPLE

Abd-al-Muttalib Muhammad's grandfather

Abdullah Muhammad's father

Abu Bakr friend of Muhammad; first khalifah

Abu Lahab uncle of Muhammad who opposed him

Abu Sufyan uncle of Muhammad who opposed him

Abu Talib uncle of Muhammad who adopted him

Adam the first created man

Aishah (Ayesha) youngest wife of Muhammad, daughter of Abu Bakr

al-Ghazzali famous Sufi mystic

Ali adopted son of Muhammad, son of Abu Talib, who married Muhammad's daughter Fatimah. Fourth khalifah (first Shi'ite khalifah)

Aminah Muhammad's mother

Azra'il the angel of death

Bilal Ethiopian slave, first caller to prayer

Dawud the prophet David, king of Israel

Fatimah daughter of Muhammad who married Ali

Hafsah Umar's daughter, wife of Muhammad

Hajar (Hajara) wife of Ibrahim

Halimah Bedouin woman who reared Muhammad

Hamzah Muhammad's uncle, a famous warrior

Harun the prophet Aaron, brother of Moses

Husayn (Hussein) grandson of Muhammad

Iblis the devil, Shaytan or Satan

Ibrahim Abraham, the 'father' of Jews and Arabs, and 'friend of God'

Isa the prophet Jesus, worshipped by Christians

Isma'il the prophet Ishmael, son of Abraham

Israfil the angel who takes souls to judgement

Jalal ud-din Rumi famous Sufi mystic

Jibril (Gabriel) the angel who transmitted revelations to Muhammad

Khadijah first wife of Muhammad

Khalid early warrior of Islam

Maryam the Virgin Mary, mother of Jesus

Mika'il angel that protects the faithful

Muawiya the fifth khalifah

Musa the prophet Moses

Nafisah famous Sufi woman mystic

Nuh the prophet Noah

Rabia famous Sufi woman mystic

Shaikh Nazim Sufi mystic

Shaytan Satan, the devil, the chief Jinn

Suleiman the prophet Solomon, son of Dawud (David)

Umar (Omar) friend of Muhammad; the second khalifah

Ummayyads one of the leading families of Makkah

Uthman (Othman) friend of Muhammad; third khalifah

Waraqa ibn Nufal Christian cousin of Khadijah

Yazid son of khalifah Muawiya

Zaid ibn Haritha adopted son of Muhammad

Zaid ibn Thabit Muhammad's secretary who compiled the written Qur'an

INDEX